Last Weapons

BERKELEY SERIES IN BRITISH STUDIES

Edited by James Vernon

Last Weapons

*Hunger Strikes and Fasts in the
British Empire, 1890–1948*

———

Kevin Grant

⊞

UNIVERSITY OF CALIFORNIA PRESS

University of California Press, one of the most distinguished university presses in the United States, enriches lives around the world by advancing scholarship in the humanities, social sciences, and natural sciences. Its activities are supported by the UC Press Foundation and by philanthropic contributions from individuals and institutions. For more information, visit www.ucpress.edu.

University of California Press
Oakland, California

Library of Congress Cataloging-in-Publication Data

Names: Grant, Kevin, 1965– author.
Title: Last weapons : hunger strikes and fasts in the British empire, 1890–1948 / Kevin Grant.
Description: Oakland, California : University of California Press, [2019] | Series: Berkeley series in British studies ; 16 | Includes bibliographical references and index. |
Identifiers: LCCN 2018057018 (print) | LCCN 2018059956 (ebook) | ISBN 9780520972155 (e-book) | ISBN 9780520301009 (cloth : alk. paper) | ISBN 9780520301016 (pbk. : alk. paper)
Subjects: LCSH: Hunger strikes—Great Britain—20th century. | Hunger strikes—Ireland—20th century. | Hunger strikes—India—20th century.
Classification: LCC HN400.H84 (ebook) | LCC HN400.H84 G73 2019 (print) | DDC 303.6/1—dc23
LC record available at https://lccn.loc.gov/2018057018

Manufactured in the United States of America

26 25 24 23 22 21 20 19
10 9 8 7 6 5 4 3 2 1

To Lisa, Anita, and Neil

The publisher and the University of California Press Foundation gratefully acknowledge the generous support of the Ahmanson Foundation Endowment Fund in Humanities.

They think it is crazy for a man to despise beauty of form, to impair his strength, to grind his agility down to torpor, to exhaust his body with fasts, to ruin his health and to scorn all other natural delights, unless by so doing he can more zealously serve the welfare of others or the common good. Then indeed he may expect a greater reward from God.

—THOMAS MORE, *UTOPIA* (1516)

I know not what the younger dreams—
Some vague Utopia—and she seems,
When withered old and skeleton-gaunt,
An image of such politics.

—WILLIAM BUTLER YEATS, "IN MEMORY OF
EVA GORE-BOOTH AND CON MARKIEVICZ" (1927)

Suffering even unto death and, therefore, even through a perpetual fast is the last weapon of the satyagrahi. That is the last duty which it is open to him to perform.

—MOHANDAS GANDHI, "WHEN IS IT POSSIBLE?" *HARIJAN,*
    18 FEBRUARY 1933

CONTENTS

ILLUSTRATIONS

ACKNOWLEDGMENTS

In July 2004, on Bastille Day, Anita and Neil arrived. Lisa and I spent three months with them in southern California, then we all moved to Bombay for most of a year. The kids have been excellent travelers ever since. They did not realize until relatively recently that their parents travel not just to talk about history, but also to do historical research. They learned even more recently that the research for this book began a couple of years before they were born. Their obliviousness to this work-in-progress for most of their lives has helped me a great deal. It provided perspective on history. Lisa, meanwhile, has provided both historical perspective and a wonderful life in the present. I dedicate this book to the three of them, who are everything to me.

Various parts of this book appeared in conferences, beginning with a memorable conference in honor of Thomas Metcalf in 2003. I subsequently presented work at the Anglo-American Conference of Historians in London and at a few versions of the North American Conference on British Studies. I first published on this topic in an essay titled "The Transcolonial World of Hunger Strikes and Political Fasts, c. 1909–1935," which appeared in 2006 in a collection edited by Durba Ghosh and Dane Kennedy.* I subsequently published an essay in *Comparative Studies in Society and History* in 2011 that is the basis of chapter 2.** In 2015 Seth Koven invited me to present a draft of chapter 5 at the Rutgers Center for Historical Analysis,

---

*Kevin Grant, "The Transcolonial World of Hunger Strikes and Political Fasts, c. 1909–1935," in *Decentering Empire: Britain, India, and the Transcolonial World,* ed. Durba Ghosh and Dane Kennedy (Orient Longman, 2006), 243–69.

**Kevin Grant, "British Suffragettes and the Russian Method of Hunger Strike," *Comparative Studies in Society and History*, 53:1 (2011), 113–43.

xiii

where I received incisive and generous feedback. I have also benefited over the years from numerous conversations with friends and colleagues who may or may not have known that they were broadening my perspective or changing my mind. Thank you especially to Faisal Devji, Nasser Hussain, Thomas Laqueur, Philippa Levine, Thomas and Barbara Metcalf, and Krystyna von Henneberg.

I am grateful to those who took a direct hand in the present book: Lisa Trivedi has informed my thinking and writing in all ways. Sudipta Sen read the introduction and chapter 4, offering insightful critiques and creative ways in which to broaden my arguments. Shoshana Keller read the whole manuscript and required me to explain myself to the general reader, which was invaluable. Richard English read the whole manuscript and offered comments and suggestions that were critically constructive and right. Seth Koven's meticulous reading of the whole manuscript enabled me to see the project anew. His comments and suggestions were transformative. In the homestretch, Holly Bridges provided thoughtful and careful copyediting. James Vernon deserves special credit for both skillful editing and editorial endurance over the life of this project. He was in the audience for my first presentation in 2003, and he has provided relentless support ever since. He has read everything that became this book, and everything was made better by his reading.

I am pleased to thank others who made this book possible. Kristin Strohmeyer, an extraordinary research librarian, helped me to think about historical sources, then find them. Robin Vanderwall, who manages Hamilton College's history department, provided me with every assistance, every day. Shoshana Keller guided me through all things Russian, and John Bartle kindly provided an English translation of a key section of Vera Figner's Russian-language autobiography. Abhishek Amar shared his expertise on ancient India and the politics of its modern representation. Jonathan Fiedler prepared an annotated bibliography of scholarship on Irish hunger strikes that guided my initial research for chapter 3. Tomás Mac Conmara and Paul Minihan graciously assisted me in learning a great deal more about the hunger strikes by Clare Volunteers.

I wish finally to express my gratitude to two institutions. Thank you to the UC Berkeley history department, where I discovered that fact is stranger than fiction. And thank you to Hamilton College for supporting my research and writing over many years.

Introduction

The hunger strike and the fast are reflective experiences, performances of death in which we see ourselves. We see the outward signs of hunger that we have inwardly felt, whether with stout annoyance or wasted despair. We see an end reminiscent of the brittle walk to death in old age. We may see an end reminiscent of famine, disease, or war, depending upon our experience, our attention to history, or, perhaps, our recollection of a passing photograph of an anonymous, impossible life. Yet there is something unfamiliar about the choice to starve to achieve a goal larger than oneself, if only because people rarely choose to starve, a torturous journey to death. People have long since fasted to different ends, generally religious or healthful, but relatively seldom in the modern era have they courted death; seldom has hunger to the death been a willful act undertaken to inspire, coerce, or atone for others. One might recall famous or not-so-famous hunger strikes and fasts outside the range of strictly religious or healthful practice, but these are few in number in the broad scheme of things in comparison with other forms of protest such as laying down tools, occupying space, rioting, or attempting to kill someone other than oneself.

In these early decades of the twenty-first century, acts of hunger in protest are rare yet seemingly ubiquitous. They appear in snippets of media coverage and persistent social media campaigns that can occasionally generate global interest in a local cause. Take the case of Irom Chanu Sharmila, a civil rights activist and poet in the northeastern Indian state of Manipur. On 9 August 2016 she ended a sixteen-year hunger strike, one of the longest on record, with a lick of honey. She had begun her strike in November 2000 to protest India's Armed Forces Special Powers Act, under which the military in Manipur had been granted extensive coercive

1

powers in law enforcement and exemption from civil prosecution. The government placed her in judicial custody and fed her through a nasal tube on the grounds that India's federal laws prohibited attempting suicide. Having decided to end her sixteen-year strike in order to promote reform through electoral politics, Sharmila secured her freedom with that lick of honey under the gaze and glare of cameras that projected the moment around the world.[1]

Groups and individuals who shared in Sharmila's tactic of self-starvation in the same period, between 2000 and 2016, were myriad and incongruous. They ranged from members of the terrorist organization al Qaeda to environmental activists of Greenpeace; from the American actress Mia Farrow to the deposed Iraqi dictator Saddam Hussein. Taking a broader view encompassing most of the twentieth century, a survey of select media sources found that between 1906 and 2004 there were 1,441 hunger strikes conducted by tens of thousands of people in 127 countries, with the numbers of protests spiking in the 1980s and 1990s, probably inspired by the widely publicized Irish republican hunger strike that left ten men dead in 1981.[2] These numbers certainly understate the total number of acts of hunger in protest across this timeframe, given that such protests tend to be conducted by common people in desperate circumstances, most often in prison, out of public view and the media's reach.

Today the stock picture of hunger in protest is that of a refugee, a subject of infinitely diverse cultures and politics displaced across borders and between states. Refugees sometimes hunger in protest if their path is blocked; they sometimes hunger for asylum or against deportation to the place from which they have come. "I prefer to die here," said Mahyer Meyari, a seventeen-year-old Iranian man who in 2011 went on hunger strike with five other Iranian men camped outside the UK Border Agency office in London. They were protesting against the British government's decision to send them home and into the grip of a regime that they had denounced in street protests two years earlier.[3] Most refugees, however, starve against the conditions in which they are held in detention centers and refugee camps, cheek by jowl, fenced, and under surveillance for weeks, months, or years as their visa applications pass from desk to desk or sit in government offices.

The detention centers are increasingly run by private companies contracted by governments, as in case of the Harmondsworth Immigration Removal Center near Heathrow Airport in west London. This is Europe's largest detention center, with a 615-bed capacity for its all-male population of asylum detainees. It holds a transitory, international population of south and east Asians, Africans, people from the Middle East, eastern Europeans, and representatives of peoples from virtually every other region of the globe. Between 2013 and 2016 the center experienced a series of mass hunger strikes, including a strike by a hundred men in 2014.[4] These strikes were largely directed against conditions such as those previously brought to light by an investigatory committee dispatched by the United

Nations High Commissioner for Refugees (UNHCR) in 2012. An advance briefing paper by the UNHCR office in London observed, "Harmondsworth IRC [Immigration Removal Center] . . . is comparable to a category B (high security) prison in its design. UNHCR is of the view that facilities designed or operated as prisons or jails should be avoided."[5] The UNHCR was unfortunately arguing against the imperatives of efficiency and profit in a private enterprise. It is no wonder that the business of detention should look to the prison as a transnational model as it grows to manage the global flight of refugees. In Great Britain most detainees were held in prisons until early in the present century.[6] What is more remarkable is that under such oppressive conditions—increasingly standardized around the world— asylum seekers of dozens if not hundreds of nationalities should all find in starvation a weapon forged by Russian revolutionaries in czarist prisons over a century before.[7]

AN EMPIRE OF HUNGER IN PROTEST

I want to explain how hunger in protest became a global phenomenon. I will do this by illuminating sources of the hunger strike and the fast, the international adaptation of hunger as a form of protest, and the ways in which the meanings of hunger have refracted across cultural and political boundaries. The proliferation of hunger in protest has followed multiple paths, sometimes disparate, sometimes overlapping. This book initially follows the transfer of the hunger strike from Russian revolutionaries to British militant suffragists in the early twentieth century. When Marion Wallace Dunlop, a Scottish artist, became the first militant suffragist to hunger strike for political prisoner status in Holloway Prison in north London in 1909, she placed the so-called Russian method within the ambit of the British Empire, where imprisoned Irish and Indian nationalists subsequently adapted it to their own political causes. These nationalists first starved against British rule and then against each other in their respective countries. In focusing on hunger strikes and fasts by prisoners convicted of political offenses in their campaigns for civil rights in the United Kingdom of Great Britain and Ireland and in India, I argue that the British transimperial network was critically important in the spread of hunger in protest around the world. That is the basic point of the book.

Hunger strikes and fasts were first broadly publicized as forms of prison protest in the context of the United Kingdom and the British Empire. The tactic was simultaneously adapted by other groups in other places, including pacifists and conscientious objectors in Britain, Ireland, and the United States, suffragists in the US, prisoners of war, communists throughout Europe and Asia, and refugees virtually everywhere. Campaigns of hunger in protest in the first half of the twentieth century then served as models that various political activists adapted later in the century, from Robben Island, South Africa, to California's Central Valley. Yet it must be

said that hunger in protest does not have a neatly sequential and articulated genealogy. While I assert that hunger in protest proliferated mainly through the British
transimperial network, I acknowledge that there were many trajectories of hunger
in protest in the twentieth century, perhaps even more than there have been home-
lands lost to refugees starving for safe passage, asylum, or, simply, dignity.

This book examines acts of hunger in protest that targeted prison systems and,
in the cases of the United Kingdom and India, the ideological principles that justified the violence of these systems in moral, paternalistic terms. In an article entitled "The Revolution of the Twentieth Century," published in 1906, the British
journalist and inveterate radical W. T. Stead declared that previous hunger strikes
by Russian women had revealed the power and potential of the "modern political
strike" against the "militaristic state." "The substitution of Suffering for Force, as
the final determining factor of this world's affairs," he observed, "is equivalent to a
subversion of the whole foundation of which States are constituted to-day." He
anticipated that hunger strikes, and strikes of other kinds, especially the boycott,
would be useful to British women in their fight for suffrage. "Woman is not so
strong as man in fighting force," he explained. "She is immeasurably his superior
in the capacity to suffer. The boycott and the strike, the new weapons of the weak,
can be wielded as effectively by women as by men."[8] The weak could wield hunger
because they required nothing more than themselves to do so. Hunger was, moreover, a weapon versatile in its conduct and effects, fluid in its meaning, and, when
wielded with determined conviction, hard to stop. This combination of qualities
facilitated its adaptation and enabled protestors to infiltrate the rigid structures of
the state's bureaucracies and laws. As Stead suggested, this process proved particularly useful to groups who did not otherwise have the ability to confront the state's
power projected through the police and the military. When, for example, British
militant suffragists—derisively dubbed *suffragettes* by the media in 1906—and
anti-imperial nationalists in Ireland and India found themselves unable to wage
their campaigns on the streets or on the battlefield, they hungered to shift their
campaigns to spaces, literal and ideological, within the state itself. Hunger strikes
and fasts placed significant strain upon prison systems and especially on the conscience, resolve, and physical capacity of key personnel such as the prison medical
officer. These protests also strained the principles of British liberalism in belying
the government's paternalistic claim to provide for and protect all of its subjects.
On the contrary, prisoners embodied the state's oppressive violence in starving
themselves to death. Their assertion of abjectness exposed a coercive force that
troubled liberal sensibilities disposed to tolerance and equity, if not equality.

Prisoners most famously, if not most commonly, used the hunger strike to
claim political prisoner status in opposition to the state's portrayal and treatment
of their political offenses as crimes without just causes.[9] The laws and prison regulations of some countries distinguished between offenses committed for criminal

or political reasons. In such countries political prisoners commonly had privileges that other prisoners did not. More importantly, from the prisoner's standpoint, governments acknowledged that their claims and actions had political motives and, thus, a measure of ethical integrity. This was not the case in the United Kingdom and India.[10] Prisoners there starved for political recognition to which the law itself was blind. In unmaking themselves through starvation, prisoners abandoned the discursive rules of engagement through which people were constructed as politically recognizable and audible subjects or citizens. Taking this tactic farther still—and beyond political prisoner status—refugees today not only hunger strike, but sew their lips shut. The six Iranian men on hunger strike outside of the UK Border Agency office in London sewed their lips shut with fishing line. Banu Bargu observes in terms illuminating of both the present and the past, "These radical practices are . . . irreducible to their goals alone. As expressive acts emanating from the margins of the political, they put forth a modality of political action that critiques conventional political subjectivity."[11] In unmaking themselves, hunger strikers attempt to challenge governmental authority and the rule of law with a gut-level question that actually displaces political subjectivity, because it gets at something more basic: Can this government be just if it inspires death?

HUNGER IN SPIRIT

Poverty, virtue, sacrifice, brutality, purity—hunger has long been the product, embodiment, and means to these and other conditions and ends. This book is specifically concerned with individual hunger reasonably accepted and endured to serve and benefit others. The deepest, clearest sources of such hunger are to be found in religion. In the book of Isaiah in the Old Testament, the Lord reprimands those who habitually undertake fasts without reflection, or with simple expectation of the Lord's reward. He enjoins his followers to fast instead in the spirit of a whole, virtuous life:

> Is not this the kind of fasting I have chosen:
> to loose the chains of injustice
> and untie the cords of the yoke,
> to set the oppressed free
> and break every yoke?
> Is it not to share your food with the hungry
> and to provide the poor wanderer with shelter—
> when you see the naked, to clothe them,
> and not to turn away from your own flesh and blood?
> Then your light will break forth like the dawn,
> and your healing will quickly appear;

> then your righteousness will go before you,
> and the glory of the Lord will be your rear guard.
> Then you will call, and the Lord will answer;
> you will cry for help, and he will say: Here am I.
>
> (Isaiah 58:6–9)

The book of Isaiah incorporates fasting into its broader emphasis on the role of individual sacrifice in achieving salvation for the whole community, a principle subsequently shared by Jews and Christians.[12] In the same spirit, more than one Irish hunger striker has quoted the Gospel of John, in which Jesus states: "Greater love hath no man, than that he lay down his life for his friends" (John 15:13).[13]

The starving subjects of this book, in Britain, Ireland, and India, grew up in communities in which fasting was practiced or at least recognized as a form of religious propitiation, penance, asceticism, or preparation for sacred ritual.[14] In all three countries, people of different faiths fasted in accordance with religious calendars, and they associated fasting with spiritual trials and visions. In Britain and Ireland, as in much of Europe and the United States, "hunger artists," people who made commercial spectacles of their own starvation, treated the forty-day fast as a benchmark, referencing Christ's fast in the desert and his temptation by Satan.[15] Hunger in protest was likewise understood as a bodily trial of spiritual, even soulful strength. The Irish republican Ernie O'Malley, who found his Catholic faith intensified by his prison experiences, wrote to a friend on the thirty-fourth day of his hunger strike in 1923: "My body is pretty weak and the doctors tell me all kinds of stupid things at times, but I tell them they have to reckon with the spirit and not the body."[16]

In India, unlike in Britain and Ireland, fasting with religious purpose was a common feature of daily life. From villages to urban households, Hindus fasted to comply with rules of caste, to propitiate a god, or to assert moral leverage in family disputes. Muslims, Christians, Buddhists, Jains, and Jews also fasted periodically in accordance with the practices and rituals of their faiths. Across the subcontinent, fasting was furthermore associated with the asceticism and mysticism of monks and traveling *sadhus*, or holy men. Mohandas Gandhi, who became more mystical with age and political power, understood fasting as an essentially spiritual, rather than corporeal, journey; it was a way toward truth and oneness with *akash*, the omnipresent space between all material things in which the transcendent soul might join "the entire creation."[17] Gandhi and other Indian political mystics of his era were typecast in British conceptions of exotic Oriental culture, of which fasting was a part. Rudyard Kipling's novel *Kim*, published in 1900–01, concludes after a mendicant Tibetan Lama, a central figure in the story, rejects food and water for two days and experiences a vision that enables him to complete his years-long pilgrimage by locating a river, sanctified by the Buddha, which cleanses him of sin. In contrast, Gandhi's fasts cleansed his soul, atoned for others, and compelled those same others to see in his suffering the sin in themselves.

The religious significance of hunger strikes and fasts is critically important, but it does not fully explain the significance of hunger in protest in the modern era. It is telling that the term *hunger strike* entered the English language in the late nineteenth century with reference to protests by Russian revolutionaries who were, in fact, atheists. The word *strike* connected the act of self-starvation to a variety of acts of protest through cessation or abstention, especially work stoppages by labor unions aiming to win concessions from employers or the state. The term is now common parlance, identifying virtually any protest in which a person refuses food to induce an authority to fulfill a demand. This catchall usage of the term obscures a funda-mental distinction that historical activists themselves sometimes drew between the meanings of hunger in protest; that is, the distinction between the hunger strike as an explicitly political, militant act and the fast as a nonviolent act infused with spir-ituality. Scholars sometimes identify Gandhi's usage of hunger in protest as a hunger strike, but Gandhi himself seldom described his self-starvation with this term. Instead, he, like many others, generally preferred the term fast. He did so for two reasons. First, the spiritual connotations of the term corresponded generally with Gandhi's personal quest for truth and, more specifically, with the principles and practices of his multifaceted, nonviolent program of *satyagraha,* or "truth force," as a social and political project bent upon *swaraj* (self-rule). Second, the term distin-guished his act of protest from those of contemporary, well-publicized, militant "hunger strikers" in not only India, but also Britain and Ireland. A "strike" could, after all, be either an act of abstention or an attack. This semantic distinction between hunger strikes and fasts was often lost upon less discriminating activists and upon British officials. For example, as Gandhi attempted to advance and manage his first mass noncooperation movement in India after 1919 as a satyagraha campaign, militant nationalists on hunger strike in Indian prisons declared themselves to be *satyagrahis* (practitioners of satyagraha), and British officials mistakenly identified such strikers as satyagrahis, much to Gandhi's chagrin. Then again, Gandhi himself occasionally blurred the distinction between hunger strikes and fasts. In his book *Satyagraha in South Africa*, published in 1928, he praised a "hunger strike" success-fully conducted by satyagrahis against an abusive jailor in the Diepkloof Convict Prison in the Transvaal, South Africa, in 1910.[18] Be that as it may, the present book employs the terms *hunger strike* and *fast* in accordance with their usage by particu-lar starving subjects. As we will see, this loose dichotomy strains against the dispa-rate sources and meanings of hunger in protest.[19]

A NEW HUNGER

Historians have tended to define hunger strikes and fasts as discrete, essentially national acts, even within the British transimperial network across which ideas and information indisputably flowed between dissident groups.[20] Although historians have increasingly emphasized the transnational and international forces at work in the British Empire and at play in the rise of the Irish and Indian nationalist movements, the treatment of hunger in protest remains limited by powerful impressions of the hunger strike and the fast as national traditions.[21] Hunger strikes and fasts by both Irish and Indian nationalists have been long represented as forms of protest derived from ancient Celtic and Hindu customs and laws that authorized public fasting, especially as means to negotiate and settle debts.[22] In the case of Ireland, a debtor who regarded his debt as unjust or who feared distraint could employ the custom of *Troscead*, or fasting upon another. The debtor would sit outside the home of the person holding his debt and not eat until the debt was forgiven. Should the subject of the fast refuse to forgive the debt, he might suffer public shame and, potentially, a ruling under Brehon Law that he should pay the debtor up to twice what he himself had been owed. In the early twentieth century, the Irish poet and dramatist William Butler Yeats represented *Troscead* in his modern revival of Irish cultural nationalism through literary arts derived from Celtic legends and lore. In 1904, the same year in which Yeats co-founded the Abbey Theatre, Ireland's national theatre, in Dublin, he published a play entitled *The King's Threshold*. The climax of the play begins with the court poet Seanchan undertaking a fast to the death in the course of a dispute with the king:

> For there is a custom,
> An old and foolish custom, that if a man
> Be wronged, or think that he is wronged, and starve
> Upon another's threshold till he die,
> The Common People, for all time to come,
> Will raise a heavy cry against that threshold,
> Even though it be the King's.

Some of the best writers on Irish republican hunger strikes have quoted this passage to suggest that Irish hunger strikers of the modern era have acted upon an innate, collective, Celtic memory of hunger in protest.[23] There is no evidence, however, of a prisoner on hunger strike or fast in Ireland who, during or after her or his protest, explained the source or significance of the hunger strike in such terms. The Irish suffragette Hanna Sheehy Skeffington, who went on a hunger strike for the vote in 1912, recalled in later years, "Hunger-strike was then a new weapon—we were the first to try it out in Ireland—had we but known, we were the pioneers in a long line."[24] Likewise, looking back on the hunger strike in South Africa in 1910, Gandhi observed, "As hunger strikes were a rarity in those days, these Satyagrahis are entitled to special credit as pioneers."[25] In India imprisoned Hindu and Sikh revolutionaries who undertook hunger strikes and fasts after 1912 couched their protests in the terms not of national traditions but of their faiths. Moreover, a significant number of revolutionaries from the Bombay Presidency in western

India to the Bengal Presidency in the east cited Irish republicans, not ancestors, as inspirations for their hunger strikes.

As a youth Gandhi had been aware of the use of traditional tactics of public fasting to exercise leverage in disputes with government officials. In the princely state of Rajkot, now part of the western state of Gujarat, he had watched his father serve both the Indian ruler and local British administrators.[26] A public fast usually augmented a *dharna*, a sit-in or occupation protest, outside the home or workplace of the person from whom the protestor sought relief. Despite this early experience, however, Gandhi recognized the potential use of hunger in protest against the British state when he attended a reception in London for a group of suffragettes who had been released from prison on hunger strike in 1909.[27] Rejecting the methods of fasting that he had witnessed in his youth, Gandhi subsequently insisted that fasting should not be used to achieve personal advantage, whether political or monetary. He observed, "A fast undertaken to wring money from a person or for fulfilling some such personal end would amount to the exercise of coercion or undue influence. I would unhesitatingly advocate resistance to such undue influence."[28] He also rejected the hunger strike as practiced by suffragettes, on the grounds that this was, according to the suffragettes themselves, an extension of political violence.

Traditions of fasting to settle disputes or negotiate debt are not irrelevant to the history of hunger strikes and fasts. The invocation of such traditions surely enhanced the nationalist symbolism of hunger in protest, but these traditions were invoked in hindsight and not by the protestors themselves. It is telling in this regard that Yeats rewrote the ending of *The King's Threshold* after Terence Mac-Swiney, the lord mayor of Cork and a commander of the Irish Republican Army, died on hunger strike in a British prison in October 1920. In the original play, the poet Seanchan came off his fast and survived. In the revised play, which was staged at the Abbey Theatre in November 1921, Seanchan's fast concluded with his death. Yeats observed before the revised play's opening, "My new tragic ending . . . I think a great improvement & much more topical—as it suggests the Lord Mayor of Cork."[29] It would appear, then, that art imitated life after death, rather than death imitating a national tradition.

The same lord mayor of Cork became famous among Indian revolutionaries. When one of their own, Jatindranath Das, a Bengali, died on hunger strike in a prison in Lahore in the Punjab province of India in 1929, he became known as "the Indian Terence MacSwiney." This is just one of many demonstrations of the refraction and adaptation of hunger as a tactic of protest within the British Empire. To understand this process, one must understand how those hungering in protest became distinctive bodies politic that were defined not only by their present cause, but also by the resonance of previous protests, sometimes local, sometimes a world away.

Following the initial adaptation of hunger in protest between Russian revolutionaries and British suffragettes, the international proliferation of this tactic seems to have accelerated after 1912, as well-publicized suffragette militancy escalated. It appears, however, that hunger in protest already had disparate sources beyond even Russia. There is no evidence that another Bengali, Nani Gopal Mukherjee, was inspired by the so-called Russian method, or by British or Irish suffragettes, when in 1912 he apparently became the first Indian revolutionary to go on hunger strike for political prisoner status in the Cellular Jail at Port Blair on the Andaman Islands of British India. He starved for seventy-two days before ending his hunger strike under pressure from a comrade, who threatened his own death by starvation should Mukherjee die. We do not know why Mukherjee chose the tactic of hunger striking. It is entirely possible that he had heard about the suffragette strikes through the predominantly educated, middle-class networks of Bengali revolutionaries.[30] However, as we will see, there is reason to ask whether this Indian revolutionary may have found his inspiration to starve in India itself.

FAMISHED HUNGER AND PROTEST

While we may argue over the sources of hunger strikes and fasts, and the explicit terms with which protesters defined the significance of their actions, it has proven difficult to capture the more subtle, contemporary meaning of a particular act of hunger long ago. One might speculate that in Ireland and India the memory of catastrophic famine informed the self-representation of starving protestors or the general public's perception of these people. Would it not have been rhetorically powerful for someone on hunger strike or fast to claim to represent symbolically the starvation of a nation as a whole, given not only the deadly effects of famine, but also its prominent place in nationalist polemics and literatures?[31] Certainly, the hunger strike or the fast might have provoked a recollection of famine, but the evidence, be it written or oral, is elusive.[32] Cormac O'Grada observes that relatives of the victims of the Great Famine in Ireland (1845–50) were reluctant to confess that a family member had died of starvation, though they would readily acknowledge that one had died of fever.[33] If, perhaps, death by starvation during the famine had been regarded as shameful, famine might not have had any bearing upon the public's understanding of a hunger strike that was regarded as courageous. Or perhaps contemporaries did not associate hunger in protest with famine because they attributed famine to poverty or environmental crisis.[34] This is unlikely. Irish and Indian nationalists asserted vehemently that famines had been exacerbated, if not caused, by British laws and policies. They saw a "conjugation of natural and man-made plagues," as Mike Davis puts it.[35]

Like famines, hunger strikes and fasts reflected a ruthless legality, but only insofar as laws and official policies provoked a person to *choose* to starve and then governed the conditions of her or his protest. So why were those on hunger strike or fast seldom if ever likened explicitly to the victims of Ireland's Great Famine or India's several "late Victorian holocausts" or the Great Bengal Famine of 1943?[36] In the case of India, at least, it is possible that major differences between regional identities, including differences between languages and religions, prevented Gujaratis in the west of the subcontinent, for example, from associating a local nationalist's fast with a famine suffered by Bengalis in the east. Or perhaps it was simply a matter of goals. The famished wanted to eat in order to survive; those on hunger strike or fast wanted to make a point for which they were prepared to starve and die.

Is it possible that memories of past famines in Ireland and India informed how British officials or the British public perceived acts hunger in protest? This is a knottier question. Images of famished Irish and Indian bodies played into the paternalistic, imperial narrative that portrayed subject peoples as generally inferior and unable to care for themselves. Skeleton-gaunt bodies were signs of contemptible weakness and compelling need, mutely entreating the British to rule as a humanitarian act. As Zahid Chaudhary observes of photographs of famine victims in nineteenth-century India: "Humanitarian aid can dispense help to suffering populations, but it also brings these populations under the sway of imperialist power, and the darker side of sympathy remains the secret sharer of contemporary liberalism."[37] Against the backdrop of famine, self-starvation in British custody may have struck some Britons as historically sardonic, an insult to their faith in their own good deeds. While there is no reference to memories of famine in British records of Irish and Indian hunger strikes and fasts, there is reason to believe, as discussed below, that self-starvation exposed a failure of British duty—specifically, a failure of the new duty to feed.

CHOOSING HUNGER

In the midst of rebellion, activists themselves did not always frame their specific protests in historical or even ideological terms. This was brought home to me in 2004, when I spoke with an Indian freedom fighter, Gunvantrai Purohit, a Gujarati, about his experience of a twelve-day fast in British custody during a satyagraha campaign in Rajkot in 1939–40. Purohit, a devoted Gandhian, undertook the fast to protest against inhumane prison conditions. I asked him if it had concerned him, at the time of his fast, that militant nationalists in Bengal had recently conducted widely publicized mass hunger strikes, and that his own fast might therefore have been mistaken for a militant act by the authorities or the public. With a wave of his hand, Purohit stated simply, "This didn't matter." What had mattered to him was the necessity of protest. Self-starvation had been the only means of protest available to him. Fasting was, as Gandhi had observed, the last weapon.

Several years later, in 2010, I asked the South African anti-apartheid activist Ahmed Kathrada about the first hunger strikes undertaken by him and his fellow prisoners on Robben Island under South Africa's apartheid regime in the mid-1960s. I asked, "Whose idea was it [to hunger strike], and did you have an international model or inspiration in mind?" Kathrada said that it had been a "group decision" and that there had been no particular model that he could recall. He conjectured that if there had been a specific inspiration, it had probably been Gandhi. I then asked him a question like the one that I had put to Purohit: If the inspiration had been Gandhi, did Kathrada see anything problematic about militants, such as he and his comrades were then, employing the tactic of a pacifist? He dismissed the question and observed that the hunger strike was "a universal form of prison protest."

It is instructive that Purohit and Kathrada treated the ideological fine points of their protests as secondary concerns, and that their common goal in starving was immediate relief from oppressive prison conditions, not the long-term realization of vaunted ideals. Scholars have tended to treat hunger in protest as an ideological and symbolic act intended to win control over law and governance. From this standpoint, the tactic may appear ineffective, if not futile. The tactic has rarely driven states to complete capitulation. The Irish republican Bobby Sands and nine of his comrades died on hunger strike in prison in Northern Ireland in 1981 without securing the British government's recognition of their political prisoner status. The hunger strike by hundreds of Chinese student civil rights activists in Tiananmen Square in the spring of 1989 did not win democratic reforms and did not deter the infamous crackdown by the Chinese government. Saddam Hussein's hunger strike in custody, following the second Iraq war, did not forestall his trial and eventual execution in 2006. To date, hunger strikes by inmates in the US detention center at Guantanamo Bay, Cuba, have resulted in no reported reforms or releases.[38] The tactic of hunger in protest has not, however, been without historical power. One might argue that some ostensibly failed hunger strikes and fasts, such as the 1981 Irish hunger strike, set the stage for subsequent political dialogue and reform. More to the point, I illuminate in this study a striking consensus among government officials—British, Irish, and Indian alike—that a concession to hunger strikers seeking release could effectively break the rule of law. The stakes of hunger striking were dangerously high for both prisoners and the governments that held them.

The problem with treating hunger strikes and fasts as means to move states is that this approach illuminates only the ideological and symbolic power of these protests, without acknowledging their critical instrumentality. An act of hunger in protest can be immensely disruptive within a prison system, a complex institution dependent upon fixed schedules, procedures, regulations, and the work of staff with standard, full-time duties of which caring for hunger strikers is not one.

A hunger strike or fast by even a small number of prisoners could place intense and sometimes debilitating pressure upon the workings of a prison. This pressure was brought to bear upon not only the institution, but also individual staff members and officials who feared that the starvation of a prisoner in their care might leave them open to punishment, even prosecution for manslaughter. For these reasons, starvation was often effective in securing changes in prison conditions, though it may not have moved governments to change policies or to concede power.[39] Of course, any successful use of starvation depended on prison staff and officials bearing professional and legal responsibility for the prisoner's life, or, to put it simply, caring. For all the brutality of the British imperial regime, it had a liberal conscience that dissidents hungered to exploit.

HUNGER AND THE NEW DUTY TO FEED

Given the long history of religious fasting and the long history of fasting as a means to settle disputes, why did hunger proliferate internationally as a tactic of protest after the early twentieth century? As James Vernon has observed, British suffragettes began hunger striking at the same time that Britons were changing their views on both hunger and their government's duties to insure the health of domestic and imperial subjects. Earlier in the nineteenth century, the growing British middle classes, the press, and government officials saw the hungry as idle, immoral subjects who had brought hunger upon themselves. The hungry poor, especially, were cast as the architects of their own misery, incapable of the moral restraint necessary to check their birth rate, which produced too many mouths to feed.[40] British evangelical Protestants were apt to regard Catholics, and particularly Irish Catholics, in these same terms. This perception, in combination with faith in the beneficent power of free trade, deterred the British government from aggressively attempting to relieve victims of the Great Famine in Ireland in the 1840s. Likewise, the British government made only limited efforts to relieve victims of famine in India, who, like the Irish, were deemed deserving of their fate.[41]

In the second half of the nineteenth century, however, several factors contributed to a new status for the hungry in the eyes of Britons.[42] Substantial advances in agricultural productivity since the eighteenth century had increased the caloric intake of the poor; lethal diseases such as plague had disappeared, while public health programs reduced exposure to the diseases that remained, leaving more poor people adequately, if not robustly, nourished for work.[43] Malnutrition among the majority of Britons was reduced, and chronic hunger became less common and therefore less acceptable in the next century. At the same time, social reformers and journalists promoted a decidedly sympathetic public portrait of hungry people at home and abroad, displaying the victims' humanity and desire for improvement. This tapped into a broader evangelical project of social reform that extended responsibility for individual hardship and even criminality to civil society and the state, which had allegedly perpetuated the systemic inequity and injustice that had left the poor with few moral paths to survival, let alone improvement. When in 1851 the "ragged school" founder and children's advocate Mary Carpenter published her influential book, *Reformatory Schools for Children of the Dangerous and Perishing Classes, and for Juvenile Offenders*, she, like other reformers, charged that poor children were dangerous and perishing not because of their intrinsic moral failing, but because of neglect, which civil society and the state had a Christian duty to remedy.[44] Toward this end, in what Boyd Hilton has called the age of atonement, the British parliament passed the Youthful Offenders Act in 1854.[45]

Advocates of the hungry, and the hungry themselves, turned to the government for relief in the heyday of late Victorian liberalism. According to Vernon, "Hunger was one of the core dilemmas of British liberalism that helped determine where the boundaries would be drawn between the market and the state, the subject and the citizen, the individual and the collective, the nation and the empire."[46] Yet the transition from a laissez-faire approach to famine in Ireland and India to more systematic government support and intervention was a slow, deadly process. When the west of Ireland experienced a "near famine" in 1879—due to a confluence of events including heavy rains that ruined that year's potato crop—the government cautiously offered a greater measure of direct assistance and loans than it had done in the 1840s, but it still left the lion's share of relief work to philanthropic organizations based in Britain, Ireland, and the United States.[47] In tragic contrast, when India experienced a major famine in 1876–78, the government responded with dogmatic faith in free trade and self-help, but without significant support from private philanthropists. Millions perished. In response, the government formed a Famine Commission, which issued a report in 1880 that generally endorsed the current policy. Yet this report included a pointed minute of dissent. This minute conveyed unprecedented criticism of laissez-faire famine policy and charged that the government, having a fundamental duty to save life, should intervene to revive local Indian economies in the absence of effective private enterprise.[48] The commission's report was put to actual effect when the commission's secretary subsequently used it in drafting the first of the Indian famine codes, which included government procedures for evaluating and responding to famine with relief services. The codes initiated more thorough attention to the nutritional needs of famine victims, giving preference to the able-bodied who could still work for what was called a living wage. "This wage [was] based," as one critic later observed, "upon the price of the cheapest food grain and the physiological minimum of nutriment necessary for health."[49] This particular period of famine in Ireland and India appears to have played a pivotal role in what Peter Gray describes as "a changing centre of gravity in British liberal thinking about famine policy in the second half of the nineteenth century."[50]

"THE WOLF AT THE DOOR."

FIGURE 1. "The Wolf at the Door," *Punch*, 18 January 1879. Reproduced by permission of *Punch* magazine.

The British liberal conscience was piqued by sympathetic portraits of famine-stricken Indians and Irish and by harrowing reports of their suffering. There was a vague sense that something should be done. In the immediate aftermath of India's devastating famine and in view of the threat of famine in Ireland in 1879, a cartoon published in *Punch* portrayed Britannia, symbol of the British nation, saving a poor, rural Irish family from starvation, the figurative wolf at the door (figure 1). In reality, the Conservative government of Prime Minister Benjamin Disraeli played only a limited role in relief efforts, for which it paid no punitive, political price. When the Liberals under the leadership of William Gladstone crushed the Conservatives in the general election of 1880, they did so by condemning Disraeli for his foreign policy and by exploiting a weak domestic economy exacerbated by a historically bad harvest in Britain in 1879, which had been caused by the same weather that contributed to Ireland's "near famine." References to Irish and Indian victims of famine had no place on the hustings, as the Irish and Indians themselves took note.

Irish and Indian intellectuals and politicians charged that the British imperial economy was literally starving their peoples of resources. The Irish developed a multifaceted historical and literary genre of criticism along these lines, built upon the writings of the Irish journalist and nationalist John Mitchel during and after the Great Famine.[51] In the late nineteenth and early twentieth centuries, Irish nationalist speakers and writers decried Queen Victoria as the "Famine Queen." In 1900 Maud Gonne, a prominent republican who later conducted a three-week hunger strike, published an essay entitled "The Famine Queen" during a visit by Queen Victoria to Dublin. Gonne speculated that Victoria herself had been marked by the Great Famine, which had reached its deadly zenith in 1847, the tenth year of her reign. "For after all," Gonne observed, "she is a woman, and however vile and selfish and pitiless her soul may be, she must sometimes tremble as death approaches when she thinks of the countless Irish mothers who, sheltering under the cloudy Irish sky, watching their starving little ones, have cursed her before they died."[52] The newspaper in which the article appeared, the *United Irishman*, was suppressed by the British government.[53]

In more restrained terms, after the 1860s, the Indian merchant and politician Dadabhai Naoroji promoted his so-called drain theory to explain how Britain systematically drained India of its wealth, all the while avowing its duties to the Indian people. A co-founder of the Indian National Congress in 1885, and the first South Asian to serve as a member of the British Parliament between 1892 and 1895, Naoroji brought his criticism into full focus in the book *Poverty and Un-British Rule in India*, published in 1901. It is no coincidence that in this same period the deprivation of India also found new, symbolic expression. The modern goddess of the Indian nation, *Bharat Mata* (Mother India), born of Bankim Chandra Chattopadhyay's novel *Anandamath, or the Sacred Brotherhood* in the late nineteenth century, was originally portrayed as a famished victim of foreign rule. As the story goes, the mother would be restored by the sacrifices of her devoted sons, whom she would then empower to seize control of the state and win independence.

British government officials recognized that famines and man-made food shortages alike could have political consequences. The Irish famine of 1879 triggered the Irish Land War, which lasted until 1882 and resulted in a combination of British coercion and British concessions of tenants' rights that set the stage for Prime Minister Gladstone's first Irish home rule bill in 1886. In India, thirty years later, the British government responded to the exigencies of the First World War with increased taxes and new trade policies that sustained the Indian army abroad at the terrible expense of Indians at home. Most Indians struggled through the war under the burdens of dramatic inflation and stagnant wages. According to Sumit Sarkar, "The 'drain of wealth' took on during the war years the character of a massive plunder of Indian human and material resources."[54] Historians dwell upon the increasing influence of nationalist political parties during the war, parties that played central roles in securing postwar constitutional reforms that began the subsequent, halting extension of Indian representation in government. Yet it is noteworthy that nationalist politics gained traction in India in the midst of wartime hardship. It was during poor harvests and food riots across the country in 1918–19 that initial constitutional reforms came to fruition and that popular protest against repressive postwar British measures developed.[55] Although postwar mass nationalism arose in India for more than economic reasons, suffice it to say that Indians' hunger for swaraj was made more acute by their hunger.

By the twentieth century, explains Vernon, "in both metropolitan and colonial settings the effectiveness of government [came] to be measured by the absence . . . of hunger and famine."[56] This was no modest proposal. In the United Kingdom, the government initiated new school meal programs, as well as milk allotments to children, pregnant women, and new mothers. In the empire, there was not a comparable investment in the health and welfare of civil societies, given the imperial priorities of security and profit making, but there was a shift in principle toward a duty to feed. One sees this humanitarian ethos reflected in Kipling's "The White Man's Burden" (1899). The third stanza begins:

> Take up the White Man's burden—
> The savage wars of peace—
> Fill full the mouth of Famine
> And bid the sickness cease.

This poem was published several months before Gonne condemned Victoria as the Famine Queen.

As the British government assumed a new duty to feed, and acted upon this duty at home, nationalists in both Ireland and India represented their people's literal or figurative starvation as proof of Britain's administrative and moral failure. In a letter to the governor-general of India, Lord Irwin, in March 1930, Gandhi demanded major administrative reforms and asserted, "If India is to live as a nation, if the slow death by starvation of her people is to stop, some remedy must be found for immediate relief. . . . Great Britain would defend her Indian commerce and interests by all the forces at her command. India must consequently evolve force enough to free herself from that embrace of death."[57] These were heavily loaded terms, for in the previous week the Indian National Congress had declared 26 January to be India's Independence Day.[58] An elaboration upon Gandhi's message to Irwin is found in a broadsheet published in Calcutta in this period (figure 2). Lord Irwin is pictured standing in England, reaching aggressively to take food from an Indian family, while the secretary of state for India, William Wedgwood Benn, looks on as the British nation's standard bearer. While Irwin and Benn are simply located in a place, England phonetically spelled, the Indian family is located in a place and a time: *Bharatavarsha*, an ancient term for India,

FIGURE 2. "*Bharat ki lut*" (The plunder of India), ca. 1930, Oriental and India Office Collection, British Library, PP Hin F56. Reproduced by permission of the British Library.

land of the heroic prince Bharata of the epic the *Mahabharata*. The image asserts that the once great land and its people have been brought low by the hand of England, a representation of the drain theory in epic scale.[59] Surrounding the image are numerous quotations by British liberals, in both English and Hindi, testifying to Britain's exploitation of India, or—as the title of the image puts it—"the plunder of India" (Bharat ki lut).[60]

As previously observed, nationalist prisoners on hunger strike or fast did not liken themselves to famine victims. Still, the new politics of hunger informed the significance of their starvation, having made hunger a political liability. Hunger weakened the moral authority of the government and thus morally empowered those who chose to endure hunger to display the government's unjust rule.

THE BOOK'S COURSE AND ITS SOURCES

Women and men of different cultures and faiths in Britain, Ireland, and India hungered against their subjugation by a liberal British regime, which, they charged, was willfully deaf to their voices. They entered upon starvation without science, ignorant of what little medical research existed on the subject, guided by hearsay, fearful imaginings, and cultural conjecture on the sources and limits of human endurance. It took courage, to be sure. Strategic representations of gender and religion played the most consistently important roles in heightening the power of hunger strikes and fasts as critiques of the ostensibly paternalistic state as an illiberal state of silence. When British and Irish suffragettes took up the "Russian method," they likened the Liberal government of Prime Minister Herbert Asquith to Russia's despotic czarist regime through hunger strikes and forcible feedings, which, they asserted, displayed the coercive power upon which male suffrage and women's "virtual representation" by men depended. They represented the hunger strike as a decidedly feminine and spiritual tactic of protest, empowered by women's special capacity and will to sacrifice. In Ireland female and male republicans represented the hunger strike in explicit terms of Catholicism, binding themselves in a shared sacrifice that unfortunately excluded Ireland's Protestant minority and only intensified mutual accusations of betrayal when republicanism broke into civil war. In India hunger in protest developed from both international and domestic sources, which together paid homage to Mother India, a Hindu goddess whose new national temple, sanctified by the blood of sons, dangerously excluded Muslims. Through it all, imperial and national states alike found hunger strikes and fasts notoriously difficult to manage. Political officials and prison staff struggled against starving inmates and attempted to reconcile extraordinary duties with the common law. The terms of the protests in Britain, Ireland, and India were differentiated by culture and politics, but the experiences of those managing hunger strikes and fasts had much in common, as they do to this day. States have yet to find a lasting answer to hunger in protest, as the process of refraction and adaptation continues, as women and men take up the last weapon.

Before proceeding to the main body of the book, a brief word on sources: In order to illuminate hunger strikes and fasts as not only metaphors and symbols, but also processes, I have relied largely on archival, unpublished sources that shed light on the intimate experiences of prisoners and prison staff and officials. These sources, located in Britain, Ireland, and India, are uneven in coverage. One catches numerous glimpses of acts of hunger in protest, but seldom is there enough information with which to create comprehensive portraits of activists and officials, or accounts of the public's responses, or even, in most cases, a basic chronology of events. Most of the women and men who resorted to the hunger strike or the fast were persons of local or regional, not national, reputation. Their biographies do not appear in the archival record, though they are remembered by their families and the descendants of comrades and enemies. The great majority of hunger strikes and fasts occurred in prisons or otherwise in official custody, often without any publicity, and lasted for several hours or a few days. Many acts of hunger in protest were not undertaken to achieve explicit political goals but instead to redress specific grievances held, not uncommonly, by prisoners with no previous record of political offense. So in most cases of hunger in protest we have only cursory references in prison documents, recorded by staff for whom the hunger strike or the fast was a burden, not a cause.[61] A small number of cases are famous, such as those of MacSwiney, Gandhi, the Indian revolutionary Bhagat Singh, and British and Irish suffragettes such as Emmeline Pankhurst and Hanna Sheehy Skeffington. The records of these protests are voluminous, and consequently they have already attracted scholarly attention. In this book, I combine the famous and the obscure, an ungainly combination with a virtue. The virtue is that a study of the famous and the obscure represents the diversity of hunger in protest, and it resituates the famous in a revealing context.

The suffragette Lady Constance Lytton grasped the importance of this perspective on the famous and the obscure in 1909 after she was incarcerated for protesting against the forcible feeding of suffragette prisoners on hunger strike. She resented the preferential treatment that she then received in prison due to her aristocratic status, particularly when the prison medical officer released her soon after she began her own hunger strike for fear that her heart might not bear the strain. Lytton returned to prison disguised as a working-class woman, a seamstress, alias Jane Wharton. Her published accounts of her subsequent treatment as a common prisoner, and especially her experience of forcible feeding on eight occasions, created a public scandal joined by supporters and detractors alike.[62] Lytton's point was simple: British justice was not blind, and therefore it was not just. Some prisoners enjoyed privileges that others did not, though they were guilty of the same offenses. This has much to do with our understanding of acts of hunger in protest and how such acts corresponded one to the other, or not. Situating privileged protesters in the context of their common comrades enables us to look past the status of icons and consider whose experience was the rule or the exception. To take two more conspicuous examples: MacSwiney's hunger strike of 1920 and Gandhi's many fasts have been treated as the quintessential acts of hunger in protest in the Irish and Indian nationalist movements of their eras. Yet these protests were anomalies in most respects, which is why, as we shall see, British government officials treated each of these men as "a special case." In their torturous journeys, MacSwiney and Gandhi, like Lytton, were better off than most who hungered toward the same ends.

1

Knowing Starvation

Science and Strange Stories

Mohandas Gandhi would, if necessary, "fast unto death." So he declared before beginning what came to be known as his "epic fast" on 20 September 1932 in the Yerawada Central Jail in Pune, in the Bombay Presidency of British India, now in the western Indian state of Maharashtra. He fasted against the British government's decision to reserve seats in provincial Indian legislatures for *dalits*, then known to the general public as "untouchables," to the government as the "depressed classes," and to Gandhi as *harijans* (children of God). Having previously divided Indian electorates between Hindu and Muslim voting blocs, the government intended to carve out a so-called communal award for dalits from the Hindu bloc. Gandhi charged that the government would use this measure to advance its traditional strategy of divide and rule, this time at Hindus' particular expense. The measure had the full support of Dr. Bhimrao Ambedkar, the dalits' political leader, who looked skeptically on imperialists and nationalists alike, finding that neither had a principled interest or practical stake in relieving the degradation of dalits in Indian society. To his mind, the communal award was the only way for his people to insure their own civil rights and welfare through direct political representation. Multiparty talks aimed at resolving Gandhi's and Ambedkar's differences reached an impasse. Gandhi chose to fast until either the impasse or his body broke.

Gandhi's secretary, Pyarelal Nayyar, recalled, "Great anxiety was felt when Gandhiji commenced his fast whether he would be able to stand the physical strain of it for any length of time."[1] Gandhi was sixty-three years old. Nayyar had worried, "He was not the same man as he was when he undertook his twenty-one days' fast at Delhi in 1924 [when he was 55, fasting for Hindu-Muslim unity]."[2] The doctors in attendance watched Gandhi with increasing anxiety. There had been few physiological studies of voluntary starvation, and there were no consistent clinical protocols or diagnostic measures for starvation in India or elsewhere.[3] Even as the use of hunger in protest proliferated between the wars, medical knowledge lagged far behind, and most medical professionals treated starvation with poorly founded guesswork. Gandhi's doctors placed their diagnostic faith in analyses of urine samples, looking specifically for increases in acetone and urea. What troubled them most was not the measurable physiological process of starvation, however, but a prospective moment in time. It was the moment at which the patient would suddenly take a turn for the worse, the seemingly unpredictable point at which the patient entered the so-called danger zone, where death became imminent.

On the sixth day of Gandhi's fast, levels of both acetone and urea in his urine increased. The doctors reported ominously, "We are definitely of opinion that this portends entry into the danger zone." News of Gandhi's failing health alarmed not only his supporters, but also leading British officials and Indian legislators who worried about the political turmoil that his death would bring. Reference to the danger zone stoked their worry into fear. In response to a legislator's inquiry, Dr. M. D. Gilder explained, "The words 'Danger Zone' . . . we have used in this sense that Mahatmaji [Gandhi] had not got much fat reserve, he has used that up; and now he is living really on his muscles and apart from an accident like a sudden collapse or a stroke of paralysis that may intervene at any time, we are of the opinion that he has now entered into that stage of his illness where every day increases the danger and where, even if the fast is broken, some danger will still remain."[4] That same evening, all parties agreed to the terms of a compromise of which Gandhi approved. He broke his fast with a sip of citrus juice.

Before the Second World War, starvation was mysterious. The dread of starvation as an inscrutable, fickle killer was shared by all, whether one hungered by accident or design, or whether one cared for the hungry as a humanitarian, missionary, an agent of government, or even as a physician. People in Great Britain, Ireland, and India perceived starvation in ways little different from those of their distant ancestors. Meanwhile, after the early twentieth century, nutritional science developed rapidly and won the confidence of governments, which incorporated it into domestic, foreign, and imperial policies, especially during and after the First World War.[5] Nutritional scientists initially conceived of nutrition as a thermodynamic process. This understanding then gave way after the 1920s to a conception of nutrition based on biochemistry and vitamins, prompting both researchers and policy makers to advocate not only the energy value of food, but also dietary balance—the now familiar "square meal."[6]

None of this helped Gandhi's doctors, however. Nutritional science had little to say about starvation, a fact that Francis Benedict, director of the Carnegie Nutrition Laboratory in Boston, had attributed "to the difficulty of securing willing human subjects."[7] Dr. Gilder and his colleagues therefore had little confidence in their clinical understanding of Gandhi's starvation. The "danger zone" was a fearful measure of their ignorance. It lay somewhere between life and death, a space willingly occupied only by those with transcendent courage or holy foolishness. This certainly played to the advantage of Gandhi, the Mahatma, the "great soul."[8]

In recounting the science and strange stories of starvation in the first half of the twentieth century, this chapter offers perspective on why prison officials responded in the ways that they did to hunger strikes and fasts, and what starving prisoners believed was happening to their bodies. Prison medical officers, those primarily responsible for prisoners' health, constituted an official transimperial network, operating with common, if wanting, medical knowledge. This network was overlaid by the informal network of prisoners who did their best to twist and skew prison regulations and the medical arts toward their goals. Both parties knew where starvation would ultimately end, but neither knew precisely when, or even how, they would arrive on the far side of the danger zone. It seemed always close, perhaps only days beyond the last meal, despite much anecdotal evidence to the contrary. This evidence was to be found in city slums, fields of famine, the so-called life reform movement, as well as prison cells. There was apparently no assurance that the weeks- or months-long endurance of one starving person provided a useful measure of the potential endurance of others who followed, particularly if those others came from more polite society. As medicine afforded no certainties about starvation, acts of hunger in protest were commonly understood as much more than physiological experiences and acts of resistance; they were spiritual trials and testimonies of faith, mordants that fixed cultures of sacrifice in the fabric of the nation.

MEDICAL RESEARCH ON STARVATION

Research on the effects of starvation on metabolism began in 1825 with a study of the urea output of an insane patient who fasted for eighteen days. Chemists and physiologists then conducted intermittent studies on fasting humans and numerous studies of starving animals until the late nineteenth and early twentieth centuries, when a series of studies examined the metabolisms and physiologies of individual "hunger artists" who performed public fasts for profit and fame.[9] The most significant of these studies employed calorimetric technologies and monitored subjects in controlled laboratory environments. The Italian hunger artist Giovanni Succi participated in seven such experiments, including a landmark study in Florence, Italy, in 1890.[10] Yet at the outset of the twentieth century, no studies of any consequence had examined subjects of involuntary starvation, despite the opportunities presented by desperate poverty in the United Kingdom and famines in Ireland and India. There had been influential dietary studies of the British poor, and of prisoners and soldiers in the United Kingdom and India, but these mainly addressed the effects of undernutrition on labor productivity and socioeconomic stability.[11] The recognition of undernutrition as a measure of general poverty, not just as an obstacle to economic development, was established by Seebohm Rowntree in his study of the working class in York, *Poverty: A Study of Town Life*, published in 1901. Following the revelation that many British men were physically unfit for service in the second South African War (1899–1902), undernutrition became a matter of national security. The British government established the Inter-Departmental Committee on Physical Deterioration, which issued a report in 1904 that laid the groundwork for new public health programs, including free school meals to improve the nutrition of British children.[12] None of these governmental projects, however, addressed the metabolic or physiological processes, or the clinical symptoms, of starvation.

Nutritional scientists in the early twentieth century regarded protein as the most important nutrient. They accordingly treated starvation as fundamentally a protein deficiency.[13] They believed that the body more efficiently digested animal proteins than proteins from grains (gluten) and green vegetables (albumen).[14] Researchers over the next twenty years came to understand that there was no distinction to be drawn between animal and vegetable proteins, but they, and physicians generally, maintained a strong preference for animal protein in feeding starving people.[15] They recognized that carbohydrates and fats were mainly responsible for the body's production of heat and energy, but they believed that only protein could restore tissue lost in starvation. They understood, furthermore, that in the long run even a protein-rich diet had to be replaced by a properly proportioned "mixed diet" that included the other three recognized groups of essential nutrients: carbohydrates, fats, and minerals. Vitamins and amino acids had not yet been recognized as essential nutrients, though research on both was well under way. Between 1910 and 1941, scientists would isolate the thirteen vitamins that we know today, and in the 1930s they would determine the nine amino acids essential to human health. In 1907, however, Carl von Noorden, a German physician and professor of medicine at the University of Vienna, could observe that there were still no studies that explained exactly why a "mixed diet" was critical to health, but, he noted, "simple clinical experience forms a sufficient guide."[16]

The most widely acknowledged tenets of early nutritional science are found in Robert Hutchison's *Food and the Principles of Dietetics*, which, after its publication in 1900, went through ten editions and was reprinted twenty times with periodic revisions by 1950. Hutchison, a physician at the London Hospital, compared the body to a steam engine: "The building material of food corresponds to the metal of which the engine is constructed, the energy-producers to the fuel which is used to heat the boiler. Where the body differs from the engine is that it is able to use part of the material of its construction (proteid) [protein] for fuel also."[17] He divided nutrients into two categories: organic and inorganic. In the former category, he placed nitrogenous nutrients, proteins and albuminoids, and non-nitrogenous nutrients, carbohydrates and fats. In the latter category, he placed minerals and water. Tissue formation depended on the combination of proteins, "mineral matters," and water. "Work and heat" were produced by proteins, albuminoids, carbohydrates, fats, and "maybe" mineral matters and water.[18] As proteins could fulfill both functions of food, Hutchison hailed their "physiological omnipotence."[19]

Hutchison's description of the body as a potentially self-consuming engine and his description of its nutritional fuel informed the limited scientific understandings of the metabolism and physiology of starvation through the 1930s. Researchers understood that the catabolism—that is, destructive metabolism—of carbohydrates or glycogen precedes the catabolism of protein in the absence of ingested food and that the store of carbohydrates or glycogen is generally sufficient for one to two weeks, after which the body continues to burn fat and protein as necessary.[20] They had observed that the breakdown of fat produces acetone bodies, which are excreted in measurable quantities by the kidneys and detectable in the smell of a fasting person's breath.[21] They understood that the breakdown of protein increases the excretion of nitrogen, and particularly urea, through the kidneys.[22] Studies further suggested that the human body could regulate its metabolism in response to either prolonged undernutrition or starvation.[23] The body presumably increased protein catabolism only after its fat stores were exhausted, but there were no long-term studies of humans to confirm this.[24] Researchers recognized that advanced starvation placed excessive strain upon the heart, leading them to conclude that the most common, immediate cause of death by starvation was heart failure.[25] They understood that the heart lost mass in response to strain and deprivation as starvation progressed, and they became concerned when variable pulse rates revealed "irritability of the heart."[26] This explains, in part, why prison medical officers worried intensely after 1909 that British and Irish suffragette hunger strikers might suffer heart attacks in only a matter of days.

Medical research did not justify this fear of the rapid demise of starving women. Prior to the 1920s, there were only two studies of the effects of long-term fasting on women; the subject of each study was a hunger artist. The first of these fasts, in June 1905, lasted fourteen days; the second, in March 1906, fifteen days. Both studies focused on the analysis of urine samples, especially nitrogen levels.[27] These studies did not indicate that fasting would precipitate heart attacks. The researchers observed that women lost 20 to 30 percent less nitrogen than men during the early stages of starvation, probably due to their greater percentage of fat, but they did not then speculate that women were likely to endure starvation longer than men.[28] Despite the dangers of fasting, researchers generally agreed that after prolonged fasts under controlled circumstances their subjects, whether women or men, experienced no long-term problems. Starving subjects could look forward to returning to normal health, if they did not first die of heart failure.[29]

Researchers recognized that the clinical symptoms of starvation developed in stages. In the first week, there were stomach pains, headaches, fatigue, and dizziness. Also, the tongue became furred, which they regarded as a general sign of declining health. Throughout the process of starvation, the subject would lose weight, but more quickly in the beginning than later, due to the initial loss of water and fat. After the second week, the subject experienced further fatigue and was prone to fainting spells. The skin became waxen and blotchy, and the blood pressure tended to drop. The subject's temperature also tended to drop, which researchers attributed to the body exhausting its fat. Starving people commonly complained of cold, increasingly after the second week, and it was clear that a cold environment worsened their condition. In the third and fourth week, while the symptoms above intensified, subjects began to lose motor control, muscles began to atrophy, and eyesight began to deteriorate. Although prior to the Second World War researchers had not run controlled experiments of more than about a month in duration, they knew that after the fourth week a starving subject would develop scurvy, if the subject had not done so already, unless he or she drank citrus juice, a prophylactic proven in practice long before the isolation of vitamin C and the discovery of its effects after 1928. All researchers recognized that starving people were likely to suffer psychological difficulties, most commonly depression. They observed that the starving human body did everything in its power to avoid compromising the brain and nervous system. Indeed, some hunger strikers remained lucid for several weeks. Even after more than seventy days on hunger strike in a British prison in 1920, the Irish republican Terence MacSwiney could reject offers of food as he slipped in and out of consciousness. Finally, researchers recognized that the process of breaking a long-term fast could be fraught with physical and psychological difficulties. At the conclusion of a study at the Carnegie Nutrition Laboratory in 1912, Agostino Levanzin broke a thirty-one-day fast in high spirits and apparent sound health, under the attentive care of Benedict and his staff, and with an initial diet of lemons, oranges, honey, and grape juice. Soon, however, he experienced severe colic and vomiting and "appeared to be utterly wretched and weak." His digestive problems continued for four days, aggravated by depressed and "mentally unbalanced" behavior, according to Benedict.[30]

STARVING FOR PROFIT AND HEALTH

At the same time that medical researchers examined starvation as a problem to be solved, there was no shortage of people who regarded long-term fasting as either a miraculous achievement or a panacea. For centuries Britain and Ireland had known of "fasting maidens" who allegedly survived for months or years with virtually no food but with an abundant faith in God.[31] There were also less-spiritual acts of starvation. In 1869 there was the controversial case of Sarah Jacobs, the "Welsh

Fasting Girl," whose parents turned a handsome profit on visitors to the bedside of their child "marvel," who apparently ate nothing. The British medical profession was skeptical of Jacobs, so it effectively compelled the parents to permit a team of doctors and nurses to watch the child and confirm or disprove her claim that she lived without eating. After seven days under watch, having consumed neither food nor water, the child died. This tragic revelation of fraud, covered extensively in the British media and in the *British Medical Journal*, appears to have curtailed the tradition of fasting maidens, at least in the United Kingdom, but it did not bring a complete end to the "human skeletons" of freak shows or the sporadic performances of hunger artists.[32] The hunger artist Succi conducted a fast for forty days in March and April 1890 at the Westminster Aquarium, watched day and night to insure that he lived on nothing but water and air. *The Times* observed that spectators paid a "very high charge" to attend the reception at which Succi sat in evening dress at a table on stage and ate "a little soup and warm water with a digestive mixture."[33] Human skeletons and hunger artists declined in popularity after the turn of the century, all but disappearing after the 1920s. Franz Kafka's short story "A Hunger Artist," published in 1922, concludes with the emaciated, dying artist alone in a cage, forgotten by his audience. It might be read as a representation of the waning days of such morbid spectacle. The performances of hunger artists had nonetheless provided the European public with markers of the outer limits of human starvation—approximately forty days, in imitation of Christ.[34]

Hunger striking in Britain and Ireland developed at the same time that "life reformers" were encouraging Britons to achieve health and beauty through non-medical, "natural" practices including vegetarianism, skin care, breathing exercises, meditation, and fasting. This movement, emanating mainly from London, was part of a broader reaction against the cramped, stifling conditions of urban life, the costly chimera of consumer culture, and anxieties over international and imperial competition. As Ina Zweiniger-Bargielowska demonstrates, the quest for "life reform" extended from the more prosperous working-class people to the middle class and appealed to both men and women. Fasting was generally practiced by male life reformers, who associated the requisite self-discipline with masculine strength and virility. Zweiniger-Bargielowska further observes that the positive masculine connotations of fasting existed alongside a contemporary "remapping of women's rejection of food as a mental disorder or disease."[35] While critics of suffragette hunger strikers exploited this representation of mental instability to undermine the suffragettes' political legitimacy, as we will see in the next chapter, the life reform movement gathered and disseminated a great deal of information about fasting on the bases of personal experiences and studies by its leading figures, who typically regarded a healthy diet and fasting as complementary.

In April 1910, the American writer Upton Sinclair, author of the novel *The Jungle* (1906), published an essay on fasting in the British periodical *Contemporary*

Review, reflecting upon his recent experience of several fasts, the longest of which had lasted for twelve days. In the following year, he published a book, *The Fasting Cure*, in which he declared, "The fast is to me the key to eternal youth, the secret of perfect and permanent health."[36] The fast was a means to purge the body of "superfluous nutriment" that had fermented in the body and become "a greater quantity of poisonous matter than the organs of elimination can handle." The secretions of this matter supposedly clogged the organs and blood vessels, causing headaches, rheumatism, arteriosclerosis, and paralysis, among other medical problems. Sinclair explained that this poisonous matter sapped the system and rendered the body susceptible to infection and diseases that ranged from colds to tuberculosis. Contrary to the metaphor of the body as an engine that must be fueled, Sinclair, in propagating the views of leading life reformers, asserted, "There is no greater delusion than that a person needs strength to fast. The weaker you are from disease, the more certain it is that you need to fast, the more certain it is that your body has not strength enough to digest the food you are taking into it." In other words, one's diet could exhaust the digestive system, and a fast could provide relief.[37] According to Sinclair, fasting could remedy both emaciation and obesity.[38] "As soon as the fast begins and the first hunger has been withstood," he explained, "the secretions cease, and the whole assimilative system, which takes so much of the energies of the body, goes out of business. The body then begins a sort of house-cleaning, which must be helped by an enema and a bath daily, and, above all, by copious water-drinking. The tongue becomes coated, the breath and the perspiration offensive; and this continues until the diseased matter has been entirely cast out, when the tongue clears and hunger reasserts itself in unmistakable form."[39] Having described the process of fasting over the course of twelve days, Sinclair advised the reader to take particular care upon ending a fast. One should drink only a little fruit juice and meat broth for two or three days, he suggested, then begin taking milk and slowly work one's way back to a normal diet.[40]

Sinclair's experience of fasting, and his firm belief in its many benefits, left him perplexed in the face of common notions that starvation could be a fast-moving killer. He informed his readers that the first danger in fasting was fear—whether one's own or that of family and friends—because this fear could break one's resolve before one achieved the fasting cure.[41] The British life reformer Hopton Hadley was likewise puzzled by fears for the survival of hunger-striking suffragettes in 1913 in the midst of controversy over forcible feeding. Writing in his periodical *Health and Strength*, Hadley observed that "fasting for much longer periods than any Suffragette has ever yet attempted has been adopted . . . for the BENEFIT of health." Men and women, he asserted, had undertaken "fast cures" of forty to fifty days, so it stood to reason that a suffragette hunger striker was likely to survive for up to two months. On these grounds, Hadley concluded that the forcible feeding of hunger strikers was unnecessary to maintain their health and was, therefore, "unspeakable torture."[42]

The medical profession responded to life reformers such as Sinclair and Hadley with derision. The *British Medical Journal* reviewed *The Fasting Cure* with open scorn. "The food fad embraces every variety from raw beefsteak to grape nuts," the journal observed. "Now there seems to be a tendency to simplify the problem by dispensing with food altogether, for longer or shorter periods of time." "Among the other qualities produced by fasting," the journal smugly remarked, "credulity would seem to occupy a prominent place."[43] Yet the reformers could not be ignored, because new dietary plans and natural cures were then finding a market in the United Kingdom. With a growing number of devotees behind them, the reformers derided the physicians for being misguided by the artifice of science and otherwise motivated by greed.

MANAGING THE DANGER ZONE

Until at least the 1930s, neither cutting-edge research in nutritional science nor the life reform movement exerted broad influence upon those who actually treated and cared for starving people. From the standpoint of healthcare providers, be they physicians or missionaries, critical questions remained unanswered, especially regarding the dreaded "danger zone." What was the percentage of weight loss that normally precipitated death? Researchers conceded that there was no mathematical formula with which to predict weight loss or to correlate weight loss to morbidity or mortality in prolonged fasts.[44] How long could a person normally survive starvation? Again, researchers had no definitive findings. They knew of cases in which people had lived for six to eight weeks without food, but they did not treat these cases as normative.[45] Life reformers such as Hadley speculated that the timeframe of survival was approximately two months, but this was hardly reassuring to those entrusted with and answerable for the lives of starving people. How, furthermore, should one feed a subject of advanced starvation who was in a precarious, fragile condition and prone to vomiting a normal diet? Researchers did not know the precise kind or amount of food necessary to maintain patients who were "markedly emaciated."[46] Moreover, in the absence of long-term empirical studies, they had little confidence in their knowledge of women's particular metabolic and physiological responses to long-term starvation.[47]

Although no one was sure how to anticipate the danger zone, experimentation on animals suggested that the temperature of a starving human might drop dramatically a few days before death.[48] Researchers generally agreed that the levels of acetone and urea in the subject's urine were probably the best indicators of imminent demise. The danger zone supposedly followed a decrease in acetone, indicating the exhaustion of fat stores, and an increase in urea, indicating the greater combustion of protein. It was then marked decisively by a drop in urea, which indicated the exhaustion of protein stores and the reduction of the patient to virtual skin and bones (you will recall that Gandhi's doctors were worried about the increase of both acetone and urea, rather than the decrease of the former and the increase of the latter). Beyond these questions and hypotheses were questions yet to be conceived or, perhaps, prioritized in the face of more obvious, pressing threats to starving subjects. The effects of starvation are determined in part, and critically, by the depletion of minerals, vitamins, electrolytes, and trace elements. The metabolic and physiological roles of these nutrients were not well understood until the 1920s and 1930s. Relevant medical research was then slow to inform the clinical diagnosis and treatment of starvation, especially advanced starvation, or the process of refeeding. For example, prison medical officers in the 1930s and 1940s conveyed no awareness that thiamine (vitamin B1) deficiency resulted in the neurological disorders and impaired eyesight that hunger strikers were apt to present after the third or fourth week, despite the fact that epidemiologists recognized that thiamine could remedy the neurological disorders and impaired eyesight associated with the disease beriberi, which was eventually determined to be a condition of vitamin deficiency.[49]

British officials who had managed famines in Ireland and India in the Victorian era had been far more interested in principles of political economy than nutritional science.[50] This began to change in India after 1880, when the British regime initiated a uniform famine code. Political economy remained paramount, but the government also began to use research on Indian prison diets to establish standard dietary scales for famine victims.[51] These dietary scales were determined by the availability of foods, the rules of religion and caste, and the government's determination to spend as little money as possible to provide famine victims with the minimal nutrition required for health—though in practice the goal or standard appears to have been survival. They reflected the influence of nutritional science. For example, in the scales issued by the government of India in 1883, the "full ration" provided protein through flour or rice, pulse, and vegetables. It provided carbohydrates mainly through flour or rice, and it provided fat through ghee (clarified butter) or oil. Salt was allotted to combine with protein to form tissue; it also enabled, in Hutchison's words, "the proper constitution of fluids."[52] The scales reflected proportional differences between the nutritional requirements of men, women, and children, and the different requirements of those who labored and those who were idle. While there were debates over the size of the rations, no one disputed that the dietary scales provided starving people with the four major, known nutrients: proteins, carbohydrates, fats, and minerals. The "penal diet" offered virtually no fat, and arguably inadequate protein and carbohydrates, but this was, as the name suggested, a punitive diet for allegedly able-bodied people who refused to work.

There was no clinical diagnosis involved in the administration of the dietary scales. Well into the twentieth century, British physicians, officials, missionaries, and journalists, whether in India or at home, addressed starvation not in clinical terms but as a look. This look was skeletal and "hollow-eyed"; it transformed its victims into "phantoms."[53] During a terrible famine in India in 1899–1900, Vaughn Nash, writing for the *Manchester Guardian*, recounted "a procession of the most pitiful phantoms, some thirty of them, starved beyond belief, their lips drawn back over their teeth, their eyes burning with fever in their deep-sunk sockets."[54] For all these recognizable symptoms of starvation, missionaries, who worked prominently in relief efforts in India, worried that they could not anticipate the danger zone, particularly in the many cases aggravated by diseases such as cholera and dysentery. The Reverend J. E. Robinson commented, "The best efforts prove futile in numberless instances."[55] In the absence of any quantitative, diagnostic measure of starvation, the danger zone appeared perpetually imminent. The Reverend J. E. Scott recalled, "The people suddenly fall in the midst of conversation, and rapidly sink."[56]

Likewise, prison medical officers and officials in charge of Irish republicans on hunger strike in prisons and hospitals twenty years later found it impossible to anticipate the danger zone with any precision. Less than a week into the hunger strike by Terence MacSwiney and eleven other Cork republicans in August 1920, a senior Irish civil servant in Dublin Castle, Mark Sturgis, wrote in his diary: "The hourly worry is still Hunger Strikers with Cork's Martyr [MacSwiney] at the top."[57] A week and a half later he wrote, "No hunger striker is yet dead. I can't believe they are not all being secretly fed but the danger is that this class of stunt brings out any constitutional weakness and one of 'em may die by mistake. A cipher telegram to-day from London demanded a full statement for issue after McS's death! But I—who bet 5/—to Winter that he would die—am really beginning to believe he won't."[58] Over a month later, senior medical officer Dr. G. B. Griffiths noted of MacSwiney: "As his condition has not deteriorated during the past few weeks as one would have expected, he is just as likely to live for several weeks longer as he was to survive the past few weeks."[59]

In Britain and Ireland, doctors in insane asylums had the most experience in treating starvation.[60] It was not uncommon for insane individuals to starve themselves. Doctors in asylums rarely worried about the danger zone, but instead employed forcible feeding, generally by stomach tube or sometimes in the form of a "nutrient enemata" administered by rectum.[61] Prison officials and medical officers also managed starvation, which they generally attributed to madness or depression. George Chesterton, former governor of the House of Correction at Cold Bath Fields between the 1830s and 1850s, recalled two "remarkable instances of fasting." In the first, a man "seized with a fit of moroseness" refused food for eleven days; in the second, a woman in an "obstinate mood" refused food for thirteen days. In neither case did prison staff resort to forcible feeding; instead, each prisoner suddenly resumed eating and, to Chesterton's eye, displayed "not the slightest ailment." These two cases prompted Chesterton to respond to future acts of hunger in protest with "well-feigned indifference."[62] In contrast, Arthur Griffiths recalled that when he was the deputy governor of Millbank Penitentiary in the early 1870s, "Obstinate refusal of food, and an attempt to die by starvation were of common occurrence, always to be overcome by forcible feeding."[63] Between 1904 and 1909 there were at least eighty-two men and thirty women forcibly fed in British prisons; one male prisoner was forcibly fed for over two years.[64] In most of these cases, the prisoners were deemed insane; in all of them the prisoners had been convicted of ordinary crimes. William Byrne, undersecretary of state for Ireland, later observed that the process of forcible feeding was "shocking only to those to whom the routine of asylum, prison or workhouse infirmary life is unfamiliar."[65]

The increasing use of hunger striking by prisoners convicted of political offenses in Britain after 1909 presented medical officers with a multifaceted dilemma. First, the treatment of many of these strikers was monitored closely by vocal supporters outside the prisons. Parliamentary advocates of the suffragettes provoked controversy by likening forcible feeding to torture, a simile supported by the life reformer Hadley. Second, many strikers were from the "respectable classes," and doctors proved far more reluctant to coerce them than working-class prisoners. It appears that prison medical officers were initially reluctant to feed middle-class and elite suffragettes due to a combination of factors. There was certainly social deference within a society strictly stratified by class. Also, there was an assumption that women of relative privilege were more fragile than working women. Their fragility was attributed to their domestic, sedentary lifestyles in which servants performed most manual labor and husbands grappled with harsh public realities. In the Victorian era, this fragility had become a quality of feminine beauty and a sign of the moral sensitivity essential to the idealized "angel in the house," who in the face of hardship or injustice was apt to collapse on cue into her man's arms or upon her "fainting couch." Prison medical officers saw suffragettes of this class as hothouse flowers transplanted into the cold world of politics and prisons at great risk. For these reasons, prison officials sometimes forbade the forcible feeding of particular female hunger strikers, prolonging starvation but eventuating early release.

Prison medical officers and officials in Britain, Ireland, and India were genuinely fearful of failing to anticipate the danger zone in caring for hunger strikers. This was largely due to their worry that the death of a striker in their care would open them to a charge of manslaughter.[66] Marion Wallace Dunlop, the first suffragette hunger striker, was released after just ninety-one hours for fear that she would be seriously harmed or killed by starvation. Doctors agreed that a fast of twenty-four hours would do no harm, but they continually debated how soon artificial feeding should begin after forty-eight to seventy-two hours. Most believed that stores of glycogen were exhausted in the first twenty-four hours of starvation, triggering the catabolism of fat and protein. Although Benedict had revised the duration of glycogen catabolism in a publication on prolonged fasting in 1915—finding that the process continued for one to two weeks—this information was slow to circulate through the general medical profession and especially among prison medical officers. It seems probable that physicians attending hunger strikers were also unnerved by the strikers' initial, significant loss of weight. For many years, prison medical officers treated twenty-four hours as a critical threshold, beyond which they watched intently for signs of "sudden collapse," especially in women.

The standard criteria of diagnosis for a hunger striker is to be found in reports on the suffragette Harriet Kerr by a prison medical officer in June 1913. The doctor evaluated her mental state at the outset of her strike on 18 June, describing her as "somewhat eccentric." On a daily basis he checked her pulse and heartbeat and evaluated the quality of her sleep. On 21 June he noted the "odour of malnutrition" on her breath: the smell of acetone. Two days later he observed that she had lost ten pounds and was experiencing pain in her limbs. On the following day, she had "gastric pains," her tongue became "furred," and again he noted the odor of malnutrition. He wrote, "I consider it would be inexpedient to detain her after tomorrow morning as she is an elderly woman [aged 54] and might have a sudden collapse."[67] Kerr was released on 25 June, after a strike of seven days.

In November 1919, as hunger strikes by militant republican men increased in Ireland during the Anglo-Irish War (1919–21), the governor of Mountjoy Prison in Dublin sent to the General Prisons Board of Ireland an excerpt from a medical officer's journal that listed the main indicators of the danger zone. According to the officer, temperature was not a significant factor, unless it indicated fever. "Acetonaemia may be expected about the end of the third or on the fourth day," he explained. "It is generally accompanied by mental hebetude and is a sign that the body tissues are being used up." He warned, "A heart which responds to normal demands when it is nourished normally may be either fibrous or fatty and only reveals the state post mortem." The "compressibility" of the pulse could indicate declining health, presumably as evidence of a shrinking heart, but the pulse rate was not significant. He finally noted that hunger striking tended "to wake up latent disease."[68] The officer's journal does not refer to urine samples and the measurement of the excretion of urea as a gauge of the body's store of protein. Medical officers generally had neither the facilities nor the time to conduct urine samples. More remarkable is the silence regarding the prisoner's weight. Given that there were no guidelines regarding weight loss and mortality, it is striking that emaciation was not a main indicator of the approaching danger zone, as it was in India. Apparently in the United Kingdom a person need not be a phantom to starve to death.

Prison medical officers in Britain and Ireland fed hunger strikers a liquid mixture of milk, eggs, beef, and brandy. There were variations, with an item removed or added. Dextrose and glucose were common supplements. In cases of advanced starvation, doctors would give strikers citrus juice against scurvy. Medical officers mainly attempted to combat starvation with protein, which, in combination with minerals and water, was believed to be the only nutrient that could restore tissue. Milk, a source of both protein and fat, appears to have been included in almost every forcible feeding, along with brandy. Taken in moderation, brandy was believed to have multiple benefits. It was a well-known digestif and a mild anesthetic.[69] Hutchison explained that in cases of disease the "volatile ethers" of brandy could have "a most valuable stimulating influence on the exhausted brain and heart."[70] Brandy was also believed to relieve hunger pangs in the stomach. When Kerr was released after her weeklong hunger strike, she was given a shot of brandy before being placed in a cab.[71]

In India through the 1920s, milk was the main, sometimes only, food forcibly fed to prisoners or provided to them after a hunger strike. This was probably a matter of economy, but it also reflected sensitivity to dietary rules of religion and caste. Sometimes medical officers supplemented milk feedings with eggs, mutton broth, glucose, and even brandy, but the eggs and mutton broth were probably reserved for Sikhs and the occasional Muslim hunger striker.[72] Hindus did not eat beef, and the vast majority did not eat eggs. All religious groups in India regarded brandy as an evil drink, so this could have been administered only surreptitiously or in complete ignorance. But everyone drank milk. In 1926 Manmathnath Gupta and other revolutionary prisoners under trial in Lucknow, capital of the United Provinces, went on a hunger strike for political prisoner status. After sixteen days the prison superintendent agreed to grant the prisoners special privileges on "medical grounds," so the prisoners suspended their strike. The prison medical officers gave them hot milk and insisted that they should not eat anything else for at least that night. After much imploring, the prisoners succeeded in persuading the doctors also to give them *khichri*, a mixture of rice and pulse cooked with salt, butter, and spices, a staple of village diets in northern and western India. One of the jailers provided the ingredients from his own home.[73]

Two cases of self-starvation in custody in India in the 1930s offer perspective upon British diagnostic measures and changing ideas regarding the dietary rules of forcible feeding between the wars. They also demonstrate the transimperial network through which medical knowledge was communicated among prison medical officers. The first case, reported in the British medical journal the *Lancet* in 1936, involved a nineteen-month hunger strike by a convict, Munshi Khan, in the central prison of Bareilly, United Provinces. According to H. Basil Rosair, a medical officer of fifteen years' experience who was then superintendent of the prison, Khan remained on hunger strike between May 1934 and January 1936. Rosair ordered occasional forcible feedings until July 1934, when he began a regular regimen of feedings that continued until the strike ended. Khan began his strike at 130 pounds, then reached a low point of 85 pounds in December 1934, after which his weight fluctuated between 85 and 105 pounds, depending, Rosair noted, "on the quality and quantity of liquid food given." The diet of this prisoner, probably a Muslim, given his name, consisted of various combinations of the following: milk, soup, raw eggs, *mung dal*, barley water, glucose D-Roboleine, orange juice, cod liver oil, and olive oil.

Between the wars, medical researchers concluded that deficiencies in vitamins and amino acids were more critical than protein deficiency in starvation.[74] The influence of nutritional science can be seen in Rosair's advice to other doctors: "In feeding hunger-strikers it is important to avoid vitamin deficiency and to remember the value of fats and carbohydrates compared with proteins." Eleven vitamins had been isolated by this time, and a twelfth, niacin (B3), was isolated in the year of the study's publication. Within six weeks of ending his strike, Khan regained almost all of his weight. "I have often had to order and conduct forcible feeding," Rosair observed, "and I am convinced that there are no permanent ill-effects either upon mental activity or muscular strength."[75]

LEARNING TO STARVE

Very few hunger strikers or their supporters demonstrated a clear understanding of the potential duration or the process of starvation. In November 1923 Ernie O'Malley, an Irish republican striker, wrote to a friend, "I really thought I should not last more than twelve days and here I am on my 22nd."[76] Four days later he reflected, "Two weeks ago the doctor gave me two days to live."[77] On the thirty-fifth day of his strike, he wrote, "I really thought I would be dead before the 21st." He then asked his friend to speak with a previous hunger striker, Mary MacSwiney, Terence MacSwiney's sister, and ask her to outline for him the symptoms of advanced starvation. "Or would it be better for me not to know?" he wondered.[78]

Recognizing that prison doctors shared their uncertainty about the duration and process of starvation, prisoners sometimes exploited the doctors' fear of the danger zone by feigning a sudden collapse. Ian Miller recounts the use of this tactic in a hunger strike by republican men in Cork Prison in 1917. One of the participants, Robert Brennan, recalled in a later interview, "When the strike was only five or six days old, we arranged that one of our fellows should collapse and be carted off to hospital, but before he could do so, another man actually did collapse. The doctor, in a panic, recommended our immediate release."[79]

Hunger strikers and their supporters, ignorant of current medical research, worried that prolonged starvation could have near-term or long-lasting negative effects, especially when the striker had a history of medical problems that might recur under the strain of starvation. Even a relatively short strike was believed to dramatically weaken the body's resistance to disease. When the Irish labor leader James Byrne died of pneumonia soon after a weeklong hunger strike in 1913, supporters charged that the hunger strike had killed him.[80] During the Irish civil war, word spread among republicans that after fifteen days on hunger strike one lived on the marrow of one's bones and so might be left a cripple.[81] Suffragettes and female Irish militant republicans undertook hunger strikes despite rumors that starvation and forcible feeding might leave them incapable of bearing children.[82] Men and women alike feared that starvation might drive them insane.[83] Nora Connolly O'Brien recalled of her father James Connolly's hunger strike in 1913, "At that time some strange stories were told of the effect it could have upon the brain and parts of the body after only a few days."[84]

Fears of the long-term consequences of starvation were probably enhanced by the ghastly effects of starvation on the prisoner's body and mind. Strikers and their supporters were alarmed by the rapid weight loss, stomach pain, and headaches in the first week. These conditions were soon followed by fitful sleep, dizziness, persecutory delusions, and occasional hallucinations. Most prisoners were bedridden by the end of the second week. When the Irish republican Joseph Campbell visited fellow prisoners on the sixteenth day of their hunger strike in a prison hospital, he was overwhelmed by the fetid smell of the ward and disturbed by the waxen skin and "yellowish" eyes of his friend Frank Daly.[85] Maire Comerford's tongue had swollen so much by the twenty-seventh day of her hunger strike that she could no longer speak.[86] After about the same length of time, Ernie O'Malley found that his eyesight was deteriorating.[87] In the second month of starvation, all strikers' muscles atrophied and lost coordination. They developed leg tremors. Sporadic dizziness became vertigo. Their bodies became skeletal. Bed sores developed and became ulcerous if not carefully treated. The striker's skin became frail and hypersensitive, so much so that it could be painful to touch one's own fingers together. Diarrhea became chronic, as the digestive system failed, which increased the importance of drinking water to cleanse the system and prevent dehydration. Strikers eventually began to vomit bile and blood. Terence MacSwiney developed scurvy and lost control over his bladder and bowels after approximately two months on hunger strike.[88] The Irish republican Michael Traynor, who endured a hunger strike of fifty-five days in the custody of the Irish Free State government in 1941, eventually lost the strength to roll over in bed. "I could smell death off myself," he recalled, "a sickly nauseating stench."[89]

Hunger strikers learned to anticipate at least some features of starvation. O'Malley asked for lemons to fend off scurvy.[90] Strikers knew that they would become cold, so they requested warm blankets. They knew that they would suffer bed sores, so they requested air beds or water mattresses—and sometimes received them.[91] They created ways to comfort themselves. C. S. Andrews recalled "the virtues of 'hunger strike soup,'" consisting of water, pepper, and salt, which "with a little stretch of the imagination . . . could taste like beef tea."[92] Experienced strikers were aware that overeating or indulging in an inappropriate diet after a long-term strike could result in serious constipation and vomiting, which would tax an already overtaxed system and possibly entail dire medical problems.[93]

Hunger striking was not for those unresolved to die for a cause. The Sikh militant socialist Sohan Singh Josh recalled the decision that he made with his comrades to hunger strike against oppressive conditions in Lyallpur District Jail in Punjab in 1922. "This was a risky plunge," he explained, "because a long hunger strike could demoralize some of the weaker prisoners, compelling them to give up the strike, and thus weaken our struggle."[94] Demoralization was neither a full description nor a full explanation of the experience of prisoners who gave up long-term hunger strikes. All prisoners found themselves at a growing disadvantage in their battle of wills with prison staff, because long-term starvation produced confusion and amnesia that undermined basic cognition, let alone morale. On the other hand, there could be moments of euphoria. Frank Gallagher wrote during his hunger strike in April 1920 that he felt "a fierce joy, a sacrificial glory, a feeling of spiritual pride . . . an ecstasy."[95] Experienced strikers attempted to guard against ecstasy, however, because it was a fleeting, precarious emotion that left them vulnerable to still greater depths of despair.

Prisoners who argued against hunger striking were consistently, primarily concerned that the collapse of a strike would leave comrades resentful, divided and in a far weaker position than the one in which they had begun to starve. Vinayak (V. D.) Savarkar, imprisoned in the Cellular Jail on the Andaman Islands in British India, opposed hunger strikes by comrades in 1912–13. This was the same person who ended Nani Gopal Mukherjee's hunger strike by threatening to starve himself to death if Mukherjee died. He declared hunger strikes to be "ruinous to the individual and ruinous to the cause." They were a waste of strength better reserved for fighting.[96] The Irish republican Sighle Humphreys recalled the failure of a mass strike in which she participated for thirty-one days in 1923: "We were flattened. . . . The tinted trappings of our fight were hanging like rags about us."[97]

Nonetheless, most of those who argued against hunger striking joined in a strike if the majority of their comrades decided to do so.[98] Pax Ó Faoláin, a republican imprisoned by the Irish Free State in 1922 and 1923, recalled that many of his comrades in Mountjoy Prison—the 'Joy, as it was known—proposed to hunger strike for release after many months of incarceration, and after a ceasefire between the Free State government and the Irish Republican Army. "I know the Army outside were very much against it," Ó Faoláin explained, "but these prisoners decided they would. I was six weeks on it, even though I objected strongly to it. Still, once they started, you felt that if you did not join in, you were letting them down. So I joined in."[99]

Hunger striking was a young person's game, or at least a game that the young were more likely to want to play. Older prisoners, especially those who had been on hunger strikes before, generally regarded hunger striking as a grave and dangerous method of protest to be avoided if at all possible. Gupta recalled that at the age of eighteen, during his imprisonment in 1926 for revolutionary activities, he had advocated a hunger strike for political prisoner status, but his older comrades had rejected the strike as premature. Gupta and two other young revolutionaries had nevertheless begun a strike, which, Gupta quickly recognized, was an ill-conceived gesture without the support of the experienced majority of his comrades. The young men gave up after only three days. "We had understood the futility of the strike," he explained. "We had to wait patiently till others were converted to our point of view."[100]

For the vast majority who hungered in protest, the experience was characterized by desperate fear, confusion, grit, and suffering. Virtually none of these protestors understood their starvation in symbolic terms; none presumed to be hunger artists. Their perspectives had been straitened by imprisonment, their focus brought to bear on miserable conditions or a reviled criminal status so intolerable that they reached for the last weapon. Yet the confusion surrounding starvation and especially the location of the danger zone, shared by prisoners and prison staff alike, opened a space in which starving bodies could be perceived as more than bodies. Whereas officials were dismayed by the endurance of some hunger strikers, the strikers and their supporters characterized their survival as a miraculous feat that defied any feeble explanation that science might offer and thus confirmed the sanctity of their causes and their own moral convictions. When suffragettes refused to characterize forcible feeding as a medical procedure and instead described it as torture, they shifted debate from clinical to moral grounds, to a contest between good and evil. Theirs was then a spiritual campaign worthy of identification with Joan of Arc, just as Irish republicans identified with Christ's mother, Mary, and Indian nationalists identified with Mother India, as we will see in the chapters that follow. The confusion over starvation probably went some way toward jostling aside ideology in the minds of many starving prisoners, who looked only to the starving comrades beside them in weighing their common goal against the prospect of death.

Beyond the prisoners' beds, beyond the ward, and beyond the prison walls this confusion made the meaning of hunger all the more malleable and discursively powerful. Although every starving prisoner did not begin her or his protest as an inspiration, the act of hunger in protest could render one inspiring, provided that one's starvation was cast and perceived as an act of sacrifice. Those against whom the sacrifice was directed usually had only the rule of law with which to defend themselves against the charge of inhumanity. The problem was that the death of the starving prisoner would prove the charge, while releasing the prisoner would certainly weaken the rule of law. Law was a gutless defense against moral indictment by holy fools. The confusion over starvation offered government officials no relief if prisoners themselves became indifferent to it. Confusion persisted even as the science of starvation advanced during and after the Second World War. This is illustrated again by Gandhi, whose exceptional status has left us with official records that chronicle the state's persistent, vain attempt to divine the danger zone.

NEW SCIENCE AND GANDHI'S STILL STRANGE STORY

The American scientist Ancel Keys, who conducted path-breaking research on starvation during the Second World War, observed in 1946 that, even during the "golden age" of nutritional science in the 1930s, "extremely little was known in detail about either chronic starvation or relief feeding."[101] This changed during and soon after the war, when Keys and other scientists examined starvation with new urgency in order to save the starving populations of occupied Europe.[102] Scientists were able to analyze data systematically gathered through two unprecedented studies. The first, directed by Jewish doctors in Warsaw's Jewish ghetto during the war, focused upon 150 starving subjects of Nazi occupation. Neither the doctors nor their patients lived to see the benefits of their findings, which were successfully smuggled out past the Nazis.[103] The second study, directed by Keys, focused on a group of 36 US conscientious objectors who volunteered to serve in a controlled experiment at the University of Minnesota in 1944–45.[104] Keys sought to replicate the famine diets of people in occupied Europe, examining the men's decline into morbidity and then their recovery through an experimental diet. Keys's findings were critically important in the subsequent development of relief feeding. He generally discounted the role of protein, and he determined that deficiencies in vitamins and amino acids were not primary factors in starvation, though they were of course essential to good health. He found that starvation was fundamentally a caloric deficiency. Contradicting long-standing medical practice, Keys stated, "In relief feeding, calories are of overwhelming importance."[105] Some other researchers and physicians had been moving toward these findings in the 1930s, but the war provided Keys with a terrible opportunity to confirm these findings through a study of greater scope.[106] His work, and that of other researchers, contributed to the improvement of famine and refugee relief programs in the new era of the United Nations, especially in the creation of standardized, nutritious rations.

The significant developments in nutritional science between the 1920s and 1940s had dramatic effects upon British social policy in the postwar era of the welfare state. As Vernon demonstrates, advances in nutritional science influenced programs for collective feeding and produced new dietary rules about which the state set out systematically to educate its citizen consumers.[107] Nutritional science, coupled with unprecedented wartime advancements in starvation science, did not, however, decisively change the ways in which health care providers and government officials managed or otherwise evaluated hunger strikes and fasts. When Traynor and three other republicans came off their fifty-five-day hunger strike in April 1941 at Saint Bricin's Military Hospital in Dublin, they were fed two poached eggs on toast, tea, milk, and sugar, followed by a dose of hydrochloric acid to aid in digestion.[108] Five years later, in May 1946, when the Irish Republican Army member David Fleming was on hunger strike in the Crumlin Road Prison in Belfast, Northern Ireland, the medical officers reportedly offered him orange juice or "vitamin tablets," which Fleming refused.[109] Fleming had commenced his strike on 20 March, then had intermittently suspended it. He finally abandoned the strike on 8 June, having gone without food for seventy-seven of the previous eighty-one days.[110] The *Irish Independent* reported that the deputy prison medical officer, in consultation with "a nutritional expert," then put Fleming on "a light diet of brandy, milk, glucose, and warm tea."[111]

At the same time that prison medical officers commonly maintained traditional views and policies on the feeding of hunger strikers—if with occasional vitamin supplements—the medical profession in general remained unable to measure a starving subject's approach to the danger zone. This was made abundantly clear, much to the frustration of British officials, when Gandhi undertook a fast in British custody in 1943, at the age of seventy-four. Months before Gandhi began this fast, British officials had anticipated the protest and conferred about it even in the cabinet in London. They agreed that when Gandhi reached the danger zone, they would release him.[112] Gandhi commenced the fast on 10 February while imprisoned under British authority in the Agha Kahn Palace, again in Pune, to protest accusations by the viceroy, Lord Linlithgow, that Gandhi himself was largely responsible for outbreaks of violence and loss of life during the Quit India movement in the previous year. Gandhi declared that this was not a "fast unto death," but a "fast to capacity"—in this case, twenty-one days. The viceroy observed privately that Gandhi received the best medical care available; there were six doctors in attendance and a daily series of urine and blood tests, blood pressure measurements, weight measurements (until Gandhi became too fatigued), and measurements of all fluids and salts consumed to the ounce. On the fourth day of the fast the surgeon general of the Bombay Presidency, Major General Candy, warned that on the following day "[Gandhi] would reach a critical point."[113] On 16 February, the sixth day, government doctors concurred that Gandhi could not last another five days.[114] Their overriding concerns were, first, that Gandhi was seventy-four years old and, second, that he had arteriosclerosis, which presumably rendered him prone to a sudden heart attack. The doctors feared that he had overestimated his capacity to fast.[115] On 17 February, the seventh day, the doctors agreed that Gandhi had reached the danger zone, but the viceroy determined that it was politically inadvisable to release him at that time.[116] Lord Linlithgow subsequently explained: "No compromise with him could, in my judgment, have been accepted on this issue save at the cost of a humiliating surrender which would have had disastrous effects on all the other communities and parties in this country; would have damaged the morale of the services . . .; and would have elevated the weapon of political fast into one against which no government of the future, whatever its composition, could hope to stand. For Gandhi and the Congress it would have represented a complete victory."[117]

The doctors panicked on 21 February, the eleventh day, when Gandhi experienced a seizure, and, in the doctors' view, appeared to be slipping into a coma.[118] Although his condition improved, the doctors warned ominously, "The heart is weaker."[119] Gandhi then stabilized on 24 February, to the annoyance of Prime Minister Winston Churchill, who had been following Gandhi's fast from his underground war rooms in London and now complained that he and other government officials had been erroneously led to believe since the fourth day of the fast that sudden collapse was imminent. Suspecting fraud, Churchill remarked, "How lucky we were not sucked in."[120] The viceroy commiserated: "The degree of nervous tension and hysteria engendered by all this Hindu hocus pocus is beyond belief." The inability of the doctors to diagnose Gandhi's condition had left the government open to—in the viceroy's words—"a wicked system of blackmail and terror," which officials had escaped only on the basis of his political calculation that release would have created an administrative crisis on such a scale that risking Gandhi's death was reasonable.[121] Gandhi broke his fast on 3 March, after twenty-one days, a duration that every doctor in attendance had previously dismissed as improbable. Afterward the government commissioned Candy to write a secret report on the "medical aspects" of Gandhi's fast. Candy recounted diagnostic methods that conformed closely to those employed by the prison medical officers who had treated the suffragettes thirty years earlier, and he speculated that the weakness of Gandhi's heart, in combination with Gandhi's age, was the primary source of his problems. Candy found only one possible explanation for Gandhi's survival after the crisis on the eleventh day. He suggested that Dr. Sushila Nayar, one of Gandhi's followers and the first doctor to attend him during the fast, "took fright, and sacrificed her principles" by beginning to add glucose to Gandhi's lime juice without Gandhi's knowledge. Candy conceded that the government would never know for sure if Nayar had saved Gandhi's life, which was to say that it would never know how Gandhi had survived a fast of twenty-one days.[122]

Although research in starvation science and relief feeding over the next decades would go a long way toward resolving confusion and misconceptions such as those displayed by prison medical officers and physicians in Ireland and India in the 1940s, it is finally, soberingly noteworthy that the practice of managing hunger in protest continued to lag behind research even through the era of Irish republican hunger strikes in the 1970s and 1980s and until recently.[123] The first edition of *Guidelines for the Clinical Management of People Refusing Food in Immigration Removal Centres and Prisons* was published by the British government's Department of Health in 2009. The process of starvation thus remained mysterious for many of those charged with caring for people on hunger strikes and fasts throughout the twentieth century.

British Suffragettes and the Russian Method of Hunger Strike, 1890–1914*

In the spring of 1878 male political prisoners in the Peter and Paul Fortress of Saint Petersburg went on hunger strike to protest against the oppressive conditions in which they were held by the czarist regime. After three days, news of the strike reached the prisoners' families, who appealed for relief to the director of military police, General N. V. Mezentsev. The director dismissed their pleas and reportedly declared of the hunger strikers, "Let them die; I have already ordered coffins for them all." It was a volatile period of repression and reprisal in the Russian revolutionary movement. The czarist regime had cracked down on the revolutionary populists, the *narodniki*, and the era of terrorism had just begun in Saint Petersburg that January, when Vera Zasulich shot and seriously wounded the city's governor. The hunger strikers were among a group of 193 revolutionaries who had been recently tried for treason and sentenced to various forms of punishment, including hard labor and imprisonment in Siberia. In these circumstances the news of Mezentsev's response spread quickly beyond the strikers' families, soon reaching a would-be terrorist and former artillery officer, Sergius Kravchinskii. Kravchinskii killed Mezentsev with a dagger on a city street, then fled Russia and made his way to Great Britain, a haven for Russian revolutionaries since Alexander Herzen had arrived in 1852 and established the first Russian revolutionary press abroad.[1] Kravchinskii likewise wrote against the czarist regime, under the pen name Sergius Stepniak, and in 1890 he became the editor of a new, London-based

*An earlier version of this chapter appeared in the journal *Comparative Studies in Society and History*. See Kevin Grant, "British Suffragettes and the Russian Method of Hunger Strike," *Comparative Studies in Society and History*, 53:1 (2011), 113–43.

periodical, *Free Russia*. Its first number chronicled a dramatic series of hunger strikes led by female revolutionaries imprisoned at Kara in the Transbaikal of eastern Siberia. These strikes had culminated in the death of one woman after she was flogged and in five suicides by female and male political prisoners who, after the death of their comrade, had ended their hunger strikes to eat poison. Having been inspired to terror by his sympathy for revolutionary hunger strikers, Stepniak, like other Russian exiles, believed that the hunger strike would win sympathy and support for Russian revolutionaries in Britain.

In July 1909 Marion Wallace Dunlop, a suffragette and member of the Women's Social and Political Union (WSPU), went on hunger strike in Holloway Prison. She protested against her treatment as a common criminal in the British prison system, having been sentenced to the system's second division. There were three divisions in total. The first division, generally reserved for the social elite, featured extraordinary privileges, such as wearing one's own clothing and enjoying meals prepared outside of the prison. The second division had considerably fewer privileges; for example, second-division prisoners wore prison attire and ate a standard prison diet. They were far better off, however, than prisoners in the third division, where common criminals were housed in the hardest circumstances.[2] While Dunlop recognized that her incarceration could have been worse, she nonetheless insisted on being moved to the first division in recognition of her conviction for a political, rather than a criminal, offense.

Prison officials and Home Secretary Herbert Gladstone fretted that Wallace Dunlop's hunger strike might kill her in only a matter of days. They contemplated the political crisis that would follow the death or injury of such a polite, if militant, prisoner: a painter and an illustrator of children's books, whose father had been a distinguished member of the Indian Civil Service.[3] Gladstone released her after ninety-one hours to a heroine's welcome by the WSPU, which regarded her hunger strike with surprise and admiration. Wallace Dunlop had commenced her hunger strike without consultation, and it initially appeared to some as a singular, militant inspiration. In the weeks that followed, however, Frederick Pethick-Lawrence, the joint editor of the WSPU journal, *Votes for Women*, published a leaflet in which he explained that Wallace Dunlop had "adopted the Russian method of the hunger strike."[4] This adoption was timely. Wallace Dunlop and other suffragettes took up this "Russian method" less than a month before Czar Nicholas II arrived in England to pay a call on his uncle, King Edward VII.

The international adaptation of the hunger strike as a tactic of political protest began with the transfer of this tactic from Russia to Great Britain in the early twentieth century. This chapter offers perspective upon early hunger strikes in the Russian and Siberian prisons of the czarist regime, and it suggests how Russian political prisoners understood the significance of their hunger strikes in the context of their revolutionary campaign to depose the czar. The primary aim is to explain how British suffragettes learned of this "Russian method" and then adapted it to their campaign for the vote. The refraction of the significance of the hunger strike across Russian and British politics is crucially important, because it placed the hunger strike in the international framework of British governance and law, and in a transimperial network of political protest and resistance to British rule, where Irish and Indian nationalists found and adapted it to their own causes.

Although the significance of the suffragette hunger strike was mainly defined by British domestic politics, it continually resonated with contemporary, critical representations of the czarist regime in the British press and with the controversial politics of Anglo-Russian relations. Russia was at this time an important factor in British foreign and imperial policies, as well as a notable influence upon British intellectuals and artists.[5] As Martin Malia explains, Britons, and western Europeans in general, had learned to regard the Russian nation "not as an alien entity but as one national culture within a common European civilization."[6] Nonetheless, British radicals, including prominent suffragists (that is, both nonmilitant and militant) vilified the czar as a despot. This vilification illustrates Malia's broader assertion that Europeans' own domestic problems primarily defined their perceptions of Russia. Indeed, WSPU propaganda demonstrated that the suffragettes saw something of themselves and their political adversaries in the Russian hunger strikes.[7]

We know little about the hunger strikes by female and male revolutionaries in Russian and Siberian prisons under the czarist regime.[8] There is fine work on the history of Russian prisons, the Siberian exile system, and "political crime" in this era, but this scholarship has not addressed specific policies pertaining to the hunger strike, such as those governing prison diet or forcible feeding.[9] There is a solid body of work on the Russian exiles in Britain who publicized Russian hunger strikes, especially among British radicals, after the 1890s.[10] These exiles persuaded influential British radicals and labor leaders that their goal was a new, apparently liberal, constitutional order for Russia. They represented Russian hunger strikers not as "terrorists," but as victims of the czarist regime, guilty of nothing more than fighting for freedom from despotism. These exiles and an American journalist, George Kennan, published the most thorough accounts of Russian revolutionary hunger strikes available to us. The present discussion of Russian strikes begins with two particular cases, both of which were known not only to Russian revolutionaries but also to members and supporters of the WSPU before the First World War.

There is a multifaceted body of scholarship on the hunger strikes by British suffragettes. Scholars have dwelled upon their strikes and the experience of forcible feeding as embodiments of gender politics. They have specifically examined how suffragettes described forcible feeding in thinly veiled terms of sexual violation and thus challenged the moral authority of the patriarchal political system.[11] Some writers have interpreted the hunger strike as a rejection of woman's maternal role, while others have conversely argued that the suffragettes represented it as a maternal act of sacrifice for the nation.[12] James Vernon suggests that the suffragette hunger strikes capitalized upon the new humanitarian sympathy for hungry people, especially women and children, who were now cast as victims of misgovernment.[13] Stepping outside of these analytical frameworks, Joseph Lennon has situated Wallace Dunlop's hunger strike within the broad cultural and political contexts of fasting in Ireland and India.[14]

The political power of the suffragette hunger strikes derived from these various connotations of a woman's self-starvation and her experience of forcible feeding. Yet the objectives of the strikers were fundamentally constitutional. Wallace Dunlop had been arrested and then sentenced to one month in prison for stenciling an excerpt of the 1689 Bill of Rights in violet ink onto the wall of Saint Stephen's Hall in the Palace of Westminster. The text read: "It is the right of the subject to petition the King, and all commitments and prosecutions for such petitioning are illegal." As Laura Mayhall explains, "Wallace Dunlop's deed connects the Edwardian suffrage movement to a long tradition of radical protest and highlights suffragettes' use of the constitutional idiom."[15] This constitutional idiom was epitomized by the Bill of Rights, and in the summer of 1909 British suffragettes found the antithesis of constitutional government in the despotism of the czar, who was soon to enjoy the hospitality of the British monarch. They accordingly articulated their constitutional claims by using the hunger strike to liken themselves to starving Russian revolutionaries and the Liberal government of Prime Minister Herbert Asquith to the czarist regime. In a WSPU leaflet published in December 1909, Henry Brailsford observed that Wallace Dunlop "adopted the method of protest which Russian 'politicals' use in a like case."[16] In fact, there was much to differentiate the Russian and British hunger strikers and their governments, but differences had been obfuscated by Russian exiles in their attempts to win British allies.

GOLODOVKA

Russian "politicals," as these political prisoners were known, conducted hunger strikes in Russian and Siberian prisons from at least the mid-1870s.[17] They referred to their self-starvation as *golodovka*, which Kennan translated as "hunger strike."[18] It is noteworthy that this term is not a literal translation of *golodovka*, a word of Russian origin traceable back to Old Church Slavonic.[19] Prior to the revolutionary period, it was used to refer to a time of famine or want. The 1880–82 "explanatory dictionary," edited by Dal', does not include a political definition for *golodovka*.[20] Significantly, native Russian speakers sometimes referred in English to the "famine strike."[21] The political connotations of *golodovka*, predominant in usage of the word today, appear in the 1935 explanatory dictionary, edited by Ushakov, which defines *golodovka* as "a refusal or abstention from food as a sign of protest."[22] It is probable that the changing definition of *golodovka* reflects a transitional era in the use of hunger as a form of protest in Russia in the early decades of the twentieth century.

Kennan and leading figures in the Russian exile community in Britain cooperated in criticizing the czarist regime and represented hunger strikes in similar terms. These terms simultaneously exposed the suffering and resistance of imprisoned Russian revolutionaries had obscured the terrorist acts for which they had been incarcerated. Kennan and the Russian exiles were aware that the US and British publics were fearful of the ongoing violence of Irish revolutionaries, known as Fenians, and anarchists at home and abroad, which culminated in the assassination of President William McKinley by an anarchist in 1901.[23] They therefore downplayed the militancy of Russian dissidents and instead fostered sympathetic support for them as victims of czarist despotism.[24] Their portrayal of victimhood was sometimes sensationalist. Kennan lectured on the Siberian exile system in the tattered uniform and shackles of a prisoner, as did the prominent Russian exile Felix Volkhovsky in Britain.[25] Stepniak eschewed such display, redirecting the British public's attention away from his militant past. He represented himself to Britons not as a revolutionary assassin, but as a staid advocate of the downtrodden Russian people. Thus, this former assassin would become a guest of the future suffragette Emmeline Pankhurst in her home in London, where he mingled with a diverse group of eminently respectable social reformers.[26]

Kennan and the Russian exiles implied that particular cases of prison abuse and hunger striking were representative of the suffering of all politicals throughout the Russian and Siberian prison systems. In fact, the treatment of politicals was both exceptional and variable. Jonathan Daly explains that the quality of one's life in a Russian prison or in exile was determined by four factors: "one's social status, the economic and social conditions of the place of confinement, the character of local officials, and the political climate in St. Petersburg."[27] The majority of politicals in the 1880s and 1890s had relatively high social status, because they came from well-to-do families and were educated.[28] They therefore received better treatment than did regular criminals, and they were rarely subjected to corporal punishment.[29] A large proportion of politicals was freed early under periodic amnesties or through appeals for clemency.[30] Nowhere in the works by Kennan and the Russian exiles does one find acknowledgment that the translation of Kennan's exposé into Russian in the early 1890s caused a public outcry in Russia and considerable embarrassment within the czarist regime.[31] The Interior Ministry urged officials to exercise leniency toward political exiles, and it enacted reforms, such as the 1893 abolishment of the practice of flogging female exiles.[32] Over the course of the 1890s, most political exiles enjoyed progressively more freedom of movement and less abuse, even as Kennan and Volkhovsky lectured in shackles.[33]

This situation changed dramatically after the failed revolution in Russia in 1905, when the number of political prisoners exiled to Siberia increased, as did the proportions of prisoners from the working class, the peasantry, and the military. The distinctions between politicals and criminals largely eroded, and the lives of all exiles became harder until the revolution of 1917 finally ended the exile system altogether.[34] As British press reports of Siberian exile after 1905 undoubtedly enhanced the narratives of suffering that Russian revolutionaries propagated in London, these revolutionaries drew no distinctions between political eras and readily allowed the present to color more darkly their own past. Because representations of Russian hunger strikes to the British public were highly selective and propagandistic, and in the absence of archival research on Russian hunger strikes in the late imperial era, this chapter offers a provisional treatment of the conduct and significance of the hunger strikes recounted by Kennan and the Russian exiles.

Kennan and Leo Deutsch, a Russian revolutionary exile in London, wrote the best-known contemporary accounts of Russian hunger strikes. In 1891, Kennan published his two-volume work *Siberia and the Exile System*, which recounted his investigations as a journalist in Siberia between 1885 and 1888. In 1903 Deutsch published *Sixteen Years in Siberia*, a memoir of his incarceration in Russian and Siberian prisons between 1884 and 1901. Helen Chisholm, the translator of Deutsch's memoir, suggested that the two works should be read together.[35] The authors refer to several hunger strikes by both women and men, the earliest being the aforementioned strike in the Peter and Paul Fortress.[36] Both highlight the hunger strikes of female politicals in Siberia, which is remarkable given the relatively small number of female politicals sent to Siberia. Politicals made up only about 2 percent of the approximately 170,000 people exiled to Siberia between 1878 and 1885, the year in which Kennan arrived. Only a small fraction of them were women; the majority were young, unmarried men.[37] One destination for political exiles in Siberia was the prison and penal colony at Kara, where the inmates labored in gold mines. When the revolutionary Katerina Breshkovkaia reported to the prison director there in 1878, he observed, "I have no cell for political women. You are the first one here," and sent her to live with a family in a nearby town.[38]

Kennan and Deutsch provide full accounts of the hunger strikes by political prisoners at Kara in 1888–89, the same strikes covered by Stepniak in the first number of *Free Russia* in 1890.[39] Their accounts merit summary here, because the "Kara Tragedy" became infamous among both Russian revolutionaries and British suffragists who followed Russian affairs. It appeared not only in *Free Russia*, which we will see had a significant suffragist readership, but also in *Votes for Women* in 1912.

According to Kennan and Deutsch, the prisoners' protest at Kara began when one of the women politicals, Elizabeth Kovalskaia, insulted the visiting Governor General Baron Korf by refusing to stand in his presence.[40] Korf ordered her transfer, which the commandant Masyukov decided to execute in the dead of night, employing a group of criminal convicts to assist the wardens in pulling Kovalskaia out of bed.[41] Outraged by this act, three other women politicals staged a hunger strike.[42] The commandant was unable to persuade them to end it, so he sought assistance from a male prisoner, Alexander Kalyushny, who was incarcerated in a nearby men's prison with Deutsch. Both Kalyushny's wife, Nadyeshda Smirnit-skaia, and his sister, Maria Kalyushnaia, were taking part in the strike.[43] The third striker was Maria Kovalevskaia, who had joined three other female prisoners in a previous hunger strike in the prison at Irkutsk in Siberia in 1882.[44] According to Deutsch, the commandant "begged Kalyushny to ... pacify the women, and induce them to give up their hunger strike, promising beforehand that he would do anything in reason to give them satisfaction."[45] Kalyushny and his male com-rades urged the women to end their strike if the commandant apologized to them, fearing that they might otherwise die in a hopeless gambit. In a concession to the men, the women agreed to eat if the commandant arranged his own transfer under some pretext. The women also asserted that if the commandant was not gone in a fixed period of months, they would resume their strike to the bitter end.[46]

The commandant's request for transfer was denied, so the women resumed their strike, now joined by four other female politicals. Although Deutsch and his comrades believed that an apology from the commandant should have sufficed, they joined the women's strike in an act of solidarity, a decision typical of the ambivalent, resigned solidarity that characterized some later hunger strikes in Russia, the United Kingdom, and India.[47] The women had not eaten for eight days, and the men for three, when the commandant presented them with a telegram confirming that his superiors had agreed to transfer him.[48] All of the politicals ended their strikes, but months later, in 1889, approximately a year after Kovals-kaia's departure, the commandant was still there. So four women decided to com-mence a third hunger strike. In an effort to preempt the suffering of her comrades, one of the women, Nadezhda Sigida, hit the commandant, anticipating that the usual procedure would follow: his transfer and her death.[49]

Contrary to expectations, the governor general left the commandant at his post and ordered that Sigida be flogged rather than executed for her offense. This news shocked Deutsch and his comrades, given that even male politicals were rarely flogged.[50] In disbelief, the men further learned that Sigida had died shortly after her punishment—perhaps of injuries suffered in the flogging, perhaps of a nervous fit, or perhaps of self-poisoning. In response to her death, the other three women poi-soned themselves and died in the prison infirmary.[51] Seventeen of the thirty-nine male politicals then attempted to commit suicide with poison, two successfully.[52] In the aftermath of this calamity, in 1890, officials in Saint Petersburg ordered the closure of the prison at Kara and transferred all of the politicals to nearby Akatoui, where the male and female politicals were henceforth subjected to the same treat-ment as common criminals in reprisal for their rebellion.[53]

The women who led these hunger strikes were narodniki, revolutionary populists committed to the violent overthrow of the czar. Most of the revolutionary
women of this generation were from privileged backgrounds and had joined
the struggle in their twenties.[54] Kovalskaia, the woman dragged from her bed,
was exceptional in being a former serf. These women shared with their male comrades a clear vision of the ideal woman, largely derived from a nihilistic ethos that
had a strong influence upon the Russian revolutionary intelligentsia after the
1870s.[55] The ideal woman displayed moral purity, recognition of duty, hatred of
compromise, and fearless sacrifice.[56] She did not treat sacrifice in symbolic, self-
aggrandizing terms of martyrdom, but as a necessary, selfless means to a principled end. She was duty-bound to resist the oppression of the people at large, rather
than the particular social or political oppression of women. The "women's question," as it was known in Britain, had been long subsumed in the broader socialist
cause.[57]

The narodniki combined their pragmatic acceptance of sacrifice with a commitment to terrorism. Although women constituted a small percentage of the
revolutionary movement, they took part in some of its most famous assassinations.[58] Sophia Perovskaia, a leading member of the revolutionary organization
Will of the People, oversaw the operations that resulted in the assassination of
Czar Alexander II in March 1881. One of her accomplices, Vera Figner, evaded
arrest until 1883, then served twenty-two years in Russian prisons, twenty of them
in the infamous Schlusselburg Fortress. Women continued to perpetrate revolutionary acts of violence, especially those who joined the secret "Battle Organization" of the Socialist Revolutionary Party after 1902. In 1905 a party operative
named Maria Spiridonova shot a general in the face.

This was the same year in which Christabel Pankhurst began the "militant"
phase of WSPU protest in Britain by persistently questioning Sir Edward Grey in
a Liberal Party meeting and then spitting in the face of a policeman to provoke her
own arrest.[59] British suffragettes in their speeches and publications drew no distinctions between Russian revolutionary populists, members of the Socialist Revolutionary Party, and themselves. Sylvia Pankhurst recalled her response to news of
female Russian revolutionaries in the summer of 1906: "And now it seemed to us
as though the spirit of revolt against oppression were flowing onward and spreading, like some great tide to all the womanhood of the world."[60]

Neither Kennan, Deutsch, Stepniak, nor any subsequent journalist or revolutionary memoirist explained the cultural or political connotations of the hunger
strikes against the czarist regime.[61] They did not refer to precedents for these strikes
prior to the 1870s, and they did not articulate the relationship between one strike
and another. Yet they referred to such strikes as "customary" or "traditional."[62] The
definition of the word *golodovka* in the early 1880s suggests that the act of self-
starvation may have customarily manifested a general condition of deprivation

attributable to famine, perhaps with the religious connotations of *dvoeverie*, a combination of Orthodoxy and pagan beliefs. Russia's rural communities commonly fasted in accordance with the calendar of the Russian Orthodox Church, but these fasts generally required abstinence from particular foods and had rules regarding the allowance of rations.[63] There were also "public fasts" observed by everyone in a town or village community. "Disasters such as epidemics and epizootics, drought, long periods of rain, etc., were the main reasons for keeping public fasts," explains Tatjana Voronina. "People kept such fasts on the permission of the priest after the local peasants' community decided to fast."[64] These fasts could have constituted direct appeals to the paternalistic duties of a landowner or government official, but this is only speculation.[65]

Although the genealogy of the Russian hunger strike remains obscure, it does appear that revolutionary populists, in particular, adapted an earlier practice of fasting to their political ends. This is not to say that the narodniki on hunger strike at Kara conceived their self-starvation in coherent ideological terms, let alone as the embodiment of a constitutional program. Unlike the suffragettes, they advocated agrarian socialism, and they did not aspire to replace the czar with a particular political regime.[66] The hunger strike became political in the sense that revolutionary populists used it as a weapon against the penal institutions of an oppressive government. The narodniki regarded it as a weak weapon, however. Deutsch states plainly that it was a "more passive means" of prison protest than breaking windows or furniture.[67] Recalling her own experiences, Figner would later characterize the hunger strike as not only ineffective but also potentially damaging to prisoner morale and camaraderie.[68] The narodniki did not see the hunger strike as an extension of the terrorist campaign beyond the prison walls, and they directed it only as a last resort against specific prison conditions and personnel.

The narodniki regarded the hunger strike as a tool, if not exactly a weapon, rather than as a symbol. The tactic was consistent with the narodnikis' commitment to self-sacrifice, but their objective was not martyrdom. Instead, they sought to defy specific authorities, disrupt the order of prison life, and secure mundane, immensely important goals: better food, the transfer of an unethical official, or, as we will see, access to books.[69] The use of hunger as leverage to ameliorate immediate conditions is something that we will see repeatedly in the United Kingdom and India, but in these contexts prisoners and their supporters also publicly represented starvation in symbolic, religiously inflected, and gendered terms. Arguably, there was a gendered symbolism in the Kara Tragedy, given the emphasis that Kennan and Deutsch placed upon the role women played. Yet one might observe in turn that Kennan and Deutsch were writing for audiences in Britain and the United States. Women led the Kara strikes, but the hunger strike was generally shared as a tactic of protest by men. More importantly, none of the strikes in Russian and Siberian prisons were directed toward a women's cause. Golodovka was not a "womanish thing," as some Irish militant republicans initially perceived the hunger strike in view of British and Irish suffragette protests.[70]

PROTEST AGAINST THE CZAR IN BRITAIN

For years the British press had covered the brutalities of the czarist regime and the swelling ranks of Russia's reform-minded and revolutionary parties.[71] After the turn of the century, the liberal press, and especially the *Manchester Guardian* and the *Daily News*, offered the most consistent and intense criticism of the czar and Anglo-Russian relations. It condemned the czar for the massacre of civilians by Russian troops on Bloody Sunday (9 January or 22 January, new style, 1905), and critically assessed his subsequent gestures toward a constitutional monarchy. It covered the czar's creation and dissolution of two intractable Dumas in 1906 and 1907, and condemned his revocation of all meaningful reforms and his turn to a repressive policy of "pacification" through censorship, incarceration, and summary courts martial.[72] Against this backdrop, the liberal press and radical members of Parliament strongly criticized Foreign Secretary Sir Edward Grey for striking an alliance with the czarist regime under the Anglo-Russian Convention of August 1907.[73] King Edward further aggravated radicals by visiting Nicholas at Reval (now Tallinn, the capital of Estonia) in June 1908 in tacit support of his government, and then by inviting the czar and his family to visit England in the following summer.[74] In the months preceding the czar's visit, radicals protested against a "liberal" British government endorsing this visit by a self-professed divine-right autocrat with blood on his hands.[75]

London was a staging ground for Russian revolutionaries, who held important meetings there in the early twentieth century. The conventions of the Marxist Social Democrats in London and Brussels in 1903 saw the split between the Bolsheviks and Mensheviks. The Social Democrats then returned to London in 1907, followed by the populist Socialist Revolutionary Party in 1908. The Russian exile community had been a vociferous lobby against the czar since the early 1880s, publishing exposés, holding public meetings, petitioning, and, finally, establishing with British radical allies the Society of Friends of Russian Freedom (SFRF) in 1890.[76] The founders of the SFRF were R. Spence Watson, parliamentarians Thomas Burt and W. P. Byles, Prince Peter Kropotkin, and Stepniak.[77] Until 1915 the society published its English-language periodical on Russian political affairs, *Free Russia*, which challenged apologists of the czarist regime and otherwise indicted the regime by enumerating its alleged atrocities.

At the same time, another Russian, Jaakoff Prelooker, published *The Anglo-Russian*, an English-language periodical devoted mainly to British commercial prospects in Russia that was not only critical of the czarist regime but also ardently supportive of British suffragists. Prelooker was not a revolutionary exile. He had immigrated to Britain in 1891 after leaving his post as the headmaster of a government school in Odessa. Along with Stepniak, he attended suffragist events at the Pankhursts' home as early as 1892.[78] In the November 1908 edition of *The Anglo-Russian*, Prelooker quoted Adela Pankhurst, who, in the face of several hundred police deployed against the WSPU in York, observed that the government "would not be able to dispense with Russian methods until women got the vote."[79] This characterization of police actions and government security measures as "Russian methods" was not uncommon among suffragettes, who recognized, according to Martin Pugh, that being likened to the Russians was "one of the worst insults for a Liberal at this time."[80] With a more nuanced understanding of Russian society, Prelooker encouraged his readers to follow the example of liberal-minded Russian men, like himself, who had long supported women's enfranchisement.[81] He regularly attended suffragist protests, joined the Men's League for Women's Suffrage after its founding in 1907, and in 1912 joined the Men's International Alliance for Women's Suffrage.[82] Remarkably, Prelooker was the first man in Britain to support the suffragist movement by refusing to pay his rates and taxes. Two representatives of the WSPU attended his hearing at the Horsham Petty Sessions in Sussex and held open-air meetings in his support.[83]

The SFRF benefited from the membership of suffragists, such as Charles Dilke, MP, and Charlotte Despard, the leader of the Women's Freedom League, as well as supporters of the militant WSPU, including Pethick-Lawrence, Brailsford, the journalist Henry Nevinson, and Keir Hardie, MP. Brailsford and Nevinson provided the liberal press with some of the most incisive critiques of the czarist regime and British foreign policy toward Russia before the First World War.[84] In cooperation with the *Daily News*, the SFRF led the public protest against the czar's visit in the spring of 1909. This protest cannot be called popular, as it never expanded beyond a small pressure group of radical activists, nonconformist ministers, and Labour Party leaders. Yet the cooperation between Russian exiles and suffragists, in particular, is significant because it forms the context in which the WSPU took up the Russian method of hunger strike.

There were two conspicuous features of this protest against the czar. The first was the illustration of his despotism through accounts of brutal prison conditions, and the second was the assertion that Britain's alliance with a despotic ruler not only undermined Britain's prestige as a leading democracy but also threatened to weaken its own democratic institutions.[85] These discourses complemented larger, radical critiques of government that had been current in Britain since the South African War (1899–1902).[86] Radicals such as J. A. Hobson had warned that the democratic bases of British domestic, imperial, and foreign policy were being undermined by the secrecy of officials and the self-serving influence of large commercial enterprises and international financiers—the "special interests" of capitalism.[87] Others had brought these points home with narratives and sometimes photographs of atrocity or "outrage," as in stories of Afrikaner women and children held in British concentration camps during the South African War, or of Congolese mutilated or killed by the infamous Congo Free State ruled by King Leopold II of Belgium.[88] There was significant overlap among the prominent participants in these campaigns. For example, suffragists including Dilke, Nevinson, Labour Party leader James Ramsay MacDonald, and the prominent Nonconformist minister Dr. John Clifford were simultaneously active in the Congo reform campaign and the protests against the czar.[89] These radicals were connected in a variety of causes by their commitment to an expanded franchise, their defense of civil society against special interests, and their insistence that government should serve and represent the needs and will of all British society in domestic, imperial, and foreign policies. Thus the interaction of the campaign for women's suffrage and the protests against the czar exemplifies a multifaceted, radical campaign for reform in the Edwardian era.

In May 1909 the protests against the czar's visit were joined by Figner, the legendary accomplice in the assassination of the czar's grandfather, who had moved to Europe after her release from prison in 1904. She had visited England twice in 1908, the first time for sightseeing, and the second to attend the Socialist Revolutionary Party's convention in London.[90] She returned to England in May 1909 to raise funds for political prisoners in Russia and Siberia, and to join in protests against the czar's visit, now scheduled for early August.[91] Yet while Figner joined British radicals in denouncing the czar, she did not necessarily endorse their vision of Russia's future. The Labour Party adopted a resolution in the House of Commons that called on the government to deny official recognition of the visit of the czar, "under whose authority and direct sanction so many terrible atrocities have been perpetrated on a people constitutionally struggling for political freedom."[92] Figner herself had engaged not in a constitutional struggle, but rather in a terrorist campaign, and, although she wanted freedom for Russia, she did not advocate the replacement of the czar with a constitutional regime.[93] Both the *Manchester Guardian* and the *Daily News* overlooked this discrepancy in their favorable coverage of her activities.

On 23 June Figner was the guest of honor at a reception at the South Place Institute hosted by the London Russian Hertsen Circle. *Free Russia* featured a summary of her speech that focused upon inhumane prison conditions and prisoners' protests. Figner gave credit for the most effective act of protest to one Mikhail Grachevskii, who had immolated himself with kerosene while in solitary confinement and thus provoked the replacement of a brutal prison director.[94] The chairman, Volkhovsky, closed the meeting with three cheers for Figner. "Then," according to *Free Russia*, "the platform was invaded by a crowd of ladies who wanted to shake hands with Mme. Figner, or have her autograph."[95]

In the run up to the czar's visit, Figner was the most famous woman in Britain to have received official political prisoner status and resisted brutal prison conditions.

In an article in the *Review of Reviews* of July 1909, William Stead treated her as the spokeswoman for Russian women of all branches of Russia's revolutionary movement.[96] Members of the WSPU were certainly aware of her presence in London, whether through reports of her activities in the *Manchester Guardian* and the *Daily News*, their affiliation with the SFRF, or personal contacts with the Russian exile community.[97] However, Figner did not cooperate with the WSPU, even as it campaigned in 1909 to secure political prisoner status for its incarcerated members. She was, after all, committed to a comprehensive socialist revolution, not to a women's movement, and she may have also learned that Emmeline and Christabel Pankhurst had resisted the influence of British socialists in guiding the WSPU after 1907.[98] Figner observes in her memoirs that she could have probably raised more money for Russian political prisoners if she "had entered into relations with the militant suffragettes." She was dissuaded from this by Kropotkin's wife, Sophie, even though the Kropotkins themselves were acquainted with Emmeline Pankhurst, and even though Christabel Pankhurst impressed Figner with her political talents.[99] Perhaps Sophie Kropotkin was troubled by the ideological divide between Figner's revolutionary populism and the Pankhursts' militant campaign for constitutional reform, or maybe she worried that Figner would be misrepresented in WSPU propaganda. In the end, Figner worked only to a limited extent with Despard, the leader of the Women's Freedom League, who unlike the Pankhursts had been a lifelong socialist and an active SFRF supporter. In June Figner recounted her prison experiences to a Women's Freedom League meeting at Caxton Hall chaired by Despard. Figner was followed by a league member, Mrs. Holmes, who made sacrifice the subject of her speech. She reportedly declared, "It was on sacrifice that the fabric of women's liberty must be built—sacrifice of money, leisure, aesthetic pleasures, of so-called womanly dignity itself. Women were out fighting for broader issues. How trifling were these sacrifices in comparison with those which women such as Mdme. Figner had been called upon to make."[100]

HUNGER AND HEROINISM

The WSPU distributed leaflets in advance of its march on Parliament on 29 June to deliver a petition to the prime minister in support of the enfranchisement of women. The leaflets quoted the Bill of Rights and asserted, "Mr. Asquith, as the King's representative, is bound, therefore, to receive the deputation and hear their petition. If he refuses to do so, and calls out the police to prevent women from using their right to present a petition, he will be guilty of illegal and unconstitutional action."[101] It was after this that Wallace Dunlop stenciled part of the text of the 1689 Bill of Rights on the wall of Saint Stephen's Hall, for which she was sentenced on 5 July to one month in prison in the second division. She insisted that she be transferred to the first division in recognition of the political nature of her offense, but the prison officials refused to comply. The British prison regulations did not recognize the category of "political prisoner;" the Home Secretary Reginald McKenna later asserted that political prisoner status was "a pure figment of modern imagination."[102] The suffragettes' imaginations had been inspired, nonetheless, by the fact that the prison system had previously given first-division treatment to a small number of convicts, such as Chartists and Fenians, whose offences were legally defined as "seditious" but were commonly regarded as political.[103] After being transferred to the first division on appeal to the home secretary in October 1906, Emmeline Pankhurst, leader of the WSPU, had declared, "We are at last recognized as a political party; we are now in the swim of politics."[104] Although Wallace Dunlop's demand for transfer to the first division had been predictable, her hunger strike was not. On 9 July the home secretary authorized her release. In its coverage of the hunger strike, *Votes for Women* declared, "The treatment which the Suffragettes receive in Holloway is , , , inferior in some respects to that which Russian political prisoners are receiving to-day."[105] Pethick-Lawrence explained in a WSPU leaflet titled *Treatment of the Suffragettes in Prison* that the hunger strike was a Russian method.

Wallace Dunlop, and those who followed her example in hunger striking, regarded this tactic of protest as effective in both instrumental and symbolic terms. Like Russian politicals, Wallace Dunlop took up the hunger strike as a weapon with which to challenge the authority of prison officials and the practical capacities of the prison system. She had declared to the medical officer at Holloway, "You may feed me through the nostrils or the mouth, but suppose you got 108 women in here on Friday all requiring to be fed through the nostrils? At this," she noted, "the doctor's face was a delightful study."[106] As this comment suggests, suffragettes quickly recognized that prison officials lacked adequate staff with which to manage hunger strikes by groups of prisoners. Twelve suffragettes went on hunger strike after Wallace Dunlop, and all were released within a week. The sheer numbers of suffragette strikers, sometimes dozens at a time, placed great burdens upon the prison system, and especially upon the medical officers who were responsible for prisoners' diets and health and for virtually all day-to-day prison conditions, as we will see in chapter 5.[107]

Unlike the Russian politicals, the suffragettes represented the hunger strike as a symbolic act of heroic martyrdom inspired by the their indomitable, feminine, "spiritual" commitment to their cause.[108] The WSPU represented strikes through speeches, posters, and numerous publications as acts of sacrifice for the nation and as embodiments of the coercion upon which the government's "virtual representation" of women depended.[109] In the former respect, the strikes tapped into the strong ethos of martyrdom that had been symbolically identified in WSPU spectacles with Joan of Arc, the divinely inspired young woman who had miraculously led French forces to victories against the English and their allies in France during

FIGURE 3. WSPU postcard of Elsie Howey as Joan of Arc, 1909. Reproduced by permission of the Museum of London.

FIGURE 4. WSPU hunger strike medal awarded to Lady Constance Lytton, 1909. Reproduced by permission of the Museum of London.

the Hundred Years War of the fifteenth century. In April 1909, for example, the suffragette Elsie Howey impersonated Joan of Arc, reportedly "clad in glistening armour, with purple, white, and green plumes on her helmet," riding a white charger at the head of a WSPU parade to celebrate the release of Emmeline Pethick-Lawrence from prison.[110] Howey's spectacle received extensive coverage in the press and was further disseminated by the WSPU as a postcard (figure 3).[111] "No one ever knew so well as Joan of Arc, that greatest of all militants, how to slay a moral fallacy," *Votes for Women* subsequently declared.[112]

Hunger strikes served much the same purpose as did the suffragettes' attempts to provoke public, physical confrontations with police in order to shame the government through the violent display of its disproportionate and allegedly despotic power.[113] The WSPU organized parades and receptions for suffragettes who had

FIGURE 5. Lady Constance Lytton wearing prison number badge and hunger strike medal, ca. 1912. Reproduced by permission of the Museum of London.

been released on hunger strike. Beginning in August 1909, they awarded them medals, symbolically honoring hunger strikers as soldiers who had sacrificed themselves in a moral, potentially mortal campaign. The medal, awarded to Lady Constance Lytton (figure 4), is typical of the WSPU medals that were awarded over the next several years. The words *Hunger Strike* are etched on the obverse side of the medal. The top bar reads, "For Valour"'; the ribbon features the colors of the WSPU (green, white, and purple); the bottom bar indicates the date on which the strike began, "October 9th 1909." On the reverse side of the medal is etched the name *Constance Lytton*, surrounded by a laurel wreath, a classical symbol of victory and authority.

Framing the significance of suffragette spectacles and material symbols were numerous published accounts of the strikers' sufferings, which the WSPU deployed mainly through its publications to inspire its rank-and-file members and subscribers.[114] Lytton's published memoir, *Prisons and Prisoners*, which recounts her experiences of prison and forcible feedings while disguised as a working-class woman, *alias* Jane Wharton, provoked controversy in the general media, largely due to her aristocratic status, rather than due to the sufferings *per se* that she shared with dozens of women who had also been forcibly fed but had received little or no public sympathy. Her photographic portrait (figure 5) combines military honor and studied, domestic femininity, represented by the juxtaposition of Lytton's prison number badge, her hunger strike medal, her delicate lace collar, and her cool gaze. The badge and the medal mark the aftermath of violence. Every other feature of Lytton's careful Edwardian propriety suggests that violence should have had no part in this woman's life. The history of violence is not concealed, however. Lytton is an open book. Her gaze further suggests that she and her comrades, represented by the WSPU medal, were resolved to play political roles larger than those to which they had been born.

LIBERALISM AND THE POLITICAL PRICE OF TERROR

Christabel Pankhurst and others asserted that the suffragette hunger strikers were shielded by the sympathies of the general public, which would presumably never stand for the death of a woman starving herself for the vote.[115] By the summer and fall of 1909, however, the British press had become generally critical of the suffragettes' escalating violence, which now included window breaking and physical attacks on government ministers. The press generally represented the hunger strike as a means to escape the just consequences of illegal and dangerous actions.[116] The liberal press simultaneously supported British protests on behalf of Russian political prisoners in the light of the czar's visit. On 12 July the *Daily News* reported that over one hundred Nonconformist churches in London and the countryside had devoted the previous day to sermons about Russian prison conditions. Nevinson had given an address at Westbourne Park Chapel, with Figner in the congregation. Figner was then present in Trafalgar Square on 25 July 1909 as a participant in the largest public demonstration against the czar's visit, organized by the SFRF and the *Daily News* and attended by a variety of prominent suffragists.[117] Sylvia Pankhurst would later accuse the liberal press of a double standard in condemning the suffragette hunger strikers at the same time that it praised Figner for once assaulting a prison official to gain better conditions for her comrades.[118]

Nicholas II visited Edward VII between 2 and 5 August at Cowes, on the Isle of Wight, under heavy security. On the day of the czar's arrival, *The Times* published a letter to the foreign secretary from the Parliamentary Russian Committee, a coalition of radicals and Labour Party MPs that had formed in the previous year. After describing the oppressive treatment of prisoners in Russia, the committee stated, "We desire to base our protest on the ground of simple humanity; but it is none the less important to remember that many of these prisoners, if guilty at all, are suffering for acts or words which in any constitutional country would be lawful, or even praiseworthy."[119] In the same issue, an editorial accused the letter's signatories of "boorishness."[120] Critics of the czar had no success in raising public protest during his visit, and it appears that no dissident voices reached his ears. The czar observed in his farewell message: "The Emperor is deeply impressed by his visit to this country. . . . The attitude of British statesmen, people, and Press are all happy auguries for the future."[121]

The contest between suffragette hunger strikers and the government intensified after 24 September, when prison medical officers began to forcibly feed the strikers with the authorization of the home secretary. This was by no means a new procedure in British prisons, as observed in the previous chapter. Medical officers had already forcibly fed criminal convicts who had stopped eating to protest their incarceration or specific prison conditions on nonpolitical grounds. Likewise, medical officers in asylums had forcibly fed people whose self-starvation was attributed to insanity. Authorities called this process "artificial feeding" and characterized it as a standard medical procedure. They subsequently resisted using the term "forcible feeding," though it quickly gained currency in the press and in parliament.[122] The suffragettes did not look to the past incidents of "artificial feeding" in prisons and asylums as precedents for their own political protests. Their entire campaign for political status in prison was designed to refute the identification of their actions with those of criminals, and they explicitly rejected any identification with the insane. In a much publicized lawsuit brought by the suffragette Mary Leigh against the home secretary and prison officials who had authorized her forcible feeding in 1909, Leigh testified that she had told the prison medical officer that it would be illegal to forcibly feed her. She had explained to him that if forcible feeding was indeed a medical operation, then it could not be performed without a sane person's consent.[123]

On 24 September, the same day on which medical officers began to forcibly feed hunger strikers, *Votes for Women* featured a front-page cartoon of Prime Minister Asquith titled, "The British Czar" (figure 6). This cartoon represents the extraordinary security precautions that had been taken against suffragettes when Asquith delivered a major speech on the controversial "people's budget" at Birmingham on 17 September.[124] The precautions included secret passages, a closed motorcar, barricades in the streets, and the deployment of hundreds of policemen. Referencing the czar's visit under heavy security in the previous month, the cartoon portrays Asquith in military uniform and guarded closely by armed Cossacks, two with sabers drawn. The subcaption, a quotation from the *Daily Mail*, observes that Asquith was "surrounded by precautions that might have sufficed to protect a Czar." Three days later, in their protests against forcible feeding, the suffragettes' supporters in parliament again likened the government to the czarist regime.

On 27 September, Hardie asked Deputy Home Secretary Charles Masterman in the House of Commons if suffragette hunger strikers in Birmingham Prison had been fed by force. Masterman replied that they had undergone the "ordinary medical treatment." Pursuing the issue, Hardie asked, "Can the hon. Gentleman say if the full operation is the food being pumped through the nostrils of these women or inserted by a tube down the throat?" Masterman answered, "I think the ordinary method is the second one." Hardie was appalled by this revelation, probably all the more so given Masterman's usage of a medical discourse that rendered normal what Hardie found extraordinary. Philip Snowden, MP, interjected and ironically invoked the Spanish inquisition and the czarist regime to reorient the terms of the debate from medical treatment to torture. Snowden said, "May I ask if the hon. Gentleman will convey the suggestion to the Home Secretary that he should make application to Spain or Russia in order to adopt the most brutal and up-to-date methods of barbarism?"[125] The final phrase, "methods of barbarism," had been coined by the former Liberal Party leader Henry Campbell-Bannerman in 1901 to describe British military atrocities during the South African war under a Conservative government. Snowden applied it here to assert implicitly that the Liberal government, having won a strong majority in Parliament in the 1906 general election, had abandoned its moral high ground. A week later Nevinson and Brailsford resigned from the *Daily News* because the editor, A. G. Gardiner, refused to denounce the forcible feeding of suffragettes. The men declared in a letter published in *The Times* on 5 October: "We cannot denounce torture in Russia and support it in England, nor can we advocate democratic principles in the name of a party which confines them to a single sex."[126]

Although the suffragettes were vitriolic in their condemnation of forcible feeding, there is little evidence in British press coverage to suggest that the general public was particularly concerned about, let alone divided over, this issue.[127] "When the process [of forcible feeding] was actually applied," explains C. J. Bearman, "almost

FIGURE 6. "The British Czar," *Votes for Women*, 24 September 1909. Reproduced by permission of the British Library.

every national newspaper applauded the decision, or accepted it as a regrettable necessity made inevitable by the suffragette's own actions. Only the *Manchester Guardian* stood apart."[128] The WSPU published powerful images of forcible feeding in an effort to liken the process to torture and to render this "method of barbarism" symbolic of the Liberal government's despotic dependence on violence.[129] However, the press generally rejected the equation of forcible feeding and torture upon which the power of the images depended.[130] The symbolic power of the image of forcible feeding was further undermined in December 1909 when the WSPU lost both Leigh's action against forcible feeding and a legal action regarding the right to petition.[131] These rulings weakened the WSPU's assertion that hunger strikers were resisting the "illegal and unconstitutional action" of the government. Following the government's victory in the general election of January 1910, Emmeline Pankhurst declared a suspension of WSPU militancy, in a "truce" that lasted until November 1911.

In March 1910, in a conciliatory gesture to suffragette prisoners, Home Secretary Winston Churchill instituted Rule 243A, which gave prison officials the discretionary authority to grant special privileges to suffragettes. This was not political prisoner status. Emmeline Pankhurst and Frederick and Emmeline Pethick-Lawrence jokingly referred to it as "one-and-a-half class," that is, a special category somewhere between the second and first divisions.[132] Two years later, Churchill's successor, Home Secretary Reginald McKenna, abrogated Rule 243A, prompting a new series of hunger strikes at the same time that WSPU violence beyond the prison walls intensified.

In late 1911 suffragettes began to employ arson, and they extended their so-called "argument of the broken pane of glass" from governmental property to private and commercial properties.[133] In this context, on 29 March 1912, the *Manchester Guardian* featured an account of the experiences of Russian "prison strikers," which on 12 April was reprinted in *Votes for Women* under the title "What a Hunger-Strike Means."[134] The account had been translated by Constance Garnett, a respected translator of Russian literature, a friend of leading Russian émigrés, and a suffragist.[135] She had rendered it from the notes of an anonymous Russian prisoner who had been held in Schlusselburg Fortress. That the prisoner was Figner can be deduced from the account's content, which corresponds to the abridged English edition of her memoirs. Garnett had befriended Figner in England and maintained a correspondence with her thereafter.[136]

Figner had left Britain in the fall of 1909, in the midst of suffragette hunger strikes and forcible feeding, to speak on the continent on behalf of Russian political prisoners. She had established the Paris Committee to Help Political Prisoners and Exiles Condemned to Hard Labor, and in 1911 she had published *Les Prisons Russes*, the most comprehensive exposé of the conditions of Russian political prisoners to date.[137] She had also been writing her memoir, in which she had begun to reflect on hunger strikes, but not those of the suffragettes. Rather, she had reflected on hunger strikes, including her own, in Schlusselburg Fortress. Figner had not publicized her experience of hunger striking while she resided in London in 1909, even as suffragettes had adopted this Russian method to secure political prisoner status. Perhaps her silence is attributable to her political distance from the Pankhursts, or perhaps, as suggested below, she was still coming to terms with one of the darkest moments in her long prison experience. It is probably not a coincidence that Figner agreed to convey at least part of the story of her hunger strike to British readers just as the WSPU renewed its hunger strikes in March and April of 1912.

The juxtaposition of the "prison strikers" article with Figner's speech in London in June 1909 is telling. The article begins by recalling the 1889 Kara Tragedy. It recounts a series of protests by political prisoners in Schlusselburg Fortress, including Grachevskii's immolation of himself with kerosene, "the most awful form of death." The article then describes a hunger strike undertaken by a group of politicals, including the anonymous author. The strike was a response to the authorities' confiscation of books from the prison library and lasted eleven days, though most prisoners gave up earlier. The author observes, "The protest ended in failure. . . . All without exception suffered even more than before in health and nerves." "This form of protest, customary in Russian prisons, is a most agonizing one," the author warns. "From its very nature this form of protest is doomed to failure. With the decline of physical strength the will grows weaker."[138]

A week later, the WSPU published a bold, column-length advertisement in *The Times* headlined "Suffragist Prisoners" and addressed to "Citizens of the British Empire!" It posed a series of rhetorical questions in support of the suffragettes' claim to political prisoner status: "Is it the wish of the Nation . . . that women should be subjected to the cruel torture of forcible feeding through the nose because they have adopted the hunger strike as a protest against receiving the prison treatment of criminals? Is it the wish of the Nation that we should follow the cruel practices prevailing in Russia?"[139] Despite the misgivings of an anonymous Russian prisoner, the WSPU employed the same tactics in 1912 that it had initiated in 1909, but this time the public responded frequently with contempt and occasionally with violence. When Sylvia Pankhurst appealed on behalf of hunger strikers at a meeting in Hyde Park in April 1912, the crowd ridiculed her.[140] On two occasions in September, WSPU members heckled the Liberal politician David Lloyd George and were then attacked by crowds, which in one case stripped two women to the waist and took home pieces of their shirts as souvenirs.[141] The WSPU continued to represent hunger strikes as symbols of sacrifice, but the avowed altruism of the women's suffering did not sanctify their militancy and did not attach to WSPU members beyond the prison walls, where many Britons regarded the organization as a threat to public order and private property.

DIVIDED LOYALTIES

Although the British public was apparently reconciled to the forcible feeding of suffragettes, prison medical officers were not. This small corps found it very difficult to attend to hunger strikers and still fulfill its many duties to the general prison population. At the end of 1912, the medical inspector of prisons, Herbert Smalley, observed that the forcible feeding of suffragettes was ultimately distinguished from previous practices of "artificial feeding" by "the persistent, great struggling and resistance of these females" and by "the want of assimilation of food administered, owing partly to more or less self-induced vomiting and partly to inhibition to digestion owing to their mental condition."[142] He acknowledged that medical officers were releasing prisoners on dubious medical grounds, which he attributed to "the natural hesitation of the Medical Officer to use force towards the opposite sex, more especially in the case of persons many of whom are cultured and of refined habits."[143] Recognizing the burdens upon the prison system, McKenna introduced the Prisoners (Temporary Discharge for Ill-Health) Act in April 1913. The so-called Cat and Mouse Act enabled the government to release hunger strikers whose health was deteriorating and then arrest them once more after their health had recovered. This gave medical officers and staff some ability to regulate their workloads in response to the exigencies of prison life, complicated as these were by the suffragettes' strikes and general recalcitrance. The game of cat and mouse continued until Britain's declaration of war against Germany in August 1914. As Britain prepared to enter the war in alliance with Russia, the WSPU again suspended its militant protest after more than 240 British and Irish suffragettes had gone on hunger strike in British and Irish prisons.[144]

Emmeline Pankhurst re-created her public image as a patriot, asserting that in advocating women's suffrage the WSPU had always fought for the good of the nation first and foremost. She assumed a variety of roles in the war effort, including that of a British emissary to Russia. After the abdication of Nicholas II in March 1917, she traveled to Russia on behalf of the British government to assist in persuading the provisional government of Alexander Kerensky not to withdraw from the allied war effort. In the capital, Petrograd, she received a private message that the czar wished to meet her, as he had heard about her leadership of the British women's suffrage campaign.[145] Pankhurst, who had herself conducted hunger strikes and endured forcible feeding, declined the request. She might have accepted, but she had been commissioned to work with the government that had replaced the czarist regime. She departed from Russia in October, having been told that the strangely quiet streets of Petrograd were the calm before a Bolshevik storm.[146]

In the meantime, Figner had returned to Russia and found herself extolled as the heroic founder of a revolution that she now found unfamiliar. She did not find in Bolshevik governance the freedom for which she had fought, yet she remained in Russia, an unquiet legend, and devoted herself to work for the poor and advocacy for political prisoners and exiles.[147] She continued to write about her own experiences of prison and exile, and in 1928 she published her finished memoir, in which she finally provided a full account of her own hunger strike.

Figner recounts in her memoir that Grachevskii conducted an eighteen-day hunger strike against prison conditions in 1886 before immolating himself in October 1887.[148] She also provides more details about her hunger strike and reflects further upon the difficulties that it created for her. She indicates that it took place in the fall of 1889 and explains that most prisoners abandoned the strike after a male comrade began vomiting blood on the ninth day.[149] Figner and a male political continued for another two days, but then reluctantly stopped after two comrades said that they would kill themselves if Figner and the other striker starved to death.[150] Not only did Figner regard the strike as a "failure,"; she found that this particular failure had made her doubt the revolutionary commitment of her comrades and question her own commitment to collective action in the future— a deeply troubling thought for a revolutionary populist. Figner had suffered, by her own account, "burning disillusionment" and a "moral catastrophe."[151]

Figner's speech in London in 1909, her account of her hunger strike published in 1912, and her account of 1928 illustrate important features of Russian revolutionary hunger strikes that were already apparent in Kennan's and Deutsch's accounts of the Kara Tragedy. Figner's hunger strike was not "a womanish thing," for she starved with men to disrupt and defy prison authorities in order to secure specific changes in prison conditions. The strike may have fulfilled Figner's commitment to self-sacrifice, but she did not see it, from a practical standpoint, as an extension of her terrorist campaign. Like Russian revolutionaries in general, she regarded the hunger strike as weak. In her speech of 1909 on prison conditions and prison protests, she highlighted Grachevskii's self-immolation as the most effective protest of her prison experience, and she did not even mention his earlier hunger strike or the subsequent strike in which she participated. In Les Prisons Russes she addressed famines in Russia and deprivation of food, hunger, and suicide in prison, but not hunger strikes.[152] When Figner finally publicized her hunger strike in Britain in 1912, she characterized it as a failure, but even then she did not convey the "burning disillusionment" and "moral catastrophe" that it had produced in her. On the one hand she regarded the hunger strike as a weak method of protest, and on the other she apparently struggled to come to terms with its powerful effect on her, the political prisoner. Figner in 1909 had been an epitome of the political prisoner in Britain, and suffragettes had thus resented that the liberal press criticized their hunger strikes for political prisoner status even as it lauded her.[153] In fact, Figner did not share in the suffragette's political priority, "votes for women," and she was skeptical of the "Russian method" as a means to this or any other political end. There is no evidence that any subsequent hunger strikers were aware of Figner's warning. Their own experiences nonetheless taught them to pay heed. Many learned to fear not only death, but the failure of a hunger strike that could demoralize and break their ranks.

INSPIRATIONS

The suffragettes' understanding of the Russian hunger strike had been primarily shaped by the Russian revolutionary exiles who had preceded Figner to Britain. They represented their revolutionary movement to British radicals as a campaign for constitutional reform in which the brutality of the czarist regime rendered the revolutionaries as sympathetic martyrs rather than terrorists. Suffragettes therefore perceived Russian hunger strikers in terms not of a contemporary anarchist threat but of their own struggle for constitutional reform. This perception was perhaps reinforced by the exiles' decision to foreground the leadership of women in the momentous strike at Kara. Be that as it may, suffragettes defined the hunger strike as a distinctly feminine tactic of protest, though a small number of men, so-called "suffragettes in trousers," employed this tactic as well.[154] According to the WSPU, women had particular qualities necessary to a successful hunger striker, such as selflessness and discipline. Sandra Holton further explains, "The suffragette identity was one built around a feminine heroic, and a rhetoric of female rebellion which the presence of men continually threatened to undermine."[155] In 1912, with the resumption of hunger strikes and the escalation of WSPU violence, the Pankhursts began to distance the WSPU from its male supporters.[156] Such a move would have been incomprehensible to Russian revolutionary populists.

Leaders of the WSPU declared in *Votes for Women* that the hunger strike was "the strongest weapon they had ever used against the Government."[157] Indeed, it served as both an instrument of liberation and a symbol of heroic martyrdom. Suffragettes adapted it to a symbolic idiom of feminine sacrifice that they had already developed in their militant campaign, especially in seeking physical confrontation, arrest, and imprisonment. Their hunger strikes and experiences of forcible feeding embodied for the British public the despotic violence of an ostensibly liberal government and their own willingness to sacrifice themselves for the nation. They represented their current sacrifice as the basis of their future vote, and they invoked the past protests of Russian revolutionaries, whose greater suffering in a presumably similar quest for political representation heightened the significance of their own. Although the Russian analogy was only one facet of the propaganda that accompanied the suffragettes' strikes, it illuminated most precisely the constitutional goals of their campaign.

These goals were obscured in the public's eye, however, by the WSPU's increasing violence. In January 1913 the WSPU began a campaign of destruction across

Britain that moved beyond window breaking and arson to include bombings, cutting telephone and telegraph lines, and destroying artwork in galleries and muse-
ums. The British press and the general public were alienated not by the constitutional goals of the hunger strikers, but by the fearful violence that had brought the
strikers to prison in the first place. This violence widened the division of the suffragist movement itself between a militant minority and the nonviolent majority.
The latter included Millicent Garrett Fawcett, president of the National Union
of Women's Suffrage Societies, who repeatedly condemned WSPU violence and
voiced support for the government.[158] As representatives of the WSPU were heckled, pelted with fruit and eggs, and sometimes assaulted by hostile crowds, the
government cracked down on the organization, now confident in its moral authority over suffragettes who in 1913 declared themselves to be "terrorists."[159] When in
June 1914 a suffragette turned to King George V in His Majesty's Theatre and
yelled, "You Russian Tsar!" her cry must have rung hollowly, if offensively, in the
ears of his subjects.[160]

The suffragettes' campaign for constitutional reform and their multifaceted discourse on rights nonetheless resonated with critics of British imperialism in the
United Kingdom and abroad. News of their hunger strikes spread through British
imperial networks of governance and communication, conveyed by official and
private correspondence, newspapers, books, and rumor.[161] These strikes inspired
or informed two distinct forms of hunger in protest in Ireland and India, the first
defined by militancy and the second defined by nonviolence, both embodying in
different cultural contexts the disparate ideologies and objectives of their practitioners. Irish suffragettes, militant socialists, and republicans, women and men,
took up the hunger strike and reframed its significance in not only spiritual, but
explicitly religious, predominantly Catholic terms of shared sacrifice and nationalism. Some Indian militant nationalists then found in Irish republican strikes an
inspiring model. Others found their inspiration to starve in India itself. Together,
both groups adapted hunger in protest to a variety of ends in building a new
national temple to Bharat Mata (Mother India).

Mohandas Gandhi, one of the most famous practitioners of hunger in protest,
had noted the effectiveness of the suffragette hunger strikes against the British
government when he was moving in suffragist circles in London in 1909.[162] He had
already begun to articulate his nonviolent program of *satyagraha*, which included
fasting as a method of self-purification and atonement. He accordingly criticized
the suffragettes' militancy.[163] Gandhi insisted that he, in contrast, conducted his
fasts with love, and that their success depended upon another's love for him.[164]
He recognized that this relationship of love was arguably sustained by the liberal
principles of British governance and the publicity of a modern media, both of
which protected him, like the suffragettes, from starvation without comment or
care. It was harder and more dangerous for prisoners to starve in isolation against

an illiberal government that was indifferent to the display of blood on its hands. Gandhi once observed, "You cannot fast against a tyrant."[165] Nonetheless, the proliferation of hunger as an international tactic of political protest began when British suffragettes took up the Russian method from the prisoners of a tyrannical czarist regime.

3

A Shared Sacrifice

Hunger Strikes by Irish Women and Men, 1912–1946

George Kennan's account of the hunger strikes, floggings, and suicides of Russian politicals at Kara in 1888–89 provoked a critical letter to the editor of the *Century Magazine*. The correspondent, identified as "C—— M——," writing from "X—— Hotel, X——, June 3, 1891," challenged Kennan's claim that Nadezhda Sigida had been flogged to death and speculated that she had probably taken her own life. C—— M—— observed, "The only evidence that the flogging, which she actually courted, was unduly severe, is that she died in three days afterward—the day when the other prisoners committed suicide." This letter troubled Kennan. He returned to it, reprinting it in full, in the second volume of *Siberia and the Exile System*, which he published later that year. It was quibbling, he observed, to assert that "Madam Sigída was not flogged to death because . . . she did not actually die under the lash." In a moment of morbid fancy and uncanny prescience, Kennan then observed:

> If Mr. C—— M——'s younger sister, a cultivated, generous, impulsive, and patriotic young Irish girl, we will say, had been sent to the Andaman Islands [a penal colony of British India] for twenty years as a hard-labor convict because she had helped to maintain a secret "Home Rule" printing-office in Belfast; if, driven to despair by cruel treatment of herself and her companions in penal servitude, she had starved herself twenty-two days in order to bring about, by the only means of compulsion open to her, the removal of the officer responsible for such cruel treatment; if, finally, she had been fed by force through a rubber tube; if, in the abnormal mental condition that would naturally be caused by so terrible an experience of hunger and outrage, she had committed a breach of prison discipline; if she had then been stripped, held by the wrists on a soldier's back, and flogged until she fainted; and if, at last, in an agony

70

of helplessness, shame, and despair, she had taken her own life, I do not think that Mr. C—— M—— would regard it as an overstatement if I should say that his sister had been "flogged to death."[1]

News of the Kara Tragedy had appeared in Irish newspapers a year earlier, in 1890.[2] Additional stories about hunger strikes in Russian prisons appeared occasionally thereafter. Following the first hunger strike by the suffragette Marion Wallace Dunlop in 1909, the Irish press covered suffragette strikes on a regular basis, and still, occasionally, covered hunger strikes by Russian politicals, both women and men.[3] The first Irish women to hunger strike did not do so for home rule, as Kennan envisioned, but for the vote. Irish suffragettes initially starved in British prisons, then, after 1912, in Irish prisons. In contrast to British suffragettes, they were not averse to men taking up the hunger strike as a tactic of protest. As Irish republican men began hunger striking after 1913, and then in increasing numbers after 1917, hunger striking became a tactic shared by women and men in closer, if unwitting, emulation of the "Russian method" than British suffragettes had ever achieved.

Between 1912 and 1946 dozens of Irish women and thousands of Irish men conducted hunger strikes in the custody of the British government and the Irish Free State, a self-governing dominion of the British Empire after 1922, renamed Éire in 1937. They used the hunger strike as a means to assert their demands for political prisoner status, to defy the authority of courts, to gain release, or to improve prison conditions. The vast majority of strikers understood their self-starvation as a militant act, a last weapon to be used after killing and the destruction of property were no longer options. There were a few pacifist strikers, but they generally sought the same goals as militants, namely, votes for women or an Irish republic.[4] This chapter begins with the first hunger strike by suffragettes under the British government in Ireland in 1912 and ends with a hunger strike by an Irish Republican Army (IRA) officer under the government of Éire in 1946. The first strike ended with release, and the last with one of the ten deaths of Irish men on hunger strike in this period.

This chapter explains how the hunger strike was adapted from protests against the male monopoly on the vote in the United Kingdom to protests against the United Kingdom as the legal, sovereign artifice of Britain's conquest of Ireland. Both of the campaigns focused on citizenship and equality, though in different political registers, the first strictly domestic and the second international. During the First World War these campaigns overlapped, if in the minds of more women than men, but they then effectively separated after the great majority of Irish and British women won the vote under the 1918 Representation of the People Act.

This chapter shows that, as in Russia and Britain, most strikers in Ireland did not think of their own starvation as a symbolic act, but as a last weapon through which to challenge the practical capacities of their prisons and to push warders and prison medical officers beyond their professional duties into the violation of law. This chapter furthermore examines how the meaning of the hunger strike refracted through the prisms of gender and religion in Ireland, and how the hunger strike became a powerful and ultimately fraught political symbol. As a symbolic weapon, the hunger strike proved to be double-edged in the hands of republicans. It cut against republicans' own goals in a couple ways. First, women and men established hunger striking as a shared sacrifice through not only their common suffering, but also through the ritualization of hunger striking in the terms of Catholicism, thus rendering hunger striking inaccessible to a critical community: Protestants. A shared nationalist sacrifice in which Protestants could not fully take part only reinforced the impression that they, a historically privileged minority, would be marginalized in the future, majority-Catholic Irish nation, despite republicans' inclusive and religiously tolerant rhetoric. Similarly, looking forward, we will see that Indian nationalists represented hunger striking in terms of Hinduism and thus rendered this tactic of protest not just inaccessible but alienating to Muslims.

The second problem for republicans was that internecine hunger strikes after the Anglo-Irish War (1919–21) deepened divisions between those who supported the subsequent foundation of the Irish Free State and the partition of Ireland and those who supported only a republic for the whole of Ireland. Former Irish hunger strikers imprisoned members of their own political generation and the next between the 1920s and the 1940s. The prisoners then proceeded to hunger strike against their Irish captors in a broader contest to realize as yet impossible dreams of national freedom. Sitting by a window at Thoor Ballylee in 1922, W. B. Yeats reflected upon the civil war that had recently arrived at his home:

> We had fed the heart on fantasies,
> The heart's grown brutal from the fare,
> More substance in our enmities,
> Than in our love.[5]

As we will see, this vexed situation was shared by Indian nationalists after their own divisions were exposed and deepened by their contests for control over Indian provincial governments in the 1930s. In Ireland and India, nationalists-turned-government-officials saw the hunger strike as a more dangerous threat to the state than they had appreciated when they themselves had once starved. Starving bodies, Irish and Indian, challenged the moral authority of self-governing nationalists and especially their liberal declarations of commitment to the whole nation on the strength of only a majority of voters. Turning their critics' own charge back upon them, nationalists elected to office in Ireland and India claimed legitimacy on the grounds that they, unlike the British, demonstrably enjoyed the consent of the governed and were thus duty-bound to enforce the rule of law to insure the nation's future. They then responded to hunger strikes in much the same ways that the British had done before them.

GENDER AND FAITH IN REVOLUTIONARY HUNGER STRIKES

Hunger strikes developed in Ireland in an era of momentous political change. In 1912 Irish suffragists, Irish labor, and the Irish home rule movement were approaching a crisis in which they would all be subsumed by a new republican politics. The United Kingdom of Great Britain and Ireland (UK), established in 1801, was threatened by the third Irish home rule bill, which was progressing through Parliament with the support of constitutional nationalists in the Irish Parliamentary Party in alliance with the Liberal government of Prime Minister Herbert Asquith. The prospect of Irish home rule alarmed members of the Irish Unionist Alliance, a predominantly Protestant party concentrated in the northern Irish province of Ulster, who regarded "home rule as Rome rule." Unionists formed militias; then, in 1913, they organized the Ulster Volunteer Force against the seemingly imminent prospect of Catholic nationalist governance. Later in the year, the nationalist Irish Republican Brotherhood (IRB) formed its own paramilitary organization, the avowedly nonsectarian Irish Volunteers, and militant socialists formed the Irish Citizen Army, bringing the UK to the brink of civil war.[6] The outbreak of the First World War in 1914 postponed hostilities, but two years later, in April 1916, Irish republicans and socialists launched a rebellion, the Easter Rising, which proved to be the pivotal event in twentieth-century Irish history. Although British forces crushed the Rising in a matter of days and executed sixteen of its leaders, civil war had arrived. Irish constitutional nationalism gave way to militant republicanism over the next two years.

By the time the Allies and Germany signed an armistice in 1918, Irish nationalism was dominated by the republican political party Sinn Féin and the Irish Volunteers, renamed the IRA in the following year. Under the leadership of Eamon de Valera, a veteran of the Rising, Sinn Féin swept into power across all of Ireland except Ulster in the 1918 general election. The party refused to take its seats at Westminster, but instead founded its own government in Dublin centered upon the Dáil Éireann (People's Assembly), which declared Ireland's independence in its first meeting in January 1919. British forces and the IRA then battled for control over Ireland until December 1921, when Sinn Féin and the London government signed a divisive treaty, bringing the UK's civil war to a troubled end. Ireland was partitioned in 1922; the southern twenty-six counties became the Irish Free State and the northern six counties of Ulster remained part of the reconstituted United Kingdom of Great Britain and Northern Ireland. Irish republicans split between those who accepted and those who opposed the partition and the Irish Free State, resulting in the state's own civil war between 1922 and 1923. This struggle ended in victory for the "staters" and concluded what historians call Ireland's "revolutionary era."

In the long aftermath of this civil war, two political parties formed, Fianna Fáil and Fine Gael, which remain at the center of politics in the republic of Ireland to this day. After forming its first government in 1932, Fianna Fáil, headed by de Valera, proceeded to draft a new constitution, ratified by a popular referendum in 1937, through which it asserted the Irish Free State's almost complete autonomy from the UK and laid unenforceable claim to a united Ireland. With that united Ireland a distant prospect, Fine Gael took power in 1948 and declared Éire to be an independent republic in 1949.

Margaret Ward once characterized republican women of the revolutionary era as "heroic subordinates."[7] This representation is supported by a large body of scholarship that recounts the collapse of the women's suffrage movement and, more broadly, Irish feminism under the weight of Irish nationalism and the relegation of women from public life to the domestic sphere under successive governments of the Irish Free State.[8] It is striking indeed to compare the Proclamation of the Irish Republic, which launched the Easter Rising in 1916, with the Irish constitution of 1937. The proclamation declared that Ireland should have a national government "elected by the suffrages of all her men and women." Irish women subsequently gained the vote not as Irish citizens, but as subjects of the United Kingdom under the Representation of the People Act, 1918. The first constitution of the Irish Free State in 1922 then guaranteed them the vote on equal terms with men. The constitution of 1937 maintained the vote of "every citizen without distinction of sex," but it furthermore prescribed married motherhood as the normative and ideal social role for women. This followed legislation that had already limited women's employment opportunities and even restricted them from juries. In sum, the suffrage secured in 1918 and the subsequent progress toward the independence of Éire in 1949 did not entail greater socioeconomic equity for women and so undermined the development of women's role in Irish public life.

A range of scholars have asserted that the key to women's marginalization was their exclusion from combat after the IRA turned to guerilla warfare against British forces in 1919 and initiated the so-called masculinization of Irish militancy.[9] Women had comparatively few opportunities to risk a blood sacrifice, which was presumably the basis of an incontrovertible claim to full citizenship. A woman's proper sacrifice for the nation was the loss of a son, a brother, or a husband; it was her duty to endure, grieve, and honor, rather than to join in a sacrificial death.[10] Scholars furthermore attribute the marginalization of women to the resurgent influence of the Catholic Church under postwar Irish leaders, especially de Valera.[11] Those republican women who refused to accept their quiescent, domestic role were famously caricatured by P. S. O'Hegarty in 1924 as "the furies."[12]

Previous studies of Irish hunger strikes in the revolutionary era have represented women's subordination in compelling cultural terms. In an argument of
long-standing influence, George Sweeney asserts that the cultural origins of the
hunger strike in Ireland rendered it a fundamentally masculine symbol that
women could not legitimately embody.[13] He explains that the revival of Celtic culture through the Gaelic language movement after the 1870s and the Irish literary
renaissance after the 1890s, combined with the growing social and political influence of the Catholic Church at this time, created a context in which Irish rebels
revived the Celtic tradition of fasting in protest and found in this practice a symbolic discourse that resonated broadly with Irish nationalists. Sweeney asserts,
moreover, that the spirit of self-sacrifice manifested in the Easter Rising was the
catalyst that gave subsequent strikes their political significance and power by val-
orizing and combining Celtic mythology, especially the hero Cuchulain, and a
Catholic conception of glorious martyrdom in the image of Christ.[14] The identification of fasting with Christ rendered the hunger strike not only moral, but essentially masculine—and all the more so in view of the martyrs of the Rising, sixteen
dead men.[15]

A closer examination of the experiences of Irish hunger strikers in the early
twentieth century reveals that these women and men were not inspired by a Celtic
tradition of fasting in protest and that they did not represent their strikes in terms
of their Celtic heritage. Irish suffragettes, the first to use the hunger strike in Ireland, recognized the Russian origins of this tactic of protest.[16] Moreover, although
Catholicism was deeply influential in Irish hunger strikes, male strikers rarely portrayed their strikes in the exclusively gendered terms of Christlike sacrifice. If there
was a man inspired to fast by Christ's example, it was Terence MacSwiney, but he
was one among thousands, and he was in other ways exceptional. As a rule, men
cooperated with women in hunger striking, as women conducted and represented
their hunger strikes in terms of their Catholic faith, specifically appealing for support to Christ's mother, Mary. Contrary to Sweeney, Catholicism offered female and
male strikers a common language with which to commiserate, inspire, and endure,
even if in the long run the institutional cooperation of the Catholic Church and
Irish nationalist governments pushed women to the margins of public life.

At the same time that republicans ritualized and represented hunger strikes in
the terms of Catholicism, they saw themselves engaged in a more broadly spiritual
cause that crossed the boundaries of Christian denomination, gender, and class.
The ecumenical quality of these spiritual notions was conveyed through the Proclamation of the Irish Republic, in which republicans pledged "[to cherish] all the
children of the nation equally."[17] However, as Richard English argues, "Catholicism
was a binding and defining force for Irish republicans," even as they sincerely
declared that they would embrace Protestants as fellow citizens of the prospective
Irish nation.[18] They were seemingly oblivious to the fact that their ecumenical

politics were imbued with Catholicism. The Catholic discourse and rituals of hunger strikes thus played into a larger republican paradox to the exclusion of Protestants across the revolutionary era.[19]

Beyond Catholicism, there were other factors, more mundane, that enforced women and men's perceptions of a shared sacrifice in hunger striking. Most important among these were experiences of incarceration in the same prisons, the coordination of strikes, and, finally, family ties. The bonds forged by these experiences were strong; so strong that survivors of strikes and the families of dead strikers in the revolutionary era became central figures in subsequent strikes by imprisoned IRA members during and soon after the Second World War. Republican strikers and their supporters and Irish government officials viewed these later strikes in irreconcilable terms of nobility and hypocrisy. Many were former comrades, or the children of former comrades, each sure that her or his adversary had forsaken their once common commitment to a united Irish republic. Hunger strikers of the past thus divided over strikers in the present.

TOWARD A SHARED SACRIFICE: IRISH SUFFRAGETTES AND IRISH LABOUR

The women's suffrage movement in Ireland was considerably smaller than the movement in Great Britain. There were perhaps 3,500 suffragists in Ireland in the spring of 1914, and the great majority of these were nonmilitants affiliated with the Irish Women's Suffrage Federation.[20] The Irish suffrage movement was split not only between militants and nonmilitants, but also between nationalists and unionists. Inspired by the Women's Social and Political Union (WSPU), two Irish suffragists, Margaret Cousins and Hanna Sheehy Skeffington, founded the Irish Women's Franchise League (IWFL) in November 1908. The core of the IWFL membership, like that of the WSPU, was middle class, educated, and urban. Like the WSPU, the IWFL asserted its political legitimacy in prison, though far fewer members were arrested—only thirty-five in all.[21] Given the similarities between these organizations, the differences were considerable. Whereas the WSPU couched its demand for women's suffrage in terms of duty and service to the British nation, the IWFL sought to incorporate women's suffrage into the Irish Parliamentary Party's political platform for home rule.[22] It was only after years of fruitless dialogue with the party that the IWFL finally turned, like the WSPU before it, to the argument of the broken pane of glass.[23]

In June 1912 Sheehy Skeffington and seven other IWFL members staged the first suffragette protest in Ireland. They broke over fifty window panes in government buildings in Dublin to protest the refusal by John Redmond, leader of the Irish Parliamentary Party, to include women's suffrage in the third home rule bill, which was then before parliament.[24] The women were arrested, prosecuted, and sentenced. As the first Irish suffragettes to be incarcerated in Mountjoy Prison, they demanded placement in the first division in recognition of their status as political prisoners. As in Britain, there were three divisions of incarceration in Irish prisons, and the government refused to recognize political status on the grounds that there was no such thing as political crime. It did, however, authorize differential treatment and, thus, de facto political status for the women under Rule 243A, which had been recently instituted by Home Secretary Winston Churchill to appease WSPU prisoners and reduce problems for prison officials and staff.[25]

Before departing from the courtroom for prison, Sheehy Skeffington had declared to her supporters in the audience, "Remember Mr. Asquith is coming in July!"[26] She was not aware that British members of the WSPU, not the IWFL, were preparing the most memorable welcome for the prime minister. They threw a hatchet at his car as he and Redmond drove into Dublin, then set fire to curtains in the theater where he was scheduled to speak.[27] Three British women, Gladys Evans, Mary Leigh, and Jennie Baines (a.k.a. Lizzie Baker) were arrested for their roles in these and other protests. The first two were sentenced to five years of penal servitude and the latter to seven months of hard labor in Mountjoy. On 14 August the three women began a hunger strike for release, and within a day four of the eight Irish women sentenced in June also went on hunger strike for release in an act of solidarity.[28] At least six of the eight Irish women imprisoned in June had been previously imprisoned in England for their participation in WSPU protests.[29] These included three of the four Irish women on hunger strike: Marguerite Palmer and the sisters Hanna and Margaret Murphy.[30] Whereas the Murphys had been forcibly fed in England, their Irishness spared them this treatment in Ireland. The Viceroy Lord Aberdeen instructed prison officials not to forcibly feed any of the Irish women, probably due to concerns that Irish medical officers might refuse to carry out the procedure.[31] In the interest of consistency, British officials did not forcibly feed the British women either—at least not while the Irish women were imprisoned with them. The Irish women were released on 19 August, as was Baines due to poor health.[32] On the following day, the prison medical officer, Raymond Dowdall, began to forcibly feed Evans and Leigh, who endured forcible feeding for 46 and 58 days respectively until they were released on medical grounds.[33] Sheehy Skeffington recalled, "They . . . looked like living and slightly decayed corpses."[34]

The experiences of suffragette hunger strikers in Ireland were consistent over the next couple of years. Officials did not forcibly feed suffragettes of any nationality again. Instead, they either acceded to their demands for privileges or released them. There were at least eighteen hunger strikes by suffragettes in Irish prisons between February 1913 and August 1914.[35] Nine of these strikes occurred in Ulster, and of these at least eight were conducted by British women. The shift in hunger striking to Ulster was provoked by the unionist leader, Sir Edward Carson, who announced in September 1913 that the Unionist Party had decided to support women's suffrage in its plans for a provisional government. Christabel Pankhurst of the WSPU promptly dispatched Dorothy Evans to establish a WSPU branch in Belfast, with the intention of pressing Carson to make women's suffrage a reality. When Carson then retracted his party's support for women's suffrage in March, the WSPU responded with violence, including attacks on party and governmental officials and an attempt to blow up the Lisburn Cathedral. Few Irish members of the WSPU participated in the violence, and all of the prisoners who went on hunger strike were released unconditionally or under the Cat and Mouse Act after a week or less.[36]

The IWFL, like the WSPU, had an idealized, heroic vision of feminine valor and sacrifice, symbolically embodied by Joan of Arc. It probably mattered more to the great majority of Irish Catholic members of the IWFL than it did to the predominantly Protestant WSPU that Joan of Arc had been beatified by the Catholic Church in 1909, setting the stage for her canonization in 1920. In April 1914, as part of the IWFL Daffodil Fete, the flamboyant republican Countess Constance Markievicz posed as Joan of Arc, and Kathleen Houston, assistant secretary of the IWFL, as a prisoner in "A Militant Tableau," one of a series of *tableaux vivants* of great women of the past. "As a finale to the tableaux," Ward recounts, "the militant Joan of Arc led on the women who had been imprisoned for the cause."[37] On 1 May, Houston was arrested for breaking a window of the post office on College Green in Dublin. Her life then imitated art as she began a hunger and thirst strike, through which she won unconditional release after several days. The cover of the next issue of the IWFL publication *Irish Citizen* featured a photograph of Markievicz and Houston's tableau (figure 7).[38] The photograph subsequently became a popular fund-raising souvenir for the IWFL.[39]

At the same time that the IWFL and the WSPU shared the symbol of Joan of Arc, the IWFL invoked a nationalist tradition that was decidedly anti-British. The conflicting interests of the two organizations became more pronounced over time, especially with the increasing power of labor in both countries.[40] While the Pankhursts simultaneously rejected cooperation with the Labour Party and, after 1912, alienated men from their organization, the IWFL cooperated closely with Irish labor, and especially militant socialists, regardless of gender. Irish suffragettes were strong supporters of labor during the Dublin Lockout of 1913, a major, violent conflict between unionized workers and their employers. In turn, they enjoyed the backing of James Connolly, one of Ireland's most important labor leaders.[41] It was not labor politics, however, but the First World War that decisively broke the alliance between the WSPU and the IWFL. Whereas the Pankhursts suspended their protests in order to support the British war effort, the IWFL joined Irish labor in denouncing the war.[42]

Although the IWFL readily cooperated with male supporters, its rhetoric, like that of the WSPU, highlighted women's superior self-discipline, spiritual resolve, and will to sacrifice. The hunger strike gave ultimate expression to these feminine

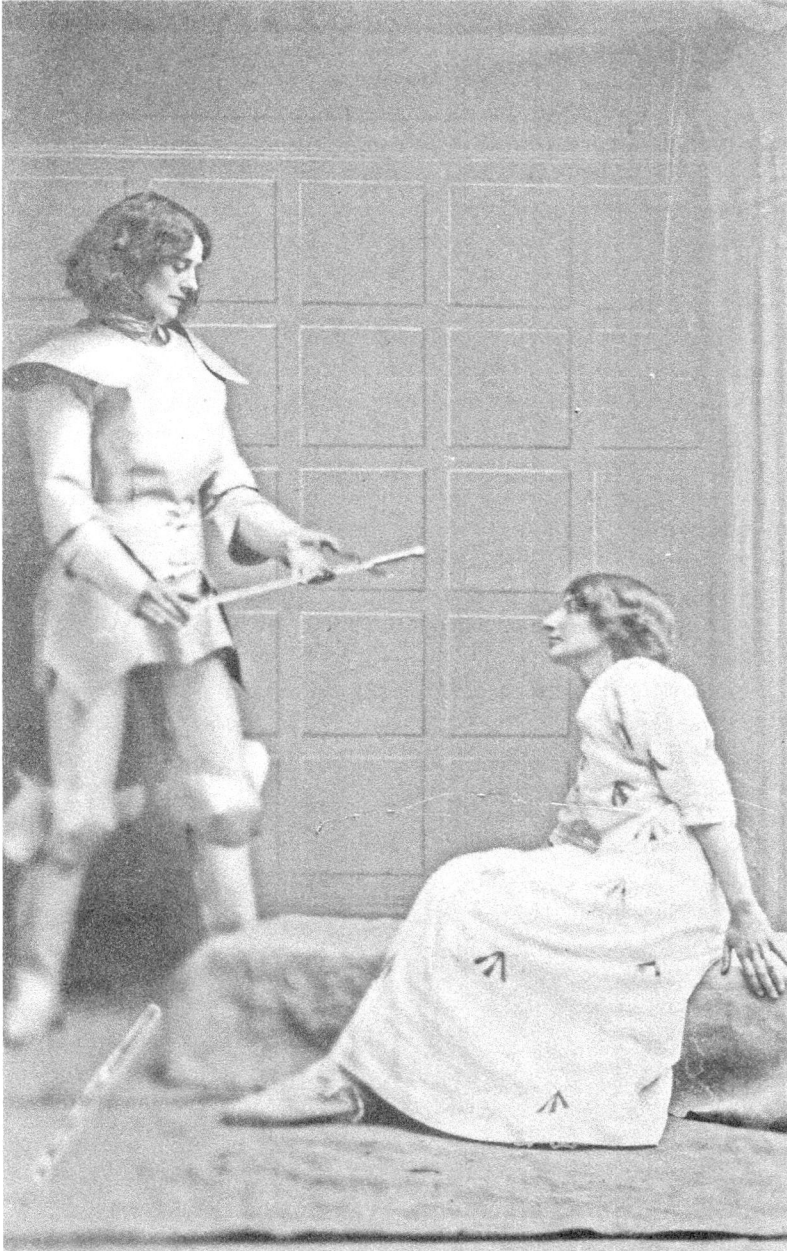

FIGURE 7. A Militant Tableau featuring Countess Constance Markievicz (as Joan of Arc) and Kathleen Houston (as a political prisoner) in April 1914. Reproduced by permission of the National Library of Ireland.

characteristics. At an IWFL meeting held in June 1913, Markievicz asked, "How many men would face the Hunger Strike for any cause on God's earth?"[43] The answer would prove to be thousands. Despite the suffragettes' representation of hunger striking as a demonstration of feminine strength, numerous men adopted this tactic in the ensuing years. A few factors enabled the hunger strike to become an act of shared sacrifice in the revolutionary era. Most importantly, the great majority of male strikers used starvation as an instrument, rather than a symbol, of prison protest. It was, for most, an extension of their rebellions against prison authority, a sequel to work stoppages, destroying furniture, breaking spy holes, and using books to wedge doors off hinges. The vast majority of male strikers saw starvation as a means to achieve their two most common goals: differential treatment and rendering prisons ungovernable. And they were aware that hunger striking sometimes worked. Considering the thousands of strikes by men, it is notable how seldom these men or their supporters represented their strikes in masculine, let alone Christlike, terms comparable to the powerful, feminine representations by the suffragettes. Over time, however, women and men developed a shared discourse on hunger striking grounded in Catholicism.

The hunger strike was initially transferred from women to men through Connolly and other labor leaders during the Dublin Lockout. On 30 August 1913 Connolly was arrested on charges of sedition for his leadership of the Dublin tramway strike and sentenced to three months' imprisonment. On 7 September he began a hunger strike for release, because the prison officials had refused to let him post bail. Fearful that Connolly's death would trigger greater violence in the city, the viceroy released him after a week into the care of his wife, Lillie Connolly, who took him to Marckievicz's home, where he recuperated for two days.[44] Although James Connolly had sometimes valorized martyrdom in his political writing, there is no evidence that he perceived his hunger strike in sacrificial, masculine terms. When asked why he had chosen to strike, Connolly replied, "What was good enough for the suffragettes is good enough for us."[45]

Subsequently, on 20 October, James Byrne, the secretary of the Kingstown (Dun Laoghaire) branch of the Irish Transport and General Workers Union (ITGWU), was arrested for assaulting a tram inspector and placed in Mountjoy. When prison officials refused to let him post bail, Byrne began a hunger and thirst strike. By the time officials capitulated and released him on bail several days later, he had contracted pneumonia in his damp cell, in his weakened state. He died on 1 November in Monkstown Hospital, leaving behind a wife and six children. Three thousand people were reported to have attended his funeral, including a thousand ITGWU members and two bands brought in by a special train. Connolly declared in a funeral oration from the roof of a cab: "[Byrne] had been thrown into a cold, damp, mouldy cell, but while in prison, so contemptuous had he been of those who put him there that he had refused food and drink."[46] Connolly charged that

Byrne had been killed by the prison authorities and the Castle, as the viceroy's government was known.

Connolly's and Byrne's hunger strikes, and Byrne's death, received relatively little coverage in the press. Neither man was likened to Cuchulain or Christ; their hunger strikes carried no masculine symbolism that we can now discern. However, Byrne's death does illuminate contingencies upon which the perception of a heroic and popular—rather than tragic and obscure—hunger strike depended. The media's indifference to Byrne's death suggests that there was no discursive context in which his death could have been elevated to public sacrifice. Byrne remained a laborer among laborers. His name appeared in the media's occasional lists of victims of the lockout, beside the names of those who had died at the hands of police. Perhaps Byrne's death might have provoked a greater response had he been a labor leader of national status, like James Larkin, who had founded the ITGWU. As Byrne lay on his deathbed, Larkin was prosecuted for sedition on 27 October and sentenced to the first division, sparking a public protest that secured his release from Mountjoy within two weeks.[47] Yet Connolly, a comparably prominent leader, had also generated only muted public protest with his hunger strike. Byrne's death was simply added to the scale of loss that inspired Connolly to call upon Irish workers to arm themselves on 14 November, prompting the establishment of the Irish Citizen Army that he would later lead in the Rising.[48]

STARVING FOR A REPUBLIC

Before and after the Rising, in the spring of 1916, imprisoned republican men turned to hunger striking.[49] Ellen (Nell) Humphreys recalled approvingly that her twenty-year-old son, Richard (Dick), who was arrested by the military during a raid of her home in April 1916, joined a hunger strike by prisoners in Mountjoy and gained release after ten days without food.[50] Following the Rising, later in the spring, two hundred Irish prisoners in the internment camp at Frongoch, Wales, successfully used the hunger strike to face down a heavy-handed commandant, Colonel F. A. Heygate Lambert, nicknamed Buckshot, who had demanded that they identify one Michael Murphy for enlistment in the British army.[51] The hunger strike did have skeptics among republicans at this time, particularly de Valera. He had been court martialed after the Rising and sentenced to death, but his sentence had been then commuted to penal servitude for life. He went on a hunger strike for a few days in October 1916 as an internee in Dartmoor Prison in England.[52] Subsequently, as an internee at Lewes Prison in England, he forbade the men under his command from hunger striking, preferring instead to employ work stoppages and other forms of resistance.[53] He observed, "You may be tempted to hunger strike. As a body do not attempt it while the war lasts unless you were assured from outside that the death of two or three of you would help the cause—as soldiers I know you would not shrink from sacrifice—but remember how precious a human life is."[54] It was not two or three but one hunger striker whose death soon revitalized republicanism into a force greater than it had ever been before.

Thomas Ashe was a leading figure in the Gaelic League, a champion hurler, an accomplished player of the Irish pipes, and a national school teacher before he joined the IRB and became a founding member of the Irish Volunteers. He participated in the Easter Rising as the commander of volunteer forces at Ashbourne, County Dublin, where he and his men seized four barracks of the Royal Irish Constabulary (RIC), making him the most successful commander of the rebellion. He was sentenced to death with de Valera, but his sentence, like de Valera's, was commuted. Following his release in June 1917, he resumed his militant activities and was consequently imprisoned in Mountjoy in September on charges of sedition. On the 17th, a committee of republican prisoners submitted a list of eleven demands for special privileges to the prison's deputy governor, stating that forty men would go on hunger strike if their demands were not met by 1 October.[55] Many prisoners then broke up their cells and created such mayhem that the warders muffled the bells with which the prisoners called them. The warders retaliated on 20 September. Tomás Ó Maoileóin recalled, "A dozen peelers broke into each man's cell and beat us up right and proper. Everything was whipped from us and we were left to lie upon the bare boards."[56] Ashe and thirty-nine other inmates led by Austin Stack, another veteran of the Rising, began a hunger strike that evening. Forcible feeding began just two days later. On 25 September, Dr. William Lowe, an inexperienced assistant to the prison medical officer, Dowdall, attempted to forcibly feed Ashe with a stomach pump but accidentally pumped milk and eggs into Ashe's lungs. The warders carried Ashe back to his cell, blue in the face and unconscious. He died that evening in Mater Misericordiae Hospital, sparking a public furor and a political crisis for the Castle.[57] In anticipation of a damning coroner's inquest, the Castle suspended forcible feeding on 29 September, then granted most of the prisoners' demands for differential treatment in what became known as the September Rules.[58]

Ashe's funeral was monumental. His remains, dressed in a Volunteer uniform, lay in state in the city hall, surrounded by an honor guard of Volunteers and boys from the nationalist scout troop, the Fianna. The funeral procession from the city hall to Glasnevin Cemetery was led by some 200 Catholic priests, followed by 9,000 Volunteers, 8,000 members of the Women Workers' Union, hundreds of members of the women's republican organization Cumman na mBan, 570 children of the Dublin Schools Hurling and Football League, 500 members of the Brick and Stone Layers Union, and representatives of many more political and labor organizations and religious orders. Also joining the procession were Dublin's Lord Mayor Laurence O'Neill and the archbishop of Dublin, Dr. William Walsh. Between 30,000 and 40,000 people marched in the procession, which took an hour and a half to pass at quickstep. Tens of thousands lined the route to pay their respects and see the coffin through the glass walls of the hearse. Before the coffin was lowered into the grave, uniformed Volunteers fired three volleys, and the republican Michael Collins gave a terse oration: "Nothing additional remains to be said. That volley which we have just heard is the only speech which it is proper to make above the grave of a dead Fenian."[59]

In death Ashe became a republican symbol, the subject of poetry and ballads, his photographic portrait a totem. In contrast to Byrne, he had been a prominent political figure who had linked himself to a national cause through his successful role in the Rising, enabling the general public, seething with resentment toward the Castle, to perceive that he had died in a good cause that was their own. He was a moral symbol sanctified by the Catholic Church. "Let me carry Your cross for Ireland, Lord" was the title of a poem that he had written after the Rising as an internee at Lewes. The poem, widely read and also set to music after Ashe's death, references the Gospels' account of Christ's staggering progress toward his crucifixion, when the Romans ordered Simon of Cyrene to carry Christ's cross on to Calvary. In contrast, Ashe volunteered to serve. It is noteworthy that he served in a secular organization, the IRB, which had remained nonsectarian since its founding in 1858, despite Ireland's religiously charged politics.[60] Ashe the symbolic martyr, with the moral conviction of his faith, fundamentally manifested spiritual devotion to the prospective Irish republic. He was a decidedly masculine symbol, given his athleticism and his courage under fire, but the hunger strike, as a tactic of protest, was not. The stalwart nationalist Timothy Healy, representing Ashe's family before the jury of the coroner's inquest, likened Ashe to the suffragette hunger strikers, who had also refused to be treated as criminals by the British state.[61] The hunger strike could be a masculine or a "womanish thing," as Sheehy Skeffington once put it. A woman could carry the cross as well.

The Volunteers created a Dublin Brigade staff to manage preparations and maintain security for Ashe's funeral, dramatically expanding and centralizing their previous organization.[62] Emboldened by the scale and success of the funeral, the Volunteer Executive made a general policy of "open defiance" and ordered each unit to drill openly after the second week of December 1917.[63] The Castle responded indecisively, having already watched most of its troops deployed to the war overseas. When the Castle sometimes made arrests, it brought problems upon itself, as hunger strikes proliferated throughout the prison system.[64]

The newly found symbolic power of the hunger strike, embodied by Ashe and blessed by the Catholic Church, was politically powerful. Ashe was from County Clare. Seventeen other men from Clare had participated in the Mountjoy hunger strike, which they followed with a hunger strike at Dundalk Prison that finally won their release in November.[65] Soon after their release, the surviving Clare men posed for a group portrait with de Valera, seated in the center of the photograph in

Peter O'Loughlin   Jas. Breene   Thos. Browne   Austin Brennan   M! O'Brien   Thos Marrman   Francis Shinners
John Minehan   M! Murray   Pat! Brennan   E. de Valera   Berly Hunt   Mich! Brennan   Francis Gallaher
W! McNamara   John Liddy   John Murnane   Jas. Madigan

FIGURE 8. Eamon de Valera and Clare hunger strikers, 1917. Permission to use this photograph from the Clare County Library was granted by Paul Minihan, grandson of John Minihan, seated at the end of the middle row to de Valera's right. John Minihan was then the vice commandant and intelligence officer of the Fifth Battalion, Clare Brigade. He subsequently fought in the Anglo-Irish War (1919–21), then in the civil war (1922–23), during which he served as divisional quartermaster and director of special services, First Western Division, IRA.

polished boots (figure 8). Having been finally released by the British in June 1917, de Valera had begun his political career by running and winning as the Sinn Féin candidate in the East Clare by-election in July. He had been unknown to the people of Clare before he had participated in the Rising. He was in many respects an unlikely national icon in the making, born in New York City to a Spanish father and a mother from County Limerick. Nonetheless, he had grown up in Ireland, and he spoke Irish fluently. The photograph says, in effect, we are all former hunger strikers, former prisoners, and, now, all men of Clare.

Republican men staged over 130 hunger strikes in Irish prisons across the country, most lasting only one to four days, in the first three months of 1918.[66] The Castle dithered then released all of the strikers under the Cat and Mouse Act.[67] Among these strikers was Terence MacSwiney, a leading republican from Cork, who went on strike for the first time in November and won release after just four days.[68] A military intelligence officer reported glumly in the same month: "As it is now evident to the parties concerned that they have only to hunger-strike for a couple days in order to get out of gaol, whether convicted or untried, it is really very little use arresting them."[69]

Despite the apparent success of hunger strikes in early 1918, the number of strikes decreased in the middle of the year for a combination of reasons. Through the mediation of Lord Mayor O'Neill, the Castle conceded a new set of "ameliorations" that further constituted de facto political status in the eyes of republicans. Also, republicans found that the Cat and Mouse Act compelled them either to serve out their sentences or waste time in avoiding re-arrest. Finally, nationalists' attention was turning from prisons to the growing conscription crisis in Ireland triggered by the Military Services Bill in April.[70] Disparate strikes nonetheless continued, including strikes by women. Following her arrest for consorting with Collins and Sinn Féin in August 1918, Sheehy Skeffington again went on hunger strike and was transferred to Holloway, from which she was eventually released under the Cat and Mouse Act.[71]

By the end of the year, Ireland had come again to the brink of rebellion, now over the prospect of conscription, which fueled Sinn Féin's numerous victories in that year's parliamentary elections after the armistice. Sinn Féin established an independent government in Dublin in January 1919, provoking the Anglo-Irish War, an atrocious conflict that featured guerrilla tactics on the Irish side and systematic reprisals against Irish paramilitary and civilian targets by the British. Historians have argued that in the course of the war Irish women were marginalized from the republican movement because they were excluded from armed combat and the potential for blood sacrifice. There is, of course, extensive evidence of women's roles in this as in previous militant campaigns, ranging from logistics to intelligence. For these acts some fifty women were incarcerated by the British, in contrast to approximately four thousand men.

Republican prisoners returned to hunger striking in growing numbers in the autumn of 1919, eight to ten months into the Anglo-Irish War, as guerrilla attacks on British forces escalated. In the spring of 1920, following a dramatic rise in republican violence, there was a series of widely publicized hunger strikes by Irish internees at Wormwood Scrubs prison in London and by prisoners in Mountjoy.[72] This occurred despite the fact that Collins, the head of the IRA, attempted to discourage striking as a waste of manpower.[73] On 5 April thirty-six men went on hunger strike at Mountjoy for "prisoner of war" status. They were joined by twenty-nine more men on the next day. Ninety men were on strike by 9 April. Mountjoy was meanwhile guarded by an infantry company and two tanks, which were surrounded by thousands of the strikers' restive supporters.[74] On 12 April the labor movement called for a general strike in solidarity with the prisoners. Two days later, the prison medical officer warned that sixty-six men were in "immediate danger," prompting the Castle to release all of the men under the Cat and Mouse

Act.[75] General Sir Nevil Macready observed that the death of a striker would have created "a situation . . . worse than anything that might happen from their release at the moment."[76] On Easter weekend, republicans burned approximately three hundred police barracks and twenty-two income tax offices.[77] This increasing violence was attributable both to general confidence among republicans and the return of former strikers to the guerrilla campaign.[78] Republicans believed that they had found in the hunger strike a last, indefensible weapon. Frank Gallagher wrote in his diary about one week into the strike: "What a fight this has become! . . . No matter how it goes now, their prison system is smashed. . . . If men die, it is smashed. . . . If men live on to political treatment or release it is smashed."[79]

In the long run, the success of these strikes played to the disadvantage of the IRA. The political and military turmoil of the spring prompted London to overhaul the leadership of the Castle and introduce new men of harder temperament. Most importantly, General Macready was appointed as commander-in-chief and John Anderson as a joint-undersecretary.[80] Under the new regime, the recruitment of Irishmen for the RIC increased, as did the recruitment of British men for a special paramilitary force to support the RIC, the so-called Black and Tans, recognizable in their motley of RIC green and British khaki military uniforms. In further response to its difficulties in an unconventional war, the Castle augmented its forces with the infamous Auxiliary Division under the authority of Major General Henry Hugh Tudor.[81] With the support of London, the Castle intensified its reprisals, which sparked controversy in Britain.[82] The government and the Castle nonetheless persisted in this course, believing that any sign of retreat would weaken what was left of their security forces' resolve to fight on.

It was in this context of political crisis and a war of reprisals that the Castle faced the hunger strike by Terence MacSwiney, the lord mayor of Cork and the commandant of the First Cork Brigade of the Irish Volunteers, who starved to protest the authority of the British courts in Ireland after his arrest in August. MacSwiney had joined a hunger strike initiated two days earlier by other republican men in Cork Male Prison. As a republican leader and a prominent public figure, he was then transferred from Cork to Brixton Prison in London, where prison officials felt confident that they could manage his starvation and keep the public at bay.[83] Recognizing that the release of republican strikers not only inspired nationalists but also demoralized British forces, the government finally drew a line and declared that neither MacSwiney nor any other republican hunger striker would starve his way to freedom. Prime Minister David Lloyd George believed that there was no alternative: "If we release him we might as well give up again attempting to maintain law and order in Ireland."[84] From this point forward, hunger strikes became a deadlier business.

MacSwiney had become the lord mayor after his predecessor and friend, Thomas MacCurtain, was assassinated in his home, in front of his wife and son, by members of the RIC on 20 March 1920. Drawing a stark contrast with MacCurtain's ignominious death, MacSwiney believed that the ideal sacrifice was clear-eyed and voluntary, an emulation of the spiritual heroes of his Catholic faith. He declared in his book *Principles of Freedom* that the Irish should "recall the old earnestness and simplicity of the early Martyrs," who "went singing to the arena" to die.[85] In his first speech as lord mayor, MacSwiney stated, "The liberty for which we strive to-day is a sacred thing, inseparably entwined with that spiritual liberty for which the Saviour of man died and which is the foundation of all just government." He thus invoked Christ's sacrifice as a model of resistance; death for freedom from British rule was, in MacSwiney's words, "akin to the sacrifice on Calvary." "It is not those who can inflict the most," he famously declared, "but those who can suffer the most who will conquer."[86]

MacSwiney broke his strike only to drink water and take communion. His sister Mary read to him from the Bible and Thomas à Kempis's *Imitation of Christ*.[87] On his thirty-eighth day without food, he dictated a press release in which he noted that his fellow strikers still in Cork had just completed a forty-day fast, equal in length to Christ's fast in the desert. MacSwiney portrayed himself as "an instrument of God" who looked forward to reaching the forty-day milestone himself.[88] On the fifty-eighth day of his strike he sent a prayer to his fellow strikers in the spirit of Christ: "I offer my pain for Ireland . . ., I offer my sufferings here for our martyred people."[89] Beyond the walls of the prison, MacSwiney's supporters embraced the religious significance of his fast and portrayed it as a spiritual quest in which the Irish nation shared.[90] It was a quest for personal and national salvation through sacrifice and prayer, whether at one's bedside or during the Sunday Mass (figure 9).

Following his death on 25 October, after seventy-four days without food, MacSwiney was honored at large memorials in London and Dublin and then a funeral in Cork, all supported by the Irish Catholic hierarchy.[91] The Castle held its breath, anticipating that MacSwiney's death and burial might trigger Ireland's final upheaval. But there was no popular rush to arms, and the number of hunger strikes in prisons decreased.[92] The Castle's desperate gamble paid off.

MacSwiney was the most famous hunger striker of the Irish revolutionary era and the most extraordinary.[93] Bear in mind that eleven men in Cork Male Prison accompanied MacSwiney toward death.[94] One of these men, Michael Fitzgerald, died on 17 October, after sixty-eight days on hunger strike. MacSwiney died eight days later. Just fourteen hours after his death, a third republican prisoner, Joseph Murphy, died in Cork, after seventy-six days on hunger strike. The remaining nine republican hunger strikers in Cork continued their protests until 11 November, when they finally resumed eating at the public request of the Sinn Féin leader Arthur Griffith. Like MacSwiney and thousands of other Irish strikers of the revolutionary era, these men had prayed and taken communion throughout their lives,

FIGURE 9. Children praying for Terence MacSwiney during his hunger strike in front of Mary Immaculate Church, Inchicore, Dublin, September 1920. Reproduced by permission of Getty Images.

then continued to do so during their strikes. Yet these other strikers did not represent themselves as martyrs in the image of Christ. Moreover, taking a broader view upon hunger strikes by republicans after 1917, one finds that MacSwiney's strike was relatively peaceful in its terrible isolation. The vast majority of hunger strikes were parts played in violent daily struggles against prison authorities. MacSwiney was a militant, but his strike was not an extension of conflict in custody. In seeking to emulate Christ in his sacrifice for the nation, MacSwiney was at once symbolic and anomalous.

Six days after MacSwiney died, de Valera was the principal speaker at a "MacSwiney demonstration" that drew forty thousand people to the Polo Grounds in New York City. Upon standing to speak, de Valera had to wait twelve minutes for the applause to subside. The *Irish Independent* reported that as he waited "three members of the Friends of Freedom for India, attired in Oriental costume, rushed across the grounds, bearing a huge Indian flag, which, with the Sinn Fein flag, they hung about his shoulders." With Sinn Féin and US flags flying at half-staff around the stadium, de Valera declared that MacSwiney had been "but a type of millions whom the British had failed to crush. He [had not gone] through the ordeal alone, and thousands of others were willing to follow, if by their death the conscience of the free nations of the world would be awakened."[95] Certainly de Valera's internationalist message was reinforced, if not a little inspired, by the Irish and Indian flags upon his shoulders, representing a long, mutual awareness and exchange of ideas and tactics between Irish and Indian nationalists.[96] The hunger strike was part of this exchange, marked again, nine years later, upon the body of another hunger striker, Jatindranath Das, dubbed "the Indian Terence MacSwiney" after his death in Lahore after a hunger strike of sixty-three days. In the meantime, after 1917, numerous other Indian prisoners took inspiration from the "Irish method" in jails across the subcontinent, generally not as a means to martyrdom, but as a last weapon with which to reform prison conditions or to gain release, as had most Irish hunger strikers before them.

A FAMILY VAULT

In MacSwiney's essay "Womanhood," published posthumously in *Principles of Freedom*, he describes the ideal republican woman as one who lays the groundwork for her future political equality by serving as the loving, unwavering helpmeet of her husband, sustaining his morals and morale, raising his children in his image, and eventually preserving his memory.[97] Accordingly, at de Valera's request, MacSwiney's wife, Muriel, and his sister Mary also traveled to New York, dressed in mourning attire, to promote and raise funds for Irish republicanism. Muriel MacSwiney had no desire to do this tour, but she felt duty-bound by her husband's memory.[98] Although Mary MacSwiney joined her in commemorating her brother, she and her sister Annie subsequently ignored their brother's prescription for republican women and took up hunger striking, as did dozens of other female republicans in their campaign against the Irish Free State during the civil war.

Mary MacSwiney remained loyal to a truncated Sinn Féin, under the leadership of de Valera, in opposing the treaty of 1921 and the Free State government headed first by Collins and then by William T. Cosgrave, another veteran of the Rising.[99] She went on several hunger strikes against the government; the two longest lasted twenty-three days in November 1922 in Mountjoy and thirty-four days in February and March 1923 in Kilmainham Gaol. Mary MacSwiney's hunger strikes have been treated as emulations of her brother's, but a closer look at this sibling relationship suggests that Mary was more a leader than a follower. Maire Comerford, a fellow republican, later recalled, "[Mary] had Terence's moral out-look on history—or perhaps he had hers, for she was the eldest of nine brothers and sisters."[100] Both Mary and Terence were devout Catholics. Like Terence, Mary represented her hunger strikes in religious terms, but with reference to Christ's mother, Mary, and, like the suffragettes, to Joan of Arc, who, as Mary knew, had been recently canonized. During her strike in Mountjoy in November 1922, her comrades built an altar beside her door, where they took turns in half-hour vigils before Our Lady of Perpetual Succour.[101] They said the rosary three times a day in Irish. Remarkably, they did not pray to Christ's mother to support MacSwiney in enduring the loss of a man, but to sustain MacSwiney in her own act of sacrifice. The Free State government and the Catholic hierarchy treated Mary MacSwiney's hunger strikes not as simple emulations of her brother's, but as methods of protest dangerously adaptable by men and women. Cosgrave stated that he did not want to release Mary MacSwiney during her strike in 1922 because he feared that the six thousand other republican prisoners, men and women, would then take up the strike for release.[102]

In the previous month, the Irish bishops had issued a pastoral letter asserting that "divine law" sanctioned the authority of the Free State government, and that opponents of the government would "not be absolved in Confession, nor admitted to Holy Communion, if they purpose to persevere in such evil courses."[103] Mary MacSwiney, like many other republicans, was refused the sacraments in prison, but what she resented even more than this was the bishops' characterization of the hunger strike as a sinful act of suicide. She wrote to Edward Byrne, archbishop of Dublin: "I can no more deny the justice of my cause than Joan of Arc could deny hers. Bishops got her burned as a heretic to please England, but the Church has now declared her one of God's saints. To God I commend my soul in all humility but in all confidence."[104]

Mary MacSwiney's hunger strikes resembled those of other female strikers. Like her, most female strikers engaged in violent prison resistance before and during their strikes. To a greater extent than men, republican women ritualized their hunger strikes with prayer, recitations of the rosary, and hymns. Nell Humphreys, who was incarcerated on a few occasions with her daughter Sighle and her sister Anna O'Rahilly, took the lead in organizing a regular schedule of prayer for all of her fellow prisoners, including Mary MacSwiney, even as Humphreys herself was on hunger strike. For her unrelenting devotion, she was nicknamed "O.C. God" (O.C. being the military acronym for Officer Commanding).[105] Women regularly invoked the Madonna as their guardian: When Mary MacSwiney's sister Annie went on hunger strike outside the gates of Mountjoy in 1922 in solidarity with her sister who was on hunger strike inside, she hung a framed picture of the Madonna and Child behind her (figure 10).[106] In 1923 another republican, Grace Plunkett, drew in crayon on the wall of her cell in Kilmainham Gaol a large picture of the Madonna and Child, to which we will return.[107]

In representing the hunger strike through a distinctly Catholic idiom, women established the moral authority and legitimacy of their participation in militant republicanism. When republican men went on hunger strike in Mountjoy in 1920, women and men stood outside the prison, singing hymns and reciting the rosary.[108]

FIGURE 10. Annie MacSwiney (right) on hunger strike outside Mountjoy Prison in 1922. She is speaking with Maude Gonne MacBride (seated) and Mary Barry O'Delany (standing), a journalist and writer. Reproduced by permission of Getty Images.

During hunger strikes by thousands of republicans in the autumn of 1923, a Sinn Féin flyer stated simply: "Why doesn't Mulcahy [the minister of defense] get the Bishops to burn us at the Stake as they did Joan of Arc? It would save him trouble and salve his conscience."[109] The flyer makes no distinction between women and men, leaving Joan of Arc to represent both. It is probable that this flyer was prepared by Mary MacSwiney, who was the head of publicity for Sinn Féin at this time.

Prisons were central arenas of republican protest, and women and men sometimes occupied the same prisons in the revolutionary era. Eithne Coyle recalled that in 1921 she was in Mountjoy when a series of republican men were executed. "It was a weird experience," she observed. "You counted the hours, and then the minutes, and unless you had a heart of stone you felt . . . drained of energy when you knew that brave men had faced the gallows or the firing squad a few yards away from you."[110] Kilmainham Gaol, where fifteen of the leaders of the Rising were executed by the British, was converted by the Free State into a female military prison in September 1922. Kathleen Clarke was imprisoned in that "chamber of horrors," where her husband, Thomas Clarke, and brother, Edward Daly, had been executed for their participation in the Rising. Three months later, Frank and Cecilia Gallagher spent their first Christmas as a married couple in different wings of Mountjoy, where women and men went on hunger strikes. Sometimes women and men conducted strikes in the same prison wings, and even in the same cells, if at different times. In October 1923 Austin Stack observed in a letter to Winifred (Una) Gordon, his future wife, that he and other men were on hunger strike in Kilmainham Gaol in the same cells that Gordon and other republican women had occupied before them. Stack happened to be in Gordon's former cell. Stack's comrade, Gerald Boland, was in Grace Plunkett's former cell, where he admired her painting of the Madonna and Child.[111] Plunkett, an artist and a cartoonist by trade, had married Joseph Plunkett, a leader of the Rising, in the chapel of Kilmainham Gaol just hours before his execution in 1916. For her, Kilmainham had also been, undoubtedly, a chamber of horrors.

During the Irish civil war, the executive council of the Free State ordered that republican women prisoners should be subject to the same prison regulations as men; one more reason why women on hunger strike perceived themselves to be engaged in the same protests as men. They were furthermore honored by republicans in comparable terms during their protests, and they were fully informed of IRA orders. In October 1923 republican men in Mountjoy went on hunger strike for political status. They were joined by thousands of men in other prisons and internment camps, and by dozens of republican women imprisoned in the North Dublin Union. Coyle recalled that the women in the union "decided to help our fellow prisoners to secure political treatment, or their release."[112]

In a related vein, the *Irish Independent* reported a well-attended public demonstration in Dublin to commemorate the death of Terence MacSwiney. A principal speaker, Michael Comyn, said "there were 10,000 of Ireland's best sons suffering for Ireland that night, and there were 60 or 70 brave women in the North Dublin Union suffering for the same cause."[113] On 30 October the paper reported that on the previous day, "A small procession, mainly composed of released internees, formed up at the Mansion House . . . and marched to Mountjoy Gaol, where they recited the Rosary. They also marched to the Dublin Union." The Sinn Féin *Daily Sheet* of 7 November even featured a male striker in womanish terms: "Amongst those fighting with the 'Women's Weapon' is Liam Pilkington, from Sligo. He fought a good fight since 1916 to the accompaniment of bomb and gun, and now, although the weapon of passive resistance must try the temper of his soul well nigh past endurance, he still endures."[114]

At the end of the strike, on 23 November, an IRA officer, Tom Derrig, came to the North Dublin Union to inform the women that the protest was over, just as he informed the men in the other prisons and camps. Sighle Humphreys awoke to see Derrig standing beside her bed. For the remaining male strikers it had been a forty-day strike, for the women it had been thirty days. Humphreys explained to her family, "Of course when we went on it was in unison with the men, so now there would be no sense in our staying on alone. . . . Tis hard and humiliating to come off, but tis not to those who inflict the most but who endure the most that victory will be given."[115]

The prevalence of family connections among militant Irish republicans is well known, so it is no surprise that republican women on hunger strike were commonly related to other republican women and to republican men.[116] There are famous cases such as those of Mary and Annie MacSwiney on hunger strike together in 1922, and Maud Gonne MacBride and her son Sean MacBride, who both went on hunger strikes in 1923. (This was the same Maud Gonne who had written "The Famine Queen." She subsequently married John MacBride, who was later executed for his participation in the Rising.) There are a variety of additional cases like that of Aileen Barry, a hunger striker in the North Dublin Union in 1923, who was the sister of the famous Cork republican Kevin Barry. He had been held in the North Dublin Union after his capture by British forces in November 1920, after which he had been hanged in Mountjoy.[117] The most extensive case of family ties is probably to be found in the Humphreys family. Dick Humphreys had been on hunger strike in prison in 1916. His sister Sighle shared her hunger strike in the North Dublin Union in 1923 with her aunt Anna, also imprisoned in the union, and with her brother, Emmet, who exchanged letters with Sighle from Gormanstown Internment Camp. He wrote to his mother, Nell Humphreys: "We are six days on the hunger strike. I do not mind it all only when I remember that Anna and Sighle are also on it."[118] Nell Humphreys (née O'Rahilly) and Sighle and Emmet's aunt, Anna, were the sisters of The O'Rahilly, killed in combat during the Rising. The family ties of hunger strikers presumably strengthened the growing national family bonded together through shared sacrifice. Frank Gallagher wrote during the mass hunger strike in Mountjoy in 1920: "Each cell is a tomb. . . . Mountjoy has become a family vault!"[119]

A SHARED BETRAYAL

In the years following the civil war, the IRA persisted in its opposition to the Free State government. At the same time, it divided over ideological questions, and especially the turn toward socialism by a significant faction of its members after 1929.[120] The majority of the IRA remained committed to realizing a unified Irish republic through physical force, but this majority was relatively small in number. In 1931 the Free State believed that there were approximately thirteen hundred IRA officers and thirty-five hundred in the rank and file.[121] Richard English makes an important observation about the mindset of IRA members and their supporters in this era. He notes that they looked not to themselves, but to martyrs of the past, the "republican undead," to define their politics and "strengthen the contemporary cult of republican violence."[122] Republicans were thus self-referential and self-reverential; they dutifully lived and died for the dead.

De Valera had split from Sinn Féin in 1926 and established a new political party, Fianna Fáil, which had a strained relationship with the IRA in its first decade. Fianna Fáil won the elections of 1932, after which de Valera's government made careful gestures toward an entente with the IRA. De Valera was unable to control the organization, however. Following two assassinations by republicans in the spring of 1936, the government arrested the IRA chief of staff, Maurice Twomey, then proscribed the IRA as a whole.[123] Among those arrested was Sean MacSwiney, the younger brother of Mary and Terence MacSwiney, who conducted an eleven-day hunger strike for release, without success.[124] De Valera had declared at the Polo Grounds in 1920, in the aftermath of Terence MacSwiney's death, that "thousands of others were willing to follow, if by their death the conscience of the free nations of the world would be awakened." Sixteen years later, de Valera himself was awake to the threat that another militant MacSwiney posed to his constitutional plans for the Irish nation.

De Valera strengthened his political hand against the IRA in the next few years through legislation and treaties that all but severed the connection between the Free State and the United Kingdom. A new constitution in 1937 rendered the Free State almost completely autonomous from Britain, while committing the Free State government to Ireland's future unification and, implicitly, its independence, the same goals as those of the IRA. In June 1939, in view of an IRA bombing campaign in Britain, de Valera secured passage of the Offences against the State Act, which included provisions for internment and a Special Criminal Court. Nine days later, the government declared the IRA an unlawful organization under this statute. It began to intern IRA members in August, as the IRA bombing campaign in Britain escalated with an explosion in Coventry that killed five people.[125] With the onset of war in Europe in September, the Irish government declared its neutrality, much to the consternation of Britain, and passed the Emergency Powers Act, which effectively suspended civil rights and gave de Valera sweeping, authoritarian powers. He used these to arrest the remaining IRA leadership. By the end of the year, seventy-six IRA members were interned, and thirty had been tried by the Special Criminal Court.[126]

The Second World War precipitated a new era of hunger striking by IRA prisoners against de Valera's government. There was much in these strikes that resembled those of the revolutionary era. Strikers again starved for release or differential treatment as political prisoners, and the government, working on the British model, refused to acknowledge political prisoner status.[127] The families of earlier strikers returned to starvation in Irish prisons and to public and private advocacy for their striking kith and kin. Women of the revolutionary generation, some former strikers themselves, played prominent roles in lobbying the government and attempting to mobilize public support for this new generation of strikers. Some women of this generation returned to prison, but this time they left hunger striking to men.[128] It is not clear why these women chose not to starve at this time. Some may have been deterred by concern for children.[129] Perhaps some doubted their fitness; Mary MacSwiney, particularly, was in poor health after 1940 and died in March 1942. These women nonetheless portrayed the strikes as evidence of not only the nobility and devotion of the IRA, but also the hypocrisy and self-serving cynicism of de Valera and his cronies, some former hunger strikers themselves. Contemporary IRA hunger strikers were cast not as Christ, but as hereditary martyrs of a vital republican faith that de Valera had lost.

Between September and November 1939, six imprisoned IRA members went on hunger strike for differential treatment as de facto political status. Two of these, Jeremiah Lynch and Richard McCarthy, were on strike for thirty-two days, but the most politically delicate case was that of Patrick MacGrath, a widely admired veteran of the Anglo-Irish War who still carried a British bullet in his body.[130] Kathleen Clarke, now the lord mayor of Dublin, used her status as a member of Fianna Fáil to urge the government to release MacGrath.[131] Margaret Pearse, mother of Padraig Pearse, the main leader of the Rising, also lobbied the government for release.[132] On 1 November the Government Information Bureau issued a press release stating that "as arrest and detention in accordance with the Powers conferred by Parliament are the only means available for the maintenance of public order and security, [the government] cannot permit the State Authorities to be deprived of these means by the policy of the hunger-strike. The prisoners on hunger-strike will, accordingly, not be released."[133] The head of the information bureau was Frank Gallagher, no stranger to MacSwiney or Pearse, and no stranger to republican hunger strikes. He had written during his own strike as a prisoner in Mountjoy in 1920: "The prison rules will not be changed. The issue is knit there, at any rate. Either that word is kept and we die, or it is broken and [the lord lieutenant of Ireland] John French goes. These are the alternatives."[134]

Armed with the 1937 constitution, de Valera asserted that there was a decisive difference between his own campaign against the Free State and the IRA's ongoing war against the current Free State government. Basically, the Free State had previously been under Britain's thumb, whereas the current state had been chosen freely by the Irish people. De Valera charged, "Those who tried, by violent means, to overthrow that state, should be held here, as in other countries, to be guilty of the most terrible crime of a public character which is known in civilised society."[135] Nonetheless, de Valera ultimately released all of the hunger strikers. He attempted to err on the side of magnanimity in the public eye. It appears that he made a calculation that the Irish public might perceive the martyrdom of these republicans as proof that the government's new authoritarian powers might be put to despotic ends. He may well have understood that the release of these prisoners would inspire more hunger strikes in the years ahead, but then he also hoped to find himself, in the years ahead, in a stronger political position.

The IRA did in fact strengthen de Valera's hand by escalating its violence at the end of the year with bombings, murders, robberies, and a brazen raid on the army's Magazine Fort in Phoenix Park, Dublin, from which it removed 1.084 million rounds of ammunition in thirteen lorries. Even as most of the ammunition was being recovered, the legislature met in emergency session and authorized the government to establish internment camps to meet the IRA threat. With solid backing in the Dáil, the government demonstrated greater resolve when it faced a new hunger strike by six republican prisoners on 24 February 1940.[136] The strikers primarily wanted differential treatment, especially greater freedom of movement in prison and to serve their sentences in military custody.[137] A few of these strikers had strong family ties to the now legendary revolutionary era. Tomás MacCurtain was the son and namesake of the lord mayor of Cork who had been assassinated in 1920. John (Jack) Plunkett, a veteran of the Rising, was the younger brother of Joseph Plunkett, one of the rebellion's leaders who was later executed, and whose wife, Grace, went on hunger strike in Mountjoy in 1923. John (Jack) McNeela was the nephew of Jack Kilroy, who had also been on hunger strike in Mountjoy in 1923. Kilroy, a member of Fianna Fáil, visited McNeela in order to persuade him to come off the strike. McNeela ordered him to leave.[138]

Maud Gonne MacBride and Mary MacSwiney, both former hunger strikers, and Áine Ceannt, widow of one of the executed leaders of the Rising, Eamonn Ceannt, and sister of two civil-war hunger strikers, Lily and Kathleen O'Brennan, made statements on behalf of the prisoners, but these were censored.[139] Censorship of the media's coverage of IRA prisoners and the battles between the IRA and the police continued throughout the war.[140] De Valera's government employed much the same tactic that had silenced de Valera himself when he had been a prisoner of the Free State during the civil war. Mary MacSwiney, then a Sinn Féin publicist, had challenged the Free State government to let de Valera speak publicly from prison. "I pity the stability of a cause," she had declared, "whose protagonists have to lock their chief opponent away from all communication, and then systematically calumniate him. Not that way lies success."[141] On 25 March the *Irish Press* published two letters in support of the hunger strikers and a response by Gerald Boland, the minister for justice. One letter, signed by five relatives of Irish men who had died on hunger strike, bemoaned the fact that twenty-three years after the death of Thomas Ashe republicans still had cause to hunger strike for political status, now under an Irish regime.[142] The second letter, signed by six relatives of men who fought in 1916, explicitly accused the government of betraying the principles of the Rising, for which the hunger strikers allegedly continued to fight.[143] Boland gave no ground in his response. He explained that the majority of the government had fought in the Rising, and that through the 1937 constitution they had successfully secured the rights for which they had previously fought. They were now proceeding, as in 1916, toward an independent, united Irish republic. "The tragedy," Boland charged, "is that there should now be people who so ignore the real character of the struggle in 1916 as to seek to pervert that Rising into a justification of attacks against an Irish government."[144]

One of the six hunger strikers, Tony D'Arcy, died on 16 April, after fifty-two days on hunger strike. On 19 April, Boland received a delegation of women led by Mrs. George Lawlor and Una Stack; the latter was both a former hunger striker and the widow of Austin Stack, with whom Boland himself had endured the forty-day hunger strike in 1923—after he had occupied Grace Plunkett's cell. The women suggested that the strike might end, and that the government and the strikers might all save face, if the government assured the strikers that their conditions would improve if they resumed eating. This proposal facilitated the ending of the strike, but not before a second striker, McNeela, died later that day.[145] His death received only cursory coverage in the press. The censor blocked resolutions of sympathy.[146] The government did not face popular protest over the deaths of D'Arcy and McNeela, and the IRA subsequently undermined whatever sympathy it might have enjoyed with a series of brutal reprisals. A month later, de Valera gained decisive political advantage over the IRA when the police, in their search for a German spy, found documents linking the IRA to the Nazis.[147]

The government's victory over the hunger strikers contributed to a new resolve with which it subsequently faced down the IRA through a combination of prosecution and mass internment. Beginning in May, the government interned over eleven hundred IRA members, who suffered both miserable conditions and internal divisions that undermined morale. That summer, the government executed two IRA members, Patrick McGrath—whom de Valera had released in 1939—and Tom Harte, for killing two policemen. The government again faced no popular protest; nor did it when it subsequently executed three more IRA men in 1941 and 1942.[148] When in 1942 and 1943 the government confronted approximately thirty hunger strikes, it refused to make concessions, and the strikes eventually collapsed, three of them on their fiftieth day.[149]

Seán McCaughey, adjutant general of the IRA, was sentenced to penal servitude for life in connection with his role in 1941 in the kidnapping and beating of the acting chief of staff of the IRA, Stephen Hayes, whom McCaughey and his comrades had believed to be a spy.[150] In Portlaoise Prison McCaughey refused to wear his prison uniform and instead wore only a blanket. Consequently, he was moved to solitary confinement, where he remained for three years. In April 1946 he went on hunger strike for release and then died, after twenty-three days, of cardiac failure.[151] At the inquest, Sean MacBride, a former hunger striker himself, representing the family, cross-examined the prison doctor and asked, "Would you allow your dog . . . to be treated in the way in which this man has been treated?"[152] After considerable hesitation, the doctor replied, "No, I would not allow my dog to be treated in this way."[153] Nonetheless, the power of the IRA had been significantly diminished, and the government faced no significant public outcry over McCaughey's death, though the inquest was mildly critical of its actions. MacBride, the son of an inveterate republican mother and a father executed in 1916 for his part in the Rising, embodied and strategically invoked the legacy and ostensibly pure moral spirit of the Rising against a government allegedly self-serving and hypocritical, with honorable blood on its hands. Speaking in the Dáil, de Valera conceded that he had combated the IRA with much the same methods that the Cosgrave government had employed against him and his republican comrades in the civil war. He added, however, that since assuming power he had learned that Cosgrave had been right.[154] Being in the right, de Valera presumed, he now enjoyed the support of the people, with the promise of the Rising still before them.

THE IRISH HUNGER STRIKE

The Russian method had been long forgotten. By the 1940s, the hunger strike had refracted so extensively through Irish culture and politics that it was reconceived as Irish itself. The transfer and adaptation of hunger in protest from Russia to Britain to Ireland displays the mutability of the gender dynamics of this tactic of bodily protest, as it displays the changing spiritual and religious connotations that may attach to and differentiate the meanings of starvation. What made the hunger strike Irish was the shared sacrifice of women and men whose acts of protest attracted popular support and profound admiration and thus became markers in the legendary narrative of Ireland's revolutionary era. Moreover, the literal and figurative familial bonds of republican women and men grounded hunger striking in kinship networks and communities.

As previously observed, however, hunger striking, as a last weapon, was double-edged. Its Catholic identification left no room for Protestants in either its practice or memorialization. Hunger striking may have become Irish, but not in the inclusive sense that republicans themselves had wished for their larger political movement and for the nation. Hunger striking reinforced charges of betrayal in the long aftermath of the partition. It furthermore served to accentuate the subordination of women in Ireland's increasingly patriarchal politics. Irish women ceased hunger striking at the same time that they were marginalized from public life between the wars.[155] By the time that militant Irish republicanism revived in Northern Ireland in the 1970s, the male republican leadership, fighting the British rather than the Irish government, regarded women's prison protests, and especially hunger striking, as an embarrassment to the masculine ethos of their movement and ordered their imprisoned female comrades to stop, but without effect.

   As the tactic of hunger in protest became Irish, it also became Indian. Its double-edged quality extended to India with remarkable parallels to Ireland before the Second World War. As in Ireland, hunger in protest became identified in India with the religion of the majority, in this case Hinduism, to the exclusion of other religious groups, especially Muslims. As in Ireland, Indian nationalists who gained self-governing power in the 1930s found themselves assailed by hunger strikers, who had previously joined them in opposing British rule and now charged them with betraying the true republic. It was a simpler thing to assert one's moral authority to take back the sovereign territory of one's own nation from a foreign power than to discredit those who were of the same national body as oneself, who had shared one's dreams and now starved for them.

4

Building the Nation's Temple

Hunger Strikes and Fasts by Nationalists in India,
1912–1948

Yama is a Hindu deity, the lord of death. In the early twentieth century, Indian prisoners bestowed the nickname Yama upon David Barry, the head jailor and self-styled god of the government of India's infamous Cellular Jail at Port Blair on the Andaman and Nicobar Islands in the Bay of Bengal. Barry managed many thousands of male criminals and a small number of men convicted of state offenses. Each of these prisoners disembarked from the four-day, six-hundred-mile voyage from Calcutta across the *kala pani* (black water), waited in quarantine in a plague camp, then stood in fetters before Barry, the squat, potbellied, crimson-nosed arbiter of his fate. Like Yama, the ruler of a multileveled, purgatorial hell, Barry determined the hell appropriate to each new inmate. He assigned accommodation and labor in accordance with the terms of the prisoner's conviction, the prisoner's physique, and whimsy. Those prisoners convicted of state offenses were assigned to "separate confinement" and the most onerous, body-breaking tasks. Once the prisoners' fates were sealed, the warders removed the fetters and distributed the jail's standard attire: a *topi* (hat), *kurta* (shirt), and "halfpants" (short pants), which many prisoners deemed immodest and suitable for boys, not men. The prisoners were next subjected to the humiliation of communal bathing, a violation of modesty and religious mores, followed by a miserable meal on oily plates. They were finally marched to their cells in the jail panopticon. This was a circular structure of seven three-storied blocks with a total of 690 barred cells facing a central three-storied watch tower. From the tower, corridors radiated to each of the blocks, presenting the only means of entry and exit. Sentries posted day and night in the tower could see into each cell at all times. Shifts of no less than twenty-one warders, overseen by sentries, patrolled each floor of each block day and night.[1]

After a few days had passed, a blacksmith came around and used iron rings to attach small, wooden "neck tickets" to the prisoners. Each ticket indicated the prisoner's number, the law under which he had been convicted, the date of his conviction, and the term of his sentence. Those convicted of state offenses preferred to identify themselves as "political prisoners," but they were not recognized as such under law or prison rules. As in Britain and Ireland, the legal category of "political crime" did not exist in India. These prisoners were nonetheless distinguished from common criminals by a patch on their kurtas featuring the letter *D*, for dangerous. The Maharashtrian revolutionary V. D. Savarkar recalled a speech with which Barry would periodically remind him and other "dangerous" prisoners of his power: "In the Universe there is one God, and He lives in the Heaven above. But in Port Blair there are two; one, the God of Heaven, and another, the God of Earth. Indeed, the God of Earth in Port Blair—that is myself. The God of Heaven will reward you when you go above. But this God of Port Blair will reward you here and now. So, ye prisoners, behave well."[2]

There was a third god at Port Blair. It was a powerful god to which Savarkar and other revolutionaries had devoted themselves in violent opposition to British rule. This god was *Bharat Mata* (Mother India), the symbolic embodiment of the new civil religion of the would-be Indian nation. The deity Mother India, derived from the Hindu mother goddess, had been popularized after the turn of the century through political protests and a song, "Bande Mataram" (Hail the Mother), which resonates to this day. Devotion to Bharat Mata was to transcend religious and regional differences and unify the peoples of the subcontinent as Indians, that is, children of the one mother: the nation.[3] In his prison memoir, Savarkar recalled, "Dear India, we, your forsaken children, ever thought of you in the dreariness and rigour of that lonely residence. We were rudely torn from your breast, Mother India, but we never forgot you; and we forgot our personal cares and sorrows in thinking of you."[4] Under Barry's ungodly regime, Savarkar and his comrades looked not to the "here and now," as Barry put it, but to the future freedom of their nation that would be realized through their sacrifice. Even within the Cellular Jail, they built the nation's temple, the then metaphorical, later brick and mortar, *Bharat Mata mandir* (Mother India temple). On the Andaman Islands or in mainland provinces, this temple was sanctified by the blood of sons. Sacrifice empowered the Mother, who then imbued her children, the future of the nation, with *shakti*, a divine, feminine power before which the British would fall. While there were many forms of sacrifice, starvation was elevated above all others in the contentious era of mass nationalism between the wars.

This chapter demonstrates that hunger in protest was more widespread and diverse in the Indian nationalist movement than historians generally acknowledge in focusing on Mohandas Gandhi's famous fasts. It examines how starvation became a multivalent symbol of militancy and nonviolence, patriotism and insurrection, unity and exclusion. Many, if not most, who starved in far-flung and disparate nationalist campaigns were, nonetheless, collectively invested in Mother India, the construction of her temple, and the assertion of *purna swaraj* (independence). Mother India was a symbol shared and contested. She not only represented but, with growing political currency, deepened India's most dangerous divides. Like Irish republicans, leading Indian nationalists found that the last weapon became double-edged. Even as they freed themselves from British rule, they empowered Mother India to discriminate between her own children and entrapped themselves in communalist politics.

Gandhi promoted *ahimsa* (nonviolence) as a moral and political imperative. He urged his followers and the Indian National Congress to reject armed revolution. Yet nonviolent and revolutionary elements of the Indian nationalist movement mixed more fluidly than Gandhi's rigid rhetoric would suggest.[5] There were supporters of the Congress, such as Bhagat Singh in his adolescent activism, who evolved into revolutionaries, and there were revolutionaries who turned or returned to nonviolence, as did Singh prior to his execution in 1931 for his role in an assassination.[6] Gandhi himself was not above turning militancy to his own advantage. It was a delicate, cynical business when he and the Congress leadership attempted cautiously after 1929 to exploit the sacrifices of revolutionaries, including Singh, to gain popular support and, especially, to appease the restive, radical left wing of the Congress itself.[7] In December of that year in Lahore, the Congress, in its annual meeting, endorsed purna swaraj for the first time, abandoning its previous goal of dominion status within the British Commonwealth. This followed vociferous protests over the British government's decision not to appoint Indian delegates to a commission dispatched to India in 1928–29 to evaluate the prospects for constitutional reform.[8] It also followed the death of the Bengali revolutionary Jatindranath (Jatin) Das in October in a jail in the same city, after a hunger strike of sixty-four days for prison privileges equal to those of Europeans. The death of Das, who had been first arrested as a Congress member years before, had charged calls among a new generation of Congressmen led by Jawaharlal Nehru for a bolder course against the British regime.[9]

While Gandhi struggled to maintain a principled yet pragmatic relationship with revolutionaries, he wholeheartedly joined them in their declarations of devotion to Mother India. This shared devotion was broadly represented in low-cost poster art and other ephemeral, visual publications of the era that capitalized on India's growing national identity. This was bazaar art in which political figures joined a visual cacophony of gods, legendary heroes, and kitsch, printed large and small, inexpensively framed or, most often, loose leaf, stacked in piles before stalls or street vendors for excavation. As Sumathi Ramaswamy explains, this art was "ubiquitous across the nation, providing it with a visual vocabulary shared by regions and communities otherwise divided from each other."[10] Christopher Pinney and Kama Maclean have further shown that this art "is indicative of forgotten or clandestine interactions between Congress and revolutionary circles" that call into question the predominant Gandhian narrative of nonviolent national struggle.[11] This chapter draws upon their work in demonstrating that while popular art represented an interaction that was real, it promulgated a visual fantasy in which Gandhi and revolutionaries were united as children of the one mother; a fantasy in which Gandhi's legitimacy depended on his support for or, at least, his tacit understanding of revolutionary violence.

The Indian nationalist movement of the 1930s was riven by conflicts. The Government of India Act, 1935, brought these conflicts into full view, as it gave Indian political parties the opportunity to compete to control provincial governments under British executive authority. In campaigns and elections in 1936 and early 1937, the Congress promised to release "political prisoners" should it win office, emboldening hundreds of revolutionary prisoners to undertake hunger strikes for release before and after the Congress and other Indian parties formed their ministries across the country. Once in office, the Congress, like Fianna Fáil in Ireland, saw "political prisoners" and hunger strikes in a new light. Their campaign slogans had not accounted for the fact that political legitimacy in office and control over government would depend on their enforcement of the same rule of law under which the hunger strikers had been prosecuted by the British for sedition and crimes of violence. The Indian ministries were perplexed by the combination of their legal duty to hold prisoners and their awareness that previous Indian hunger strikers, such as Das, had been elevated to the symbolic status of martyrs to Mother India. If they released the strikers, they would weaken the rule of law and prove themselves unfit to govern. If they held the strikers, as Taylor Sherman has shown, they would equate themselves with the British and risk expulsion from the nation's temple.[12]

In August 1937 Gandhi began calling for the release of hunger striking revolutionary prisoners, provided that they gave up their hunger strikes and renounced violence. Gandhi's motivations and goals were complex. He hoped to appease the left wing of the Congress, to co-opt militant heroes as satyagrahis, and to relieve pressure on Congress ministries fearful that revolutionaries might starve to death on their watch. There was more to it than that, however. In championing hunger strikers in the Bengal Presidency, in particular, Gandhi and his Congress allies attacked their political adversaries, a predominantly Muslim coalition ministry headed by the Krishak Praja Party (KPP) and the Muslim League. As they called upon the KPP-Muslim League ministry to release political prisoners, they alienated Muslims who perceived the Congress attempting to undermine their authority as the religious and political majority in Bengal. This perception was enforced by the fact that the Congress, with Gandhi's support, was at that same time proposing to make "Bande Mataram" India's national anthem. Since taking office, Congress ministries had made a quick tradition of singing "Bande Mataram" in their legislatures and at official functions, much to the consternation of not only British officials, but also Muslims, who by then had reason to regard the song as the anthem of a menacing Hindu-majority nationalism. Thus, Gandhi and the Congress's support for revolutionary hunger strikers at the expense of the KKP-Muslim League ministry in Bengal in 1937 was effectively set to the tune of "Bande Mataram." A decade later, with communal violence escalating on the road to partition, Gandhi finally heard "Bande Mataram" from the standpoints of both a child privileged and a child disowned. He could not then distance himself from Mother India's temple, however, even after he had deemed the temple profane and left for a Muslim's home.

HUNGER FOR VIOLENCE AND FAITH

A small number of Indian revolutionaries, generally middle-class, educated, upper-caste Hindus, organized themselves into secret societies to fight against British rule in the early twentieth century. While militancy percolated in Punjab and the United Provinces, hotbeds of rebellion were to be found in the Bengal Presidency, the Bombay Presidency, and London.[13] There were several high-profile acts of terrorism in this period. In 1908, men affiliated with the revolutionary newspaper *Jugantar* attempted to assassinate a British magistrate in Bengal and instead accidentally killed the wife and daughter of another British official. In 1909, Madanlal Dhingra, an engineering student and a member of a secret society in London led by Savarkar, who was then a law student, assassinated Sir Curzon Wyllie, the political aide-de-camp to the secretary of state for India. In 1912, there was a nearly fatal assassination attempt on the viceroy, Lord Hardinge, during a state procession into Delhi. These attacks were exceptions to the rule, however. The police were generally successful in infiltrating India's revolutionary organizations, so most of the revolutionaries prosecuted and sentenced to imprisonment for sedition or "waging war against the king emperor" were captured in the act of conspiring, rather than after successful operations.[14] Prior to the First World War, the government did not fear a full-scale rebellion in India and remained more concerned about external threats, especially the Russian Empire to the north.

As members of small, militant factions of the burgeoning nationalist movement in India, revolutionary prisoners continued their rebellion in the Cellular Jail by both traditional and new means. The most common, traditional means were individual and collective work stoppages. In 1912, revolutionaries began a "general strike" against work and made three demands: proper food, release from hard labor, and freedom of association.[15] Prison authorities responded by reducing the prisoners' diets, placing them in fetters, and handcuffing some of them to the ceilings of their cells. Among these prisoners was Nani Gopal Mukherjee, a Bengali who was about twenty-years old.[16] He had been imprisoned for throwing a bomb at the motor car of a high-ranking police official in Calcutta in the previous year.[17] Incensed by the punishments meted out to him and his comrades, Mukherjee turned to greater rebellion. According to the prison medical officer, he broke his neck ticket and refused to wear prison clothing, bathe, or even walk on command.[18] Mukherjee reportedly declared, "We are . . . political prisoners and not thieves, robbers and dacoits [armed bandits]."[19] He was transferred to a smaller jail on nearby Viper Island, where he went on hunger strike, apparently the first Indian revolutionary to do so. We do not know where Mukherjee found his inspiration to starve. Regardless, it is noteworthy that in 1912 the hunger strike was simultaneously deployed as a last weapon in Britain, Ireland, and India.

The authorities transferred Mukherjee back to the Cellular Jail, put him in chains, and began to forcibly feed him milk through the nose. Reduced to "skin and bones," Mukherjee continued his hunger strike for several weeks, in conjunction with the ongoing work stoppage by his fellow inmates.[20] The prisoners expanded their demands to include "political prisoner status" and transfer back to the mainland for the durations of their terms, setting a precedent for the demands of hunger strikers in the Cellular Jail twenty years later. Despite the prisoners' physical isolation, they exerted pressure upon the government through smuggled reports published in the Indian press.[21] Fearing for Mukherjee's life, Savarkar urged him to quit his hunger strike, asserting that a militant's strength was better reserved for battle. Savarkar's appeals were unsuccessful until he pledged to starve himself to death if Mukherjee died. Mukherjee consequently concluded his hunger strike after seventy-two days on 6 December 1912.[22] "From this time onwards," Savarkar recalled, "we had our two meals and had plenty of coconuts to eat in addition to them."[23] The government subsequently conceded that it would return to the mainland all political offenders who had not been transported for life, including Mukherjee, who had been sentenced to fourteen years.[24] All of the prisoners returned to work.

During the First World War, as the War Office in London redeployed much of the Indian army overseas, and as inflation and relentless taxation brought misery to many of the Indian people, Indian revolutionary activity changed and, with it, so did the tactic of hunger in protest. The most serious threat to British rule in India during the war came mainly from Punjabi Sikhs, but not from Punjab. These rebels were members of the international *Ghadar* movement, founded in San Francisco, California. The term *Ghadar* means mutiny or revolt. The *ghadris* were mainly Punjabi Sikh immigrants, concentrated in the US and Canada, who had committed themselves to the overthrow of the British in India as racist, illegitimate occupiers. Recognizing Britain's vulnerability during the war, thousands of ghadris returned to India and, with assistance from Bengali militants, launched a violent liberation campaign, the Ghadar, in February 1915.[25] The British quickly suppressed the uprising and imprisoned many of the rebels. They then discovered that it was harder to control the ghadris inside, rather than outside, the prison system. In the Cellular Jail, Savarkar was shocked when in 1915 a recently arrived ghadri hit the head jailor, Barry, in retaliation for an insult.[26] Across India in the ensuing years, ghadris regularly faced down prison officials and occasionally starved for their faith and nation.

Acts of self-starvation by Sikh prisoners commonly had religious connotations, as exemplified by Randhir Singh, imprisoned in Punjab in 1915 for his participation in the Ghadar. Between 1916 and 1921, he conducted several fasts, as he termed his protests, in different prisons. He fasted in order to gain dietary privileges in accordance with his religion and to retain the symbols of his faith. He began his first successful fast in Lahore Prison in 1916, when the warden would not allow him to cook his own food or have it prepared by another Sikh.[27] Subsequently, in Multan Central Prison in Punjab, he fasted successfully for dietary privileges and for the right to keep his turban, iron bangle, comb, *kachhahird* (underwear), and other Sikh symbols as prescribed by the Khalsa code.[28] Singh attributed the success of his fasts to his religious devotion, as reflected in his singing of sacred hymns (*gurbani*) throughout his protests. Singh observed in his memoirs that had the prison system respected his religious practices he would not have fasted in the first place. Imprisoned gadhris like Singh continued to go on fasts in protest over diet and clothing throughout the 1920s, but their lists of demands for special privileges would significantly expand and become overtly political.

Prison officials commonly attempted to quell rebellion among the gadhri prisoners by transferring them between provinces. This practice introduced problems of its own, because under the Prisons (India) Act, 1894, provincial governments had separately developed their prison rules. Hence, transfer entailed new dietaries and other changes in daily prison life, which the prisoners resented. Unfamiliar environments outside the prisons exacerbated difficulties inside the prisons, especially if prisoners could not communicate across linguistic and religious boundaries to win sympathy and support through visitors and smuggled messages. Prisoners repeatedly resorted to hunger strikes and fasts to secure privileges in one province that had been previously granted to them in another. The government's policy of transferring prisoners therefore inadvertently spread hunger striking across the length and breadth of India, from the Northwest Frontier Province to the Madras Presidency in the south, from the Bombay Presidency in the west to the Bengal Presidency in the east.

India's provincial prison systems were tested by the unrest generated not only by ghadris, but also by Bengali militants at this time. Consequently, in 1917, the Home Department of the government of India converted the Hazaribagh Jail in the province of Bihar and Orissa into a "political prison" for the incarceration of seditious and state prisoners from Punjab and Bengal. Ujjwala Singh observes, "This was probably the first instance in the history of the modern prison system in India that a jail had been converted into a 'political prison.'"[29] In this way the British facilitated the forging of bonds between these militant movements. According to Singh, in March, thirty-three men convicted for their participation in the Ghadar were transferred from Punjab to Hazaribagh. In October, forty-seven state prisoners from Bengal were sent to join them. An additional twelve were then transferred from Punjab in November.[30] These prisoners went on hunger strikes and fasts for a range of objectives. Randhir Singh, transferred to Hazaribagh in 1917, went on another fast to protest dietary restrictions imposed by the jail superintendent, Mr. Husband. Singh's account of this fast is particularly interesting, because he alleges that the fast divided the prison officials and undermined the authority of the superintendent. When Husband ordered the warders to forcibly feed Singh, the head warder, a Sikh, the medical officer, a Bengali, and another doctor, a Maratha, refused to comply. It is noteworthy that the head warder was probably a fellow prisoner, as it was common practice to draw warders from the ranks of prisoners with records of good behavior. According to Singh, the medical officer went over the head of the superintendent and reported to the inspector general of prisons that Singh had refused to eat on religious grounds. In response, the inspector general ordered that Singh and other Sikhs should be given a special diet and allowed to cook their own food.[31]

Singh's account of his successful hunger strike stands in stark contrast to an official record of another hunger strike by a group of twelve ghadris in April 1918. It appears that Singh's hunger strike, though undated in his memoir, preceded this second strike, perhaps by several months. It is possible that this second hunger strike was conducted by the twelve prisoners who arrived at Hazaribagh in November. According to official records, these strikers issued a list of demands that were much more diverse, and explicitly political, than those of Singh. The superintendent reported to the inspector general of prisons that the prisoners were refusing food for the following reasons:

1. They want their fetters to be removed.
2. They want to be allowed out of their cells and yards for exercise into the adjoining.
3. They want to remain during the day in a general ward and be only placed in the cells at night.
4. They want to be given cotton clothing night and day.
5. They want 'transportation', food, clothes and other privileges and not the food etc., ordinarily given to ordinary prisoners.
6. They want 'Maha Prosad' and 'Kara Prosad' [sacred foods] twice per week.[32]

Most of the prisoners then had individual demands as well. So, for example, Button Singh wanted to be transported to the Andamans or get the same privileges as if he were there. Harnam Singh wanted "two *dhoties* [cloth garments covering the legs and tied at the waist] and long coats, etc.," and "'political' food valued Re. [rupee] 1 daily."[33]

The inspector general dismissed the prisoners' grievances upon review. He insisted that the prisoners, although from Punjab, had to abide by the jail rules of Bihar and Orissa: "They cannot be allowed any liberty which is not consistent with their safe custody nor can they be given any food which is not authorized by the Jail Code rules." He asserted that the strikers were bluffing, and he ordered the medical officer to forcibly feed by stomach tube any prisoners who appeared weak.[34] The record does not indicate that the prisoners were forcibly fed, nor does it indicate the outcome of this particular strike. It is probable that the strike collapsed and that the superintendent took a stronger stand going forward. In May, prompted by this strike, the government of Bihar and Orissa revised the Bengal Jail Code, 1910, to authorize forcible feeding. According to the new rule: "If a prisoner abstains from food and thereby is, in the opinion of the Medical Officer, endangering his health or his life, the Medical Officer may administer food to him in such manner as the circumstances appear to the Medical Officer to warrant.'"[35]

There is evidence that contemporary hunger strikes in Ireland inspired some revolutionaries to hunger strike in India during and after the First World War. Scholars have observed that hunger striking was a tactic conveyed from Ireland to India through the print media.[36] Indeed, on the very day that Thomas Ashe died, the *Bombay Chronicle* carried a short notice regarding allegations by Irish nationalists that republican prisoners in Dublin and Cork were being subjected to forcible feeding.[37] In 1918 local officials in both the Bombay Presidency and the Bengal Presidency reported that they faced hunger strikes by prisoners inspired by the Irish. It stands to reason that these prisoners had learned about the regular release of Irish hunger strikers in the several months after Ashe's death.[38] Then again, the twelve prisoners who went on hunger strike in April 1918 in Hazaribagh were more likely inspired by their fellow prisoner, Randhir Singh, than by the Irish. Granted, the Ghadar movement was keenly aware of Irish political struggles and regularly covered events in Ireland in its publications, noting that Irish soldiers in the imperial armies might be allies in rebellion.[39]

A few points need to be made regarding the influence of Irish hunger strikes on prison protest in India. The first and most obvious is that Nani Gopal Mukherjee went on hunger strike in 1912 and numerous ghadris, including Randhir Singh, were imprisoned in 1915 before Irish republican strikes proliferated. The ghadris then undertook fasts at approximately the same time that republicans began to hunger strike after the Easter Rising in 1916—when there was as yet no press coverage of the hunger strikes by Irish internees, whether in the United Kingdom or India. It is finally noteworthy that the most colorful public expressions of mutual support by Irish and Indian nationalists, such as Sikhs in green turbans marching in the Saint Patrick's Day parade in New York City in 1920, generally occurred *after* the declaration of a provisional Irish government in Dublin in 1919.[40]

It is probable that Irish republican hunger strikes exerted influence in India after Ashe's death because they appeared to have worked. There was also inspiration in failure. Terence MacSwiney was valorized in India as a martyr after he died on hunger strike in 1920, probably because his months-long, clear-eyed starvation met the highest cultural standards of sacrifice in India—a point to which we will return. He was an inspiration to leading revolutionaries, including Das and his comrade Bhagat Singh, who both made blood sacrifices and are still commonly honored with the title *shahid*, denoting, in the simplest sense, a martyr, but more specifically one who bears witness to injustice.[41] Yet for all the influence that Irish hunger strikes may have had in prompting Indian revolutionaries to continue hunger striking after 1917, the use of hunger in protest in India had not only different sources, but also dramatically different cultural and political significance.

Sikhs were not the only revolutionaries to hunger for their faiths, or to couch the political ends of starvation in religious terms. Virtually all communities in India associated voluntary starvation, or fasting, with religious devotion. It was probably for this reason that imprisoned revolutionaries turned to the hunger strike and fast in contesting sacred privileges, including religious texts and symbols, diet, and clothing. For many prisoners, their faiths constituted both moral conviction and leverage, as in the case of Randir Singh's fast against Mr. Husband. However, a fast such as that against Husband in Bihar and Orissa may not have worked against another medical officer in another province. Although Indian prison systems generally accommodated different religious practices and rules of caste, prisons under different provincial governments did not govern religious practice in a uniform manner.[42] The Bengali revolutionary Barindra Ghose recalled that when he began his incarceration in the Cellular Jail in December 1909 he found "all caste distinctions . . . clean wiped out." As a Brahmin, Ghose was supposed to wear a thread across his torso as a sacred symbol of his caste position, but the prison staff took the thread from him, as it did from all Brahmin inmates. In 1918 a Punjabi Brahmin named Rama Raksha went on a hunger and thirst strike for four days to protest the removal of his sacred thread. This protest won Raksha forcible feeding with a stomach pump and then, in his weakened state, a lethal case of consumption. Only after Raksha's death did authorities in the Cellular Jail permit Brahmins to keep the sacred thread.[43]

HUNGER FOR THE ONE MOTHER

The diverse religious goals and connotations of hunger strikes and fasts came together in the principle of sacrifice to the new, ostensibly universal deity Mother India. This deity can be traced to the novel *Anandamath*, published by the Bengali writer Bankim

Chandra Chattopadhyay in 1882.[44] It is a story of Hindu devotion and empowerment based loosely on the historical events of the great Bengal famine of 1770, but also resonant of a more recent famine in 1876–78. At the outset of the novel, a Hindu couple, Mahendra and Kalyani, and their daughter abandon their famine-stricken village in search of relief. They are separated in a forest ridden with bandits, but then all are saved by the warriors of a Hindu monastery devoted to the Mother. "Who is this Mother?" Mahendra asks. A monk answers, "She whose Children we are." The monk shows Mahendra three iconic forms of the Mother: The mother as she was, the mother as she is, and the mother as she will be.[45] These are recognizable as forms of the Great Goddess of Hinduism, Devi, deity of the feminine power *shakti*, the essential energy of the universe. The mother-as-she-was is the beautiful Mother Earth (Bhu Devi). The mother-as-she-is is the horrible goddess Kali, naked and emaciated, holding a club and begging bowl. The monk observes, "Blackened and shrouded in darkness. She has been robbed of everything; that is why she is naked. And because the whole land is a burning-ground, she is garlanded with skulls." The mother-as-she-will-be is the magnificent, ten-armed Durga, the paramount form of shakti. Mahendra asks, "When will we be able to see the Mother in this form?" The monk replies, "When all Mother's children recognise her as the Mother, she will be gracious to us." Before each image Mahendra prays, "Bande Mataram," which is also the refrain of a poem in the novel.[46] The monk attributes the Mother's current hardship, marked by famine, to the rule of the Mughals, that is, Muslims. He asks Mahendra to join the warriors in defending and restoring the Mother, and Mahendra agrees to do so.

The poem in the novel, an ode to the Mother, begins with two stanzas that anthropomorphize the land of India and testify to the Mother's natural beauty. These and the following stanzas are drawn from a translation of the poem from Bengali into English by the revolutionary intellectual and guru Aurobindo Ghose:

> Mother, I bow to thee!
> Rich with thy hurrying streams,
> Bright with thy orchard gleams,
> Cool with thy winds of delight,
> Dark fields waving, Mother of might,
> Mother free.
>
> Glory of moonlight dreams
> Over thy beaches and lordly streams;
> Clad in thy blossoming trees,
> Mother, giver of ease,
> Laughing low and sweet!
> Mother, I kiss thy feet,
> Speaker sweet and low!
> Mother, to thee I bow.

Subsequent stanzas testify to the Mother's strength in arms and her power to cast off invaders such as the Mughals. The identification of the Mother with the Hindu goddess Durga is made explicit in later stanzas, such as that below.

> Thine the strength that nerves
> the arm,
> Thine the beauty, thine the charm.
> Every image made divine
> in our temples is but thine.
> Thou art Durga, Lady and Queen,
> With her hands that strike and her
> swords of sheen,
> Thou are Lakshmi lotus-throned,
> And the Muse a hundred-toned.[47]

The Bengali writer and future Nobel laureate Rabindranath Tagore set the poem to music and sang it at the twelfth session of the Indian National Congress in Calcutta in 1896. "Bande Mataram" then became a nationalist slogan in 1905 during mass protests against the partition of Bengal.[48] To Britain's political and administrative advantage, the government divided Bengal between a predominantly Hindu west and predominantly Muslim east. Thinly veiling their strategy of divide and rule, government officials suggested that the partition would enable them to better manage famine. Bengali nationalists rejected this humanitarian rationale and initiated the first *swadeshi* movement, that is, a campaign for economic self-sufficiency from Britain, which served as the model for Gandhi's later campaign under the same name. The protests over the partition of Bengal also generated a new nationalist symbol, inspired by the Mother. In that year of crisis, Aurobindo Ghose published a pamphlet titled *Bhawani Mandir*, in which he called for a *mandir* (temple) to be erected to the Mother, in this case Bhawani, another form of the goddess and an incarnation of *shakti*. Through devotion in *Bhawani Mandir*, the nation's children would rejuvenate the Mother, who, according to Ghose, would then prove herself "the Eternal Religion which is to harmonise all religion, science and philosophies and make mankind one soul." Ghose called for an elite group of devotees, who, "having the fire of Bhawani in their hearts and brains, will go forth and carry the flame to every nook and cranny of our land."[49] The influence of Bhawani was not only harmonious, however. Bhawani was the patron deity of the legendary Maratha hero Shivaji, to whom she allegedly gave her blessed curved sword to wield in his war against the Mughals. The fire of Bhawani was therefore both inspirational to her devotees and potentially deadly to her opponents.[50]

In attempting to promote a civil religion focused upon a unified, imagined Indian nation, revolutionaries and moderates alike were working against larger historical forces that had been creating and enforcing religious divisions in Indian society for decades. Harjot Oberoi observes that a century beforehand, popular religious belief and practice in India had been a dynamic bricolage. The ensuing century had then witnessed the development of "uniform, centralized, religious (communities) possessing . . . fixed canon and well-demarcated social and cultural boundaries."[51] As these communities gained support, they became reified in history and effectively rendered separate and singular. For the first time, religions were given distinctive names, such as Sikhism and Hinduism. Cultural elites codified and guarded traditions.[52] This shift from pluralism and inclusivity to singularity and exclusivity was largely driven by the imperial regime through its religious taxonomies of administration.[53] As we shall see, the ostensible inclusivity of Mother India was increasingly seen by Muslims as something insidious, and by the imperial regime as something dangerous, but also potentially, divisively advantageous. Even Tagore himself worried as early as 1907 that "Bande Mataram" was becoming a hymn to Hindu communalism.[54]

A great variety of Indian revolutionaries invoked their service to Mother India. Savarkar fostered the ideal of blood sacrifice to Mother India among young Indian men in London after his arrival to study law in 1906.[55] Before hanging for the assassination of Wyllie, Dhingra declared, "Neither rich nor able, a poor son like myself can offer nothing but his blood on the altar of Mother's deliverance. . . . May I be reborn of the same Mother and may I redie in the same sacred cause, till my mission is done and she stands free for the good of humanity and to the glory of God."[56] Twenty years later, in 1929, some twenty members of the Hindustan Socialist Republican Association began a series of hunger strikes for political prisoner status while under trial for acts of war against the King Emperor.[57] Haggard with hunger, their leader, the Punjabi Bhagat Singh, his comrades, and their supporters chanted in court, "Bande Mataram!"[58] By popular acclaim, one of the prisoners, the Bengali revolutionary Jatin Das, joined the elite devotees of Mother India's temple when he died in September 1929 after a hunger strike of sixty-four days. The *Bombay Chronicle*'s headline read, "Jatin Lays Down Life at Altar of Motherland—Glorious Martyrdom Crowns a Youthful Career of Service & Sacrifice."[59] Fifty thousand people marched in honor of Das's sacrifice in Lahore. When the train carrying Das's body from Lahore pulled into Howrah station in Calcutta, the crowd roared "Bande Mataram!"[60] Hundreds of thousands of people then joined in Das's funeral procession in Calcutta, crying "Bande Mataram!" along the way.[61] Bhagat Singh and another two comrades, the Punjabi Sukhdev Thapar and the Maratha Shivram Rajguru, subsequently joined the elite as martyrs when they were hanged in March 1931 for the assassination of a police official.

Das and Singh assumed prominent roles in a complex, nationalist visual culture. Popular images were sometimes created by political parties, but more often by barefoot artists catering to a popular market. Their work was designed for mass

FIGURE 11. *"Bhandan mein Bharat Mata ki bhent"* (Chained Mother India's Sacred Offering), ca. 1931, National Archives of India, no. 1789 (Proscribed Literature Hindi). Reproduced by permission of the National Archives of India.

distribution, and it often crossed party lines.[62] This barefoot image was published in Lahore circa 1931, after the hangings of Singh, Sukhdev, and Rajguru (figure 11). To the left is Mother India, holding the Hindu goddess Durga's trident. Her hands are chained, symbolizing British despotism. Above, Lord Krishna, an avatar of the god Vishnu, blesses the scene; to the right, revolutionary comrades are transported to prison on the Andaman Islands. The four central figures are Das, Singh, Sukdhev, and Rajguru. They offer their heads in a historical, symbolic gesture.

Giving one's head to the goddess had been regarded as a supreme act of devotion by Hindus and Sikhs in Bengal and Punjab since at least the eighteenth century.[63] Hence, the heads are here described as *bhent*, a sacred gift or offering. In Bengal, decapitation was mainly associated with a historical cult of devotees to the goddess Kali. In Punjab, decapitation was associated with martyr saints, often Muslim, who continued to be propitiated by Hindus and Sikhs.[64] According to the British administrator and ethnographer Richard Temple, writing in 1883, "the notion of cutting off the head, and so making a martyr to faith is, as regards the

FIGURE 12. Roop Kishore Kapoor, "*Azad Mandir*," Kanpur: Shyam Sundar Lal Publishers, ca. 1931, Oriental and India Office Collection, British Library, PP Hin F68. Reproduced by permission of the British Library.

Sikh religion, derived from the Hindu rites of Durgá and Deví" and from "Bráh-
manical fables."[65] It is noteworthy that although this image of supreme sacrifice
was published *circa* 1931, the first place is still given to Das, who died two years
earlier on hunger strike.

The act of sacrifice was believed to generate shakti, that essential feminine
energy, for the goddess and the devotee.[66] This is illustrated in another image (figure 12), which commemorates the death of the revolutionary Chandra Shekhar
Azad, a mentor of Bhagat Singh's, who died in a gun battle with police before Singh's hanging in 1931. The image is titled *Azad Mandir,* or Freedom Temple, and it
includes a collection of revolutionary martyrs from different parts of India, posi-
tioned as temple icons to be venerated.[67] Their relationship with the viewer is
reciprocal in the terms of Indian and especially Hindu religious belief and practice. Their pictures offer *darshan,* the sight of a revered or sacred person or object
that brings a blessing upon the viewer. The power of the blessing depended not on
the men's courage, but on the subject of their devotion. These men were united in
their sacrifice for Mother India; hence, this temple named for a man, Azad, effectively represents devotion to the one Mother. Again, Das, the hunger striker, is
given a privileged position, here atop the cupola, where one would usually find the
symbol of the god or goddess of the temple.

GANDHI'S FASTS

Neeti Nair has observed that Das's martyrdom in 1929 "brought every leading political thinker on the same platform, except Gandhi."[68] In his article "The Bomb and
the Knife" Gandhi denounced militants such as Das and Singh for advocating only
"mad revenge and impotent rage."[69] He consistently criticized hunger strikes by
militants as "political," coercive acts. In contrast, he saw fasting, as he called his own
self-starvation, as an integral component of satyagraha (truth force), his comprehensive program of self-improvement, social reform, and liberation. He described
his fasting as an act of ahimsa, self-purification, and love.[70] "While individuals
might be unequal in their ability to kill," Faisal Devji explains of Gandhi's conception of fasting, "they were all equally capable of dying, demonstrating therefore the
universality of suffering and sacrifice over violence of all kinds."[71] Like the hunger
strikes by Russian politicals, Gandhi's fasts were not directed toward a particular
form of government, such as a liberal democratic or a socialist republic. He fasted
instead, as Devji observes, to realize and display a transcendent morality that constituted the basis of the individual's sovereignty, which collectively and coopera-
tively constituted the state's sovereignty.[72]

Yet Gandhi's advocacy of nonviolence was regularly undermined by his own followers, who undertook hunger strikes in prison for much the same reasons that
revolutionaries did, perhaps because there were significant numbers of former and

current revolutionaries in Gandhi's campaigns.[73] Between June and October 1930, for example, prisons in the Bombay Presidency were overwhelmed by satyagrahis arrested in civil disobedience protests. Most of these prisoners were common people, not elites, so they were relegated to C-class—that is, the lowest—prisoner status. Major M. G. Bhandari, superintendent of the Nasik Road Central Prison, informed the provincial inspector general of prisons on 27 June that one Motibas Das, a C-class prisoner, had begun a "hunger strike" that morning for a variety of demands. Das insisted that spinning materials should be given to all prisoners who wanted them, that all prisoners should have access to writing materials and newspapers, and that the vegetables given to C-class prisoners should also be given to criminal prisoners. Bhandari subsequently reported that fourteen C-class prisoners, also participants in the civil disobedience movement, had gone on hunger strike because "the additional jailor had been rude to them." In October, Bhandarai stated that his prison had been overwhelmed by C-class prisoners associated with Gandhi's movement and asked that no more be transferred there.[74] For Gandhi, these undisciplined satyagrahis, fasting for objectives indistinguishable from those of militant hunger strikers, were both morally reprehensible and a political liability. This is probably one reason why Gandhi discouraged his followers from fasting in protest, though he encouraged them to fast for their physical and spiritual health.

Gandhi nonetheless found himself joined with revolutionaries in the work of barefoot artists, as in an image *circa* 1930–31 (figure 13). In the upper left, there is Gandhi; in the upper right, there is Jawarhalal Nehru, Gandhi's protégé and the past president of the Congress. Note that each one wears a hat that was then known as the "Gandhi *topi*" or the "Gandhi cap," symbolic of Gandhi and membership in the Congress.[75] Both watch over Singh and other revolutionary martyrs. The visual combination of revolutionaries with Gandhi and Nehru became common at this time, as in figure 14, published probably a year or two earlier. Nehru offers the gift of Jatin Das's head to Mother India, here in the form of Rhada, the consort of Lord Krishna. Behind Nehru, Bhagat Singh, in the trilby, and his militant comrade B. K. Dutt look on. The hunger striker, once more, is the supreme gift to the nation, hallowed even in the eyes of Singh. This image furthermore represents a political difference between Nehru and Gandhi. Nehru had praised the hunger strikers and called for commuted sentences; he had furthermore pushed the Congress to commit itself to purna swaraj after Das's death, thus earning the privilege of presenting Das's sacrificial gift to the Mother.

As Gandhi spurned militant nationalists, he embraced Mother India. In 1936 he presided over the inauguration of the first actual Bharat Mata Mandir (Mother India Temple) in Banares. Gandhi observed, "The temple contains no image of any god or goddess. It has only a relief map of India made of marble stone."[76] In contemplating the map, the Mother's body, Indians could presumably find their place in the nation and forget all that had fragmented them before.

FIGURE 13. "Sadar Bhagat Singh, on the Scaffold," Lahore: R. L. Behal Tawalud, Rattan Printing Press, ca. 1930–31, Oriental and India Office Collection, British Library, PIB 42/18. Reproduced by permission of the British Library.

FIGURE 14. Roop Kishore Kapoor, "*Swatantrata Ki Bhent: Amar Shahid Yatindranath Das*" (Freedom's Sacred Offering: Immortal Martyr Yatindranath Das), Kanpur: Shyam Sundar Lal Picture Merchant, ca. 1929. Author's collection.

BRITISH PERSPECTIVES ON ONE MOTHER DIVIDED

The British perceived Mother India in less nurturing terms. They were fully aware of her novel origins and her development through Aurobindo Ghose's pamphlet *Bhawani Mandir* after 1905.[77] While they recognized her as an intractable threat, they hoped that the potential range of her threat could be limited. They saw plainly that a map in a temple could not encompass all of India's sacred and political geographies. In a series of articles published in the *The Times* in 1910, the journalist Valentine Chirol identified the revival of the "Shakti cultus," focused on the goddess Kali, as an attempt by Hindu Brahmins, especially in Bengal, to reassert their power in Indian civil society, which had been undermined by the civilizing influence of British rule.[78] In 1917 James Campbell Ker, personal assistant of the director of criminal intelligence in Delhi, issued a confidential report in which he dwelled particularly on Bengali militants' devotion to Kali, a deity who they did indeed venerate and incorporate into their oaths of loyalty. In a striking visual representation of his analysis of Indian militancy, Ker reproduced a picture of Kali as the frontispiece of his report (figure 15). Kali here does not embody famished suffering or political oppression—this is Kali on a famous rampage, calmed only when she stepped upon her consort, Lord Shiva, who lay down in her path to prevent her from destroying the world.

Through the 1920s and 1930s, British officials continued to represent revolutionaries as members of a Hindu cult—maternal, bloodthirsty, and perverse. In 1927 the American writer Katherine Mayo published a disparaging treatment of Indian society in her book *Mother India* that was an extension of this British view. As Mrinalini Sinha demonstrates, Mayo acquired the central thesis of her book— that India remained poverty-stricken and backward due to the oversexed culture of Hindus—from a British officer in Indian Political Intelligence.[79] Mayo later acknowledged that she could not have written the book without the British government's support.[80] As Sinha deftly observes, "Mayo's equation of Hinduism with sexual immorality was an especially pointed response to the cultural-nationalist appropriation of the domain of religion in India as proof of India's superiority to the West."[81] That this "domain of religion" was the civil religion of Mother India is apparent in Mayo's ironic appropriation of Mother India to the title of her book. In focusing upon Hinduism in her criticism of India, Mayo, and arguably her British consultants, furthermore rejected the representation of Mother India as the one mother of all.

In 1918 the East India Sedition Committee issued an influential report in which it explained that wartime revolutionary outrages in India "were all the outcome of a widespread but essentially single movement of perverted religion and equally perverted patriotism."[82] The committee further acknowledged that militants had called on all faiths to join in serving the one Mother, but it concluded that this was

FIGURE 15. "Kali," in James Campbell Ker, *Political Trouble in India, 1907–1917* (Calcutta: Superintendent Government Printing, India, 1917), frontispiece. Reproduced by permission of the British Library.

unlikely to happen, because the Mother's temple had no room for Muslims.[83] This perception was reinforced by a growing revolutionary strain of Hindu nationalism articulated powerfully by Savarkar, who was transferred from the Cellular Jail to Ratnagiri Jail in Maharashtra in 1921. Two years later, while still imprisoned, he completed his most influential work, *Hindutva: Who is a Hindu?*, a treatise on the cultural hegemony and the past and future political dominance of Hindus in India. While Savarkar and Gandhi both heard "Bande Mataram" as a sacred call to unity, if of different kinds, the British observed with some equanimity that Muslims heard a call to assimilation and a promise of political marginalization.

PARTISAN HUNGER

Following the suppression of Gandhi's civil disobedience movement in 1932, the British made a strategic decision to ward off future rebellion by bringing Indian political leaders into government.[84] This strategy was implemented through the Government of India Act, 1935, which provided for the election of Indians to form ministries to run India's provincial governments under the supervision of British governors. The governors had a delicate task in supporting the Indian ministries without overtly guiding them. The hope was that Indian elected officials would invest themselves in "responsible government" if they felt empowered to govern under a discreet British rule. Elections began in 1936 and ran into 1937, redirecting the energies of Indian political parties from conflict with the British to competition with each other. Despite misgivings about collaboration with the British government at the possible expense of eventual independence, victorious parties took office across the subcontinent. Between July and September 1937 the Congress assumed power in seven provinces: Bihar, Bombay, the Central Provinces, Madras, Orissa, the United Provinces, the Northwest Frontier Provinces, and Assam. The ministry in Bengal was formed by a coalition of the KPP and the Muslim League. In Punjab, the ministry was formed by the Unionist Party, an interfaith party representing the interests of landlords.

Political prisoners—as they were called in common parlance—had been vexed subjects in the partisan campaigns. Neither the KKP nor the Muslim League in Bengal nor the Unionist Party in Punjab had advocated the release of political prisoners, which they saw as a precipitous act that would likely threaten civil order and thus their political control. Central to the Congress's provincial campaigns, in stark contrast, had been its promise to release political prisoners once in power. Through this promise the party had hoped to make political capital of the symbolic power of political prisoners, even though many such prisoners were militants. Sherman explains, "Congressmen—and especially Gandhi—were ambivalent about the crimes of their violent comrades, but they were willing to employ the symbol of these political prisoners to keep the more confrontational strand of the nationalist project alive, even as the mainstream Congress party moved to the right as it entered government."[85] The symbolism of the political prisoner had been effectively defined in recent years by militants such as Das and Singh. Political prisoners were not, however, merely symbols, but people with objectives and wills of their own. Before and after the Indian ministries were formed, prisoners in the Cellular Jail and in jails in several mainland provinces began hunger strikes for release, transfer, or improvement in prison conditions. This placed Congress ministries, in particular, in an awkward position, having laid claim to political legitimacy in elections by promising to release these same prisoners. They were now concerned not only about their voting constituents, but about the loyalty and morale of the police and the judiciary upon which they, along with the British, depended.[86] Once in power, they could see as never before the point of the viceroy Lord Linlithgow's warning to the governor of the Bombay Presidency on 11 August 1937: "Jail discipline throughout India would be imperiled if it were demonstrated that a body of prisoners, by resorting to a concerted hunger strike could dictate the place of their incarceration and the conditions under which they are to be detained."[87]

By the end of July 1937, some two hundred prisoners in the Cellular Jail were on hunger strike. These prisoners were then joined in their strike by others in jails in multiple provinces, many of these having been transferred from their home provinces in order to quell prison unrest. Given that the Cellular Jail fell under the administrative authority of the central government in Delhi, Indian politicians quickly saw their opportunity to establish their nationalist credentials by supporting this particular protest. Nehru treated these strikes as a symbolic means to forge national bonds. He did not condone the hunger strike as a method of protest, but he readily acknowledged its constitutive power. On 6 August 1937, speaking as the president of the Indian National Congress in Allahabad, Punjab, Nehru demanded release or repatriation into custody on the mainland for the prisoners in the Cellular Jail, as well as immediate improvement in their prison conditions. Recognizing that most of the prisoners in the Cellular Jail were Bengalis, Nehru alluded ominously to the Government of India Act, 1935: "Constitutions are as dust in the scale if they cannot give us the power to protect our own people. This is not a matter concerning Bengal only but one which affects the whole of India and which touches the honour and dignity of every Indian."[88] Nehru thus spoke for Bengal in Punjab, both provinces in which the Congress struggled to claim leadership as an opposition party. He was not the last politician to play the nationalist card on the body of a hunger striker.

Debates over hunger striking prisoners in the Cellular Jail were politically simple in comparison with those involving hunger strikers under the direct authority of Indian ministries. Of the various issues that challenged Indian ministers, including the rise of labor under increasing communist influence and the political organization of peasants demanding land reform, hunger strikes were the most thoroughly interconnected across provincial borders. As hunger strikes proceeded in multiple provinces, under separate prison rules, their politics became intertwined. Any concession made by one ministry opened other ministries to criticism if they refused to concede. This situation was further aggravated by the fact that hunger strikes took place under the separate jurisdictions of competing parties. The Congress, supported by Gandhi, attempted to diffuse pressures upon its ministries by simultaneously advocating for a methodical system of release for "political prisoners" and discouraging hunger strikes for allegedly undermining that advocacy. At the same time, the party conspicuously supported hunger strikers in Bengal, in particular, in order to attack the KPP-Muslim League ministry, provoking concern among British officials that communal violence might ensue.[89]

The British governor of Bengal, John Anderson, the former undersecretary of state in Ireland, informed the viceroy that "the most critical events of the last fortnight of August [1937] have . . . been those connected with the Andamans hunger strike."[90] It was at this time that Gandhi joined in negotiations with the government as a self-designated representative of the hunger strikers. He appealed to the prisoners, on behalf of the nation, to give up their hunger strike and renounce violence. He asserted to both the strikers and the government that this renunciation should then qualify them for release. In a message to the strikers conveyed via a telegram to the viceroy, Gandhi stated: "I would be grateful on your part yield to nationwide request. You will help me personally if I could get assurance that those who believed in terrorist methods no longer believe in them and that they have come to believe in non-violence as the best method."[91] The strikers were not demanding immediate release, but rather a process through which they might be released or at least transferred to their home provinces on the mainland. They also asked that all prisoners be given "second division" privileges. The government in Delhi was prepared to accede to these requests, provided that the prisoners renounced terrorism, as Gandhi had asked them to do. It appears that the strikers were assured of the government's good faith not by Gandhi, however, but by the Bengal ministry, which also participated in the negotiation.[92] On 28 August, after five weeks, two hundred prisoners ended their hunger strikes, while seven continued.[93] By January 1938, all of the prisoners had been transferred from the Cellular Jail to the mainland.

Gandhi persisted in negotiating on behalf of political prisoners over the next year, committing himself to securing release for all those who renounced violence and, thus, implicitly endorsed his program of satyagraha. In mid-February, in support of this process, he drafted the following resolution, which was passed by the All-India Congress Committee: "The Congress wishes to make it clear that it strongly disapproves of hunger-strikes for release. Hunger-strikes embarrass the Congress in pursuit of its policy of securing release of political prisoners."[94]

Later in the month, hunger strikes by revolutionary prisoners in the United Provinces and Bihar pushed India to a constitutional crisis. Under increasing political pressure, the Congress ministries in these two provinces issued orders to release all of their remaining political prisoners, forty-one in all. The British governors, under orders from the viceroy, used their executive authority to block the release, prompting the Congress ministers to resign. This raised the prospect of a collapse of "responsible government" not only in the United Provinces and Bihar, but across the country, which might then have been followed by a return to mass civil disobedience.[95] A flurry of correspondence among governors, ministers, and the viceroy ensued, focused upon coordinating a solution to this crisis across provincial boarders and partisan divides. The Bengal ministry, which was opposed to the release of its hundreds of political prisoners as a grave threat to public order, was deeply concerned that the British might authorize the release of prisoners in the United Provinces and Bihar, exposing it to damaging political indictment by revolutionaries and the Congress alike. Gandhi increased the pressure upon the British to do just that by publicly misrepresenting the Government of India Act as a system in which governors had authority only to advise and consent. In these terms, the governors' move to block the release of political prisoners became not an exercise of executive authority, but a betrayal of principle. In the end, the crisis was resolved by a mutually face-saving measure. The British government proposed, and the Indian ministries accepted, a process of "progressive release" of prisoners after individual examination. This process, ostensibly overseen by the British governors, enabled Indian ministries to hold those "political prisoners" guilty of violent offenses. This outcome was a minor victory for the Congress insofar as the greatest concessions were made by the KPP-Muslim League coalition in Bengal and by the Unionist Party in Punjab, which had both been reluctant to release any "political prisoners" at all.[96] If there had been any doubt about Gandhi's partisan motives in exploiting this political crisis provoked by hunger strikes, it was removed by his subsequent decision to abandon further negotiations with the Bengal ministry. As Sherman recounts, the home member in the KPP-Muslim League ministry, Khwaja Nizamuddin, indicated to Gandhi and Gandhi's Congress allies that although he would not guarantee the release of all political prisoners, he would promise to release most and then undertake a systematic review of others prosecuted for "murder and serious violence." In exchange for what the ministry saw as a major concession, he asked Gandhi to agree that, henceforth, "the matter shall cease to be a political issue." Faced with only a partial release of "political prisoners," Gandhi ended his negotiation with Nizamuddin. He stated, "It would be a breach of promise on my part if I submitted without demur to anything less than almost immediate unconditional discharge."[97]

At the same time that Gandhi and the Congress were using hunger strikes to gain a tactical political advantage in Bengal, they made a grave strategic error in fomenting communal tensions. Commenting on the Congress campaign for hunger striking political prisoners, the governor of Bengal observed in September 1937: "If the instigators of the campaign should succeed in what is presumably their immediate object—the defeat of the present Ministry—the effect of this on the relations between the two communities [Hindu and Muslim] will be most serious and the district authorities will be faced with the distasteful task of protecting the [Hindu] community whose self-constituted leaders will have deliberately created the situation from the result of their machinations."[98] Two days later, the viceroy informed the secretary of state, "I have felt very apprehensive all through the later stages of this Andamans discussion that we were confronted with an endeavor to mobilize a Hindu mass attack against the Muslim Government in Bengal."[99]

It was lost upon neither Muslims nor the British that as the Congress attacked the Bengal ministry it sang a paean to the nation as a Hindu goddess. Congressmen sang "Bande Mataram" at legislative and political functions across the country. Some even proposed that the song should be adopted as India's national anthem. The governor of Bengal observed in September 1937 that this proposal was strongly resented by Muslims in the province.[100] In October, two months after Gandhi had joined in the constitutional crisis created by hunger strikers, the Muslim League strongly objected to "Bande Mataram" in a resolution passed at the twenty-fifth session of the League at Lucknow. The league characterized the would-be anthem as "not merely positively anti-Islamic and idolatrous in its inspiration and ideas, but definitely subversive of the growth of genuine nationalism in India."[101] The Congress was not indifferent to this criticism of "Bande Mataram," especially given that, as Tanika Sarkar observes, the Muslim League "focused on the communal elements in the song and criticized its stature in Congress circles as evidence of the communal nature of the Congress itself."[102] In an effort to calm the growing controversy, the Congress established the Congress Working Committee on Bande Mataram. On 28 October the committee recognized "the validity of the objection raised by Muslim friends to certain parts of the song." As a compromise, the committee recommended, "Wherever the Bande Mataram is sung at national gatherings only the first two stanzas should be sung."[103] This policy was widely condemned by Congress supporters and the broader nationalist press as an insult to Mother India, because it limited her children's expression of devotion. Meanwhile, Muslims, especially in Bengal, were still not reconciled to a mother so clearly derived from a Hindu goddess.[104] Subhas Chandra Bose, among other Congress leaders, nevertheless remained optimistic. He wrote to Nehru in December, "It is difficult to say categorically what the nationalist Muslim reaction in Bengal will be if the two stanzas are adopted as the National Anthem. But, on the whole, I feel inclined to think that if we proceed with due tact and caution, nationalist Muslim opinion will fall into line with it."[105] The British thought otherwise. The government in Delhi recognized both the short-term benefit of a divided nationalist movement and the long-term threat of communal conflict. The viceroy wrote to the secretary of state: "A considerable Muslim agitation has developed against the use of 'Bande Matram' as a 'National' anthem and resolutions on the subject have been passed at the recent Muslim League Conference. This is all to the good from our point of view, for it is clearly preferable that the pressure should come from independent quarters rather than from Government and I am glad to think that the Muslims should appear to be waking up to the significance of the song, given its history, from their point of view."[106]

THE NAKED SWORD, THE LAST WEAPON, AND THE BURDEN OF SACRIFICE

Upon learning of Jatin Das's death on hunger strike and the transportation of his body to Calcutta, Mary MacSwiney sent the following cablegram to the city's lord mayor, J. M. Sen Gupta: "Family Terence MacSwiney unites patriotic India in grief and pride on death of Jatin Das. Freedom will come." Likewise, Eamon de Valera cabled, "Jatin Das has not died in vain. He is the Indian MacSwiney. Freedom is certain."[107] Mary MacSwiney and de Valera, then going their separate ways in Irish republican politics, each recognized the power of the hunger strike. While Mac-Swiney had personally suffered for it, and de Valera had politically capitalized upon it, they both saw something familiar in Das's protest and death that provoked their expressions of solidarity with the distant mayor. Granted, this familiarity was on their own cultural terms rather than on those of Indians with whom they were united by a common enemy. They were moved nonetheless by the visceral, common experience of starvation, of a body wasting and a mind wandering away. They may also have shared a belief, confident or just bitterly hopeful, in the effect of hunger in protest on the British liberal conscience. De Valera had observed in 1920 in a speech he delivered at a dinner hosted by the Friends of Freedom for India in New York: "We have never been able to achieve anything except when we compelled England to rule us with the naked sword. It is, of course, always by the sword that she has maintained herself in Ireland, as in India, but she prefers to maintain herself with the sword in its scabbard if she can. The English are very sensitive to what the world thinks of them."[108] MacSwiney and de Valera, like Das, never claimed to love British officials as had Gandhi, but they all recognized the power of starvation as the last weapon with which to turn the British regime's violence upon itself.

Fianna Fáil and the Congress struggled similarly against hunger strikers after they assumed substantial administrative authority from the British in the 1930s. There is no indication that the respective party leaders were aware of this coincidence. De Valera might have seen an unflattering reflection of himself and his party in Gandhi and Congress leaders who invoked the rule of law to hold prisoners incarcerated by the British. Mary MacSwiney, for her part, would have understood the indignation and resentment of hunger strikers and their families who found themselves under the thumb of nationalist ministries that emulated their imperial predecessors. Whereas de Valera generally played defense against the hunger strike, Gandhi used his calculated advocacy for hunger strikers as an offensive political weapon, especially in Bengal, where he tried to undermine a Muslim-led coalition ministry. He and the Congress thus aggravated communal tensions, even as they sang "Bande Mataram" to affirm their devotion to Mother India as the one mother of all India's children.

Gandhi heard in "Bande Mataram" a new message as he fought to end the catastrophic violence between Hindus, Muslims, and Sikhs that preceded and followed independence and partition in 1947. He declared of the song, "That was no religious cry. It was a purely political cry."[109] The sacred had become profane in the cries of Hindu and Sikh communalists who joined in terrible conflict with Muslims, especially in Bengal and Punjab. In a profound departure from the Mother India temple, on 13 August 1947, two days before India's independence, Gandhi moved into the abandoned home of a Muslim widow in a neighborhood of Calcutta recently devastated by communal violence. Gandhi moved into this home without police protection, but with the Muslim chief minister of Bengal, H. S. Suhrawardy, with whom he hoped to pacify Calcuttans by demonstrating that a Hindu and a Muslim could live as brothers even under the same roof.[110] On 15 August, India's day of independence, Gandhi celebrated a fragile peace in Calcutta. "Indeed," he observed, "Hindus were taken to the *masjids* by their Muslim brethren and the latter were taken by their Hindu brethren to the *mandirs*."[111] Within a couple of weeks, the peace was broken. To preempt an escalation of violence Gandhi determined to fast. He characterized fasting as "the weapon which has hitherto proved infallible for me."[112] This was one of over a dozen public fasts that Gandhi undertook in India, and it was arguably his most successful, for after only three days, on 4 September, Calcutta had returned to peace and he ended his fast with a glass of orange juice. Calcutta subsequently remained free from the communal violence that continued to sweep over other Indian cities.

This fast was remarkable in two respects, aside from its peaceful effect. First, in the course of the fast Gandhi never made reference to the great Bengal famine of 1943, in which an estimated three million people had died, though he might have used this to articulate and embody the injustice of British rule borne by Hindus, Muslims, Sikhs, and all Indians. Gandhi overlooked the original narrative of Mother India as the famished victim of unjust, foreign rule, and he chose instead to burden Indians of all faiths with responsibility for their own self-rule, or swaraj. The fast was furthermore remarkable in its conclusion. Gandhi made the leaders of Calcutta's different religious communities swear in a written oath that they would die to prevent any return to communal violence. He promised that, if they did not do so, he would fast unto death, and his death would be on their hands.[113] The same man who condemned militants' hunger strikes as coercive was here engaged in coercive tactics of his own, comparable to the threat with which Savarkar ended Mukherjee's hunger strike in the Cellular Jail in 1912. Gandhi and Savarkar had followed different paths in their service to Mother India in the intervening years, Gandhi as an avowed satyagrahi committed to religious harmony and Savarkar as a Hindu nationalist who regarded Gandhi's cooperation with Muslims as contemptible, needless appeasement. Savarkar was later tried for conspiracy in the assassination of Gandhi in January 1948. Although he was a known associate of the assassin Nathuram Godse and the other defendants, Savarkar was acquitted in February 1949. Upon his return to his home in Bombay, he was garlanded at the train station by his supporters, then paraded through the streets, bearing the burden of sacrifice for the one Mother.

5

The Rule of Exceptions

Hunger Strikes and Political Prisoner Status in
Britain, Ireland, and India, 1909–1946

In 1920 an Irish republican hunger striker in Mountjoy Prison observed, "Hunger-striking is different. They don't know how to meet it. . . . I admit the Castle would gladly shoot us all out of hand if they got the chance. But letting us die by inches frightens them."[1] In the first half of the twentieth century, militant suffragists in the United Kingdom and nationalists in Ireland and India took up the hunger strike as the last weapon with which to advance their causes in prison. In contrast to *satyagrahis* or other nonviolent prisoners, militants often starved to secure "political status" in prison in order to challenge the government's attempts to criminalize their violence. Whereas the previous chapters have examined the perspectives, goals, and experiences of such hunger strikers, this chapter turns to the prison officials and politicians who struggled against them. They were sometimes frightened, but not by the spectacle of the striker inching toward death. Instead, they feared that hunger strikes undermined general prison discipline and that the release of strikers could weaken the morale of not only prison staff, but also police and army beyond the prison walls. Prison medical officers, the central authorities of day-to-day prison life, furthermore feared that a striker's death could open them to an indictment for manslaughter. From this perspective, and in the context of widespread unrest or open rebellion in Ireland and India after the First World War, a hunger strike was indeed a frightful thing. This chapter, then, follows the coordinated efforts of prison officials and politicians in imperial and nationalist governments in Britain, Ireland, and India to master hunger strikes through the rule of law and prison regulations. What they achieved was a masterful rule of exceptions that regularly undermined their own liberal claims upon uniform, impartial justice.

During a hunger strike by Irish suffragettes in 1913, the chief secretary of Ireland observed correctly that "political prisoner" was "a category unknown alike to the law and to the prison regulations."[2] There was no political status for offenders under common or statutory law in the United Kingdom, nor was there in British India.[3] Those officials who confronted hunger strikes for "political status" also found that prison rules did not adequately account for this form of protest, unlike traditional prison protests, such as refusal to work. So they adapted old rules and created new ones, while politicians and bureaucrats attempted to create corresponding laws and policies. Although governments in Britain, Ireland, and India did not recognize de jure political status, a critical number of strikers succeeded in winning privileges forbidden to ordinary criminals because the burden of their starvation proved unbearable for prison staff and the elected or appointed officials who depended on that staff to enforce the rule of law. In these cases, strikers and their supporters equated their differential treatment with de facto political status, much to the frustration of their captors.

Prison staff and officials appealed to their governments for relief from hunger strikes and the legal quandary of political status. In 1920 the British government in Ireland, the Castle, notified the Home Office in London that the republican hunger striker Terence MacSwiney, the lord mayor of Cork, then starving to death in Cork Prison, required extraordinary treatment as a "political prisoner." Doctors and prison officials had determined that they could not forcibly feed MacSwiney without risking both his life and violent protest by his supporters outside of prison. The government had therefore to choose between release or continued detention, starvation, and possible death. The Home Office transferred MacSwiney to England, then used his case to make a virtue of necessity by establishing a flexible policy on hunger strikes. Henceforth, the government would make what it called a "political decision" about whether a striker should be forcibly fed, released, or held until he or she starved to death. Meanwhile, the efforts of the government of India in Delhi to establish a uniform policy on the treatment of hunger strikers was being impeded by its own provincial governments, which, under the Prisons (India) Act, 1894, controlled their own prison systems and observed disparate rules. Officials in Delhi nonetheless tried to promote consistency through recommendations based on British and Irish legal precedents and administrative practices. In 1922, spurred by a controversial hunger strike in the Madras Presidency, the government of India looked to the case of MacSwiney and advised provincial governors that they should also make "political decisions" in treating hunger strikers. Thus the proliferation of hunger in protest across political boundaries was paralleled by transimperial interpretations of law.

The governments of the United Kingdom and India responded differently to the threats posed by hunger strikes. The Home Office understood that the hunger strike was a form of protest, but it publicly characterized the prisoner's starvation as a medical condition. When critics likened forcible feeding to torture, the Home Office countered that forcible feeding was not a punishment but a means to save the prisoner's life. In India, in contrast, British officials explicitly identified the hunger strike as a form of mutiny, the most serious category of offense against prison authority. As in other cases of mutiny, such as assaults on prison staff, they sometimes punished strikers with whipping, as sanctioned by law and prison rules. This difference in the treatment of strikers in India was attributable to a combination of factors, including the comparative vulnerability of the Indian prison system to rebellion, the rationale of a state in crisis, and racism.[4]

In both Ireland and India between the wars, nationalists assumed new governmental roles during political storms of their own making. In 1922 Irish men and women assumed leadership of the Irish Free Sate. In 1937 provincial ministries were formed across the subcontinent by Indian men elected by a propertied, literate franchise of men and women. Each group found at the center of its storm mass hunger strikes for political prisoner status, now conducted by competing nationalist parties. Irish and Indian elected officials, like imperial officials, foresaw no future for their civil societies without a functional state. They argued that if individuals or groups could render themselves immune from state punishment by hunger striking, then the state would cease to function and any progress toward independence would come to nothing. Confronting hunger strikes by revolutionaries in Bengal in 1939, Gandhi declared, "Hunger-strike has positively become a plague."[5] Later in the same year, Eamon de Valera, head of the Irish Free State, denounced hunger strikes by republican prisoners in terms that resonated with the rhetoric of imperial governments before him:

> We all know that there is a body in this country with arms at its disposal. We know that in the last year their activities have taken a new turn, that the body has definitely proclaimed itself as entitled . . . to act in the name of our people. . . . Is the Government of this country to be deprived of the only power that it has to prevent things taking place here which are going . . . to rob us of the independence which has been got so far . . ., and, in so doing, to rob us of the fruits of all the efforts that have been made for the last 25 years? That is what is at stake.[6]

THE BURDEN OF CARE IN BRITAIN AND IRELAND

Prison officials and staff in the United Kingdom confronted hunger strikes in an era of prison reform following the Prison Act of 1898, a statute designed to render British prisons reformatory rather than merely punitive.[7] This statute added a new division of incarceration to the prison system, a "second division" between the social elite and the poor, thus constituting the three divisions described in chapter 2.[8] The statute also instituted shorter sentences, curtailed corporal punishments such as whipping, and even provided for the installation of netting in prison interiors to prevent prisoners from jumping to their deaths.[9] Previously the prison dietary had been regarded as a punitive element of prison discipline. Prisoners had normally lost weight. The statute initiated the systematic improvement of the prison dietary after 1900 and ameliorated weight loss among prisoners. Officials pointed to this change as evidence of their more humane administration, but then prisoners belied the benefits of reform by starving themselves.[10]

The British suffragists who turned to militancy in 1905 generally came from Britain's respectable classes, so they were initially incarcerated in the first division. As the number of suffragette prisoners increased, however, it became clear that there were structural limitations upon the prison system's ability to grant all of them first-division privileges. In 1912 the governor of Holloway Prison, where suffragettes were regularly held, commented that there was simply no way for prisons to provide multiple prisoners with separate, furnished rooms, as stipulated for the first division.[11] Between 1900 and 1911 the annual totals of male and female first-division prisoners in England and Wales fluctuated between 16 and 55, except for the year 1906–07, when the number rose to 160 due to the suffragette campaign.[12] Throughout 1907 magistrates continued to sentence most convicted suffragettes to the first division.[13] However, the growing numbers prompted the courts and the Home Office to relegate most suffragettes to the second and third divisions after January 1908, which prompted Emmeline Pankhurst to initiate a disobedience campaign by the WSPU for political status in prisons in October.[14] In this context, Marion Wallace Dunlop began the suffragettes' first hunger strike for political status in July 1909.

From the outset, Dunlop understood that the hunger strike was not only a symbol, but also an instrument with which to challenge the functions and capacities of the prison system. This is why she challenged the medical officer to imagine attempting to forcibly feed 108 more women through the nostrils in the event that he chose to begin with her.[15] Prison officials recognized a basic truth in Dunlop's scenario. The Prison Act of 1898 had greatly expanded the medical officer's duties, which now included, among other tasks, dietary management and the observation of "feeble-minded prisoners." Yet this greater measure of administrative responsibility had not been accompanied by additional staff support.[16] Herbert Gladstone, the home secretary, authorized the forcible feeding of suffragettes in September because prison officials believed that ongoing hunger strikes and releases with full remission of sentence would undermine general prison discipline. Forcible feeding was nothing new to British prisons, and, as we have seen, Gladstone's policy faced little public opposition.[17] Yet the government struggled against hunger strikes because the strikes continued to produce problems in prison management. In early October, Sir Evelyn Ruggles-Brise, chairman of the Prison Commission, warned the Home Office that a medical officer, already overburdened, could not properly care for multiple hunger strikers for even five days.[18]

The Home Office did periodically consider whether or not to resolve this matter by instituting political prisoner status. After Winston Churchill became the home secretary in 1910 he wrote to the undersecretary, Sir Edward Troup:

> I am anxious to prescribe a special code of regulations dealing with the treatment of Political Prisoners in His Majesty's Prisons. A political prisoner should, in my judgment, be defined as a person who has committed an offense, involving no moral turpitude, with a distinct political object. It should be in the power of the Secretary of State . . . to classify any person as a political prisoner.[19]

Permanent officials persuaded Churchill that it would be poor policy to alter the entire prison system for a particular group of prisoners, in this case the suffragettes. Churchill instead instituted Rule 243A, which enabled prison authorities to grant special privileges to respectable convicts who had not engaged in violent or otherwise ordinary criminal activity. This half-measure did not ultimately resolve the conflict over political status. After a lull in protest, the suffragettes resumed hunger striking in 1912. The subsequent Prisoners (Temporary Discharge for Ill Health) Act of 1913, the so-called Cat and Mouse Act, was another attempt by politicians to help prison staff overwhelmed by suffragette strikes. This act authorized the temporary release of prisoners in ill health and then the reincarceration of these prisoners after they recuperated. According to the Home Office, this act was to create a process that would relieve prison staff of both administrative and legal pressures, but without remitting the sentences of strikers or conferring political status.

Hunger strikes undermined the morale and resolution of prison staff. Time and again, prison officials complained that prisoners' resistance to feeding *made* the process "forcible" and different from standard "artificial feedings." Suffragettes recalled wardresses leaving during forcible feedings because they felt faint.[20] The misgivings of male prison staff were most serious in the cases of female strikers, especially those of "cultured and . . . refined habits," as one official put it.[21] The British regime in Ireland never forcibly fed Irish women after they began to hunger strike in 1912, probably because officials believed that Irish medical officers would refuse. Having admitted frankly that the Cat and Mouse Act was not a complete solution, a Home Office report observed, "The Home Secretary will be able . . . at any rate greatly to diminish the number of cases in which that repulsive duty [of forcible feeding] is forced upon prison officers by the action of the suffragettes."[22]

The effect of violent resistance to forcible feeding was compounded by the fact that suffragettes and then Irish republicans after 1916 often conducted hunger strikes in groups. Acts of self-starvation had generally been individual before 1909; the sheer numbers of later suffragette and republican strikes placed major strains upon the prison system, and especially upon the medical officers. One or two medical officers and one or two deputy medical officers found it virtually

impossible to oversee the welfare of hundreds of convicts in a given prison, moni-
tor the vital signs of multiple hunger strikers, forcibly feed some or all of them,
keep up with mandatory paperwork, and respond to inquiries from government
officials. In April 1912 it took the medical officer of Aylesbury Prison three hours
and forty-five minutes to forcibly feed twenty-three suffragettes—and this was just
one meal in the day.[23] A "Preliminary Report on the Forcible Feeding of Suffrage
Prisoners," published four months later in the *British Medical Journal*, suggests
that the medical officer at Aylesbury was remarkably efficient. "In the majority of
cases," the report stated, "the feeding has . . . been resisted to such a degree that two
doctors and four to six wardresses were required for each operation, and in several
instances the officials were held at bay for periods varying from ten minutes to
over an hour."[24]

In Ireland the government faced problems in recruiting qualified prison medical officers and staff to manage hunger strikes. The most infamous result of strikes
in an overburdened Irish prison system was the death of Thomas Ashe in 1917,
following his forcible feeding in Mountjoy Prison on 25 September. Ashe had been
the ninth or tenth of twenty-eight prisoners fed by stomach pump that day.[25] He
died that evening of heart failure and "congestion of the lungs" attributable to the
mixture of milk and eggs that had accidentally passed down his windpipe. The
man who had fed Ashe, Dr. William Lowe, had been hired in response to an appeal
by the head medical officer, Raymond G. Dowdall, after he declared that he could
not administer more than one meal a day to over two dozen prisoners by himself.[26]
The jury of the subsequent coroner's inquest found, "the assistant doctor called in
having no previous practice in such operations administered unskillfully forcible
feeding."[27]

The death and funeral of Ashe served as a catalyst for public defiance by militant republicans, while the subsequent release of Ashe's comrades inspired many
more hunger strikes by republican prisoners. To the government's dismay, Irish
prison medical officers regularly refused to forcibly feed these prisoners, partly
due to fear of reprisal, but mainly due to fear of prosecution for murder. The Home
Office, by its own admission, had not considered forcible feeding in litigious terms
before the autumn of 1909.[28] So it was not unreasonable for medical officers to
wonder if they could be held criminally liable for the death of a hunger striker. In
the case of *Leigh v. Gladstone* in 1909 the court had ruled that a medical officer had
a duty to preserve the life of a prisoner; nonetheless, officials remained uncertain
about criminal liability in particular circumstances.[29] If a medical officer improp-
erly exercised any of his other powers, he was liable for action under common
law.[30] In reply to an inquiry from the Home Office on forcible feeding, the law
officers of the crown determined in July 1920 that if a prisoner died, both the medical officer and the prison governor would be open to indictment for manslaughter. A jury would decide if the prisoner had died of neglect, or if he or she had died

despite the reasonable actions of the doctor in fulfilling his duty to attempt to preserve the prisoner's life.[31] Medical officers were not prosecuted in the five cases in which hunger strikers died in British and Irish prisons between 1917 and 1920, but anxiety over this issue continued.[32]

The burden of the hunger strike upon prison staff, and the uncertain legal position of medical officers, induced these officers to release a significant number of prisoners sooner rather than later. In 1912, of 240 suffragettes imprisoned, 83 went on hunger strike. Twenty-six of these were released without being fed due to "preexisting medical conditions." Fifty-seven strikers were forcibly fed, and of these 23 were released early on medical grounds.[33] At the end of the year, Sir Bryan Donkin, the director of convict prisons and honorary medical advisor to the prison commissioners, called for an end to forcible feeding, which he deemed a failure due to inconsistent practice. The same concern arose among prison officials in Ireland after 1917. "Of the 148 people tried by courts martial in 1917," explains Peter Hart, "24 per cent were released after hunger strikes and 61 per cent had their sentences remitted. Only one in ten served out their sentences."[34]

Looking beyond politically motivated prisoners, the Home Office had long worried that the release of suffragette strikers might inspire the general prison population to strike, and, indeed, after 1912 Home Office records refer to hunger strikes by ordinary criminals seeking release.[35] In Ireland this problem became common, especially after the death of Ashe and the government's concessions to his republican comrades. In March 1918 the lord lieutenant sent a letter to the lord mayor of Dublin in which he listed various ordinary criminals who had gone on hunger strike for release. The lord lieutenant declared, "Your Lordship . . . cannot but be aware of the conspiracy which is on foot to subvert all law in this country by means of the hunger strike."[36]

In Ireland between 1913 and 1918, the government made five unsuccessful policy changes in its attempts to stop hunger strikes by republican men. The policy toward hunger strikers was unclear until September 1917, when the forcible feeding of Irishmen began in earnest and resulted in the death of Ashe. On the day after Ashe's death, the Prisons Board instructed prison governors that "artificial feeding [was] a necessary duty of the Medical Officer." Following the public furor over Ashe's death, and an embarrassing inquest, the Castle issued a new policy in October, indicating that forcible feeding should take place only by special order of the lord lieutenant. In November the Castle authorized prison officials to release strikers in imminent danger of collapse without awaiting approval. In February 1918 the chief secretary declared that strikers would neither be forcibly fed nor released before the end of their sentences. The Prisons Board protested against this new policy, asserting that it was unfair to the medical officers who might be left open to a charge of manslaughter if prisoners died in their care. The board called for legislation to protect medical officers who carried out the directions of the executive, but the government refused to support this.[37] In November 1918 the government resumed releasing republican men under the Cat and Mouse Act.[38]

The government's indecisive response to hunger strikes and the many releases of republican prisoners undermined the morale of the Royal Irish Constabulary (RIC) and the army. The inspector general of the RIC observed, "In cases of organized illegality the lawbreaker is able to defeat the law by hunger-strike, and the constitutional methods of prosecution and imprisonment no longer have any deterrent effect."[39] With the onset of the Anglo-Irish War in 1919 and the IRA's turn to guerrilla warfare, the release of strikers was all the more damaging to the morale of government forces. The combined pressure of strikes and escalating violence coincidentally came to a head for the British regime when Terence MacSwiney commenced his hunger strike in August. The chief secretary told the home secretary, "If the Lord Mayor were released the military would mutiny and the police would cease to function."[40] Prime Minister David Lloyd George then issued a telling public statement:

> The Cabinet are responsible for preserving to the best of their ability the machinery upon which the protection of life and good order depend in the country. If the Lord Mayor were released, every hunger-striker, whatever his offense, would have to be let off. A law which is a respecter of persons is no law. If the Cabinet, therefore, departed from this decision, a complete breakdown of the whole machinery of law and government in Ireland would inevitably follow. Whatever the consequences, it cannot take that responsibility.[41]

The government determined that it had no choice but to attempt to break the hunger strike as a weapon and run the risk that MacSwiney's martyrdom might inspire, rather than deter, strikes in the future. In the end, MacSwiney's death in October proved to be a deterrent. Republicans no longer went on strike against the British regime in significant numbers.[42]

From the case of MacSwiney onward, the government chose strategically whether to release, to forcibly feed, or to let a prisoner starve to death—in other words, it attempted to strike a balance between legal principles, the duty to maintain civil order, and the imperative of maintaining its power. The government henceforth responded to all hunger strikes with political decisions, arguably undermining its own resistance to the strikers' claims upon political status. Official discussion of the new, political criteria was generally confined to internal correspondence, so republicans were not able to exploit this effective recognition of political status. They did, however, represent the differential treatment of strikers as an acknowledgment that they were, after all, political prisoners. As Ashe had informed the members of a visiting justices committee during his hunger strike in 1917, "I am a political prisoner and I claim to be treated as such. I do not ask to be released, but I ask to be treated differently to the pick-pocket and other criminals."[43]

Republican prisoners resumed hunger striking in large numbers against the Irish Free State during the Irish civil war (1922–23). Upon the conclusion of the Anglo-Irish War under treaty in December 1921, republicans had divided between a majority that supported the formation of the Irish Free State in 1922 and a minority that refused to accept anything less than a unified republic of Ireland. Members of the Irish Free State government under William T. Cosgrave, who had themselves fought for political status in prison, now denied this status to their former comrades, who found the new regime more consistent and uncompromising in response to hunger strikes than the British had ever been. In November 1922, Cosgrave faced calls for the release of two republican prisoners: Eamon de Valera and Mary MacSwiney, Terence MacSwiney's older sister, who was then on hunger strike. He stated in language reminiscent of Lloyd George, "They are responsible for the shedding of blood in Ireland, and for its continuance cannot themselves claim immunity. We on whom the Irish people have placed the responsibility of asserting their authority will not allow the discharge of that duty to the Nation to be hampered by consideration of any individuals, be they who they may."[44] Ultimately, the Cosgrave government was not prepared to be the first to let a woman die on hunger strike, so it released MacSwiney. It took a harder line against both men and women in 1923, when thousands of republican prisoners, including dozens of women, staged a mass strike in Irish prisons and internment camps, as discussed in chapter 3. Taking its stand upon the rule of law, the government followed through on its decision neither to forcibly feed nor release strikers. It successfully broke the strike and left two men dead.

Many republicans who had suffered through the failed strike in 1923 celebrated de Valera's return to public politics at the head of the Fianna Fáil party in 1927. Fianna Fáil won the election of 1932, de Valera became the *taosaich* (prime minister), and militant republicans were soon disappointed. De Valera wanted to lead a united Ireland to independence from Great Britain, but he chose to do so through legislation rather than by force of arms. In 1936 he outlawed the Irish Republican Army. In late 1939, in response to a resurgence of IRA activity, the government imprisoned a significant number of republicans, whose supporters then denounced members of the government as traitors. The government rejected this charge and invoked a higher duty to uphold the rule of law. Behind this noble rhetoric, however, de Valera attempted to strike a political balance in what he characterized as a time of peril. These were early days in Ireland's "Emergency" during the Second World War. The government had to face down the IRA at the same time that it consolidated its wartime neutrality under the suspicious gaze of the British. De Valera wished to avoid republican martyrdoms that might simultaneously provoke public sympathy and strengthen opposition to sweeping executive powers that he had recently acquired under the Emergency Powers Act, 1939. So, in response to hunger strikes for political status by four republican prisoners, Patrick McGrath,

Jeremiah Lynch, Richard McCarthy, and Charles McCarthy, the government chose to release the men—as it did every other republican who subsequently went on hunger strike in 1939. By the new year, however, the government perceived that it had reached the political limit of conciliation, and it passed the Emergency Powers (Amendment) Act, 1940, which gave it the power to intern Irish citizens. In the course of parliamentary debate over the bill, Gerald Boland, minister of justice, was asked if an internee who went on hunger strike would be released. Boland replied, "I can assure this House that we are not going to let people take the law into their own hands."[45] Seven more IRA men chose to test the government's resolve and began a hunger strike on 25 February. This time, like Cosgrave before him, de Valera left two men dead.[46]

THE BURDEN OF CARE IN INDIA

Before the First World War, neither courts nor provincial prison systems in British India recognized the category of "political prisoner," although officials referred to "political offenders," whose crimes they regarded as politically motivated. On Christmas day 1919 the king-emperor himself granted a royal clemency to "political offenders" in India.[47] Prison systems acknowledged the category of "state prisoner," which had been established throughout India by adoption of the Bengal State Prisoners Regulation III of 1818. The utility of this category for crimes against the state was limited by two factors, however. First, state prisoners were entitled to extraordinary privileges, such as the right to wear their own clothes, so they had legal grounds upon which to demand improvements in their conditions if these did not meet regulations. Second, state prisoners were interned, so they fell outside the purview of the civil courts.

During the First World War, the regulations regarding state prisoners were supplemented by two other measures for internment: The Ingress and Foreigners Ordinances (1914) and the Defence of India Rules (1915). The government of India employed these measures in its wartime battles against, first, the Ghadar Party, primarily in Punjab, and then against militant socialists in Bengal. In 1917, as discussed in chapter 4, the government converted the Hazaribagh Jail in the province of Bihar and Orissa into a "political prison," mainly for ghadris and Bengali terrorists. By 1918 the Bengal jail code, at odds with central government policy, explicitly identified "political prisoners" as those interned as state prisoners or *detenus* under the two wartime measures.[48]

State prisoners were few in number. Most prisoners were divided between the categories of "ordinary" and "special class," the latter being reserved for Europeans and the Indian social elite who were not guilty of violent offenses. Prisoners convicted of so-called political offenses that did not involve violence were generally sentenced to special class and held in the "civil ward." It was only after the war, in response to militant rebellions and the expansion of Gandhian nationalism below the Indian middle class, that British officials questioned their association of political offenses with a respectable class position.[49]

The Indian Jails Committee report of 1920 called for a uniform jail code for India and argued against any distinction between ordinary and political prisoners. British officials across India and in London evaluated this part of the report with an eye toward Gandhi's noncooperation movement, which had purposefully flooded the Indian prison system with satyagrahis. Although protests were generally nonviolent, the prison system simply could not give special class privileges to thousands of satyagrahis, and certainly not to the many who were not members of the respectable classes. The provincial governments initially took a variety of approaches to this problem, none of which proved satisfactory.[50] Eventually, in the summer of 1922, the government of India and all provincial governments reached a consensus: There would be no political prisoner status, but there would be a "special (or separate) division" for prisoners—in practice, satyagrahis—selected by local governments for "differential treatment." Prisoners guilty of violence or sedition would be excluded from this division, while the eligibility of others would be evaluated in terms of their "status, character, education, and the nature and motives of the offense."[51]

Indian militant nationalists conducted hunger strikes in the Cellular Jail at Port Blair on the Andaman Islands after 1912. There was a surge in hunger strikes by Sikhs of the Ghadar Party after 1916, then a notable spreading of hunger strikes through prisons across India in 1918, perhaps inspired by reports of releases of republicans on hunger strike in Ireland.[52] In confronting hunger strikes, prison officials in India faced far more complicated factors than did their counterparts in Britain and Ireland. The prison system had for decades observed religious and caste differences between prisoners, though policies on these matters varied from province to province. Tensions persisted, however. After the war, according to David Arnold, "attempts to define the essential requirements of caste and religion . . . increasingly became a source of friction between prison authorities and political or religious leaders."[53] Religion and caste became entwined with demands for political status and regularly prompted prison officials to make concessions to hunger strikers. There was the case of Nanibala Devi, a Bengali *detenu* who went on hunger strike after an abusive interrogation in Benaras Jail in 1918. In an attempt to break her isolation, she demanded food appropriate to her caste position as a Brahmin, and she demanded that her food should be prepared by another Brahmin. The superintendent gave in to her demands, and, as Devi had hoped, removed one of her comrades, Dukaribala Devi, from hard labor to serve as her cook.[54]

It appears that more often than in Britain and Ireland officials in India feared that an offense to a prominent hunger striker could provoke violent protest outside the prison walls.[55] In Ireland this fear generally focused on prisoners of national or regional political stature. In India, by contrast, officials especially feared that an offense to the religion of a striker could become in effect a violation of the sanctity of the individual's religious community. In July 1920, for example, Pir Mahbub Shah, a Muslim religious leader, was imprisoned in Hyderabad in the Bombay Presidency for making a seditious speech in which he told his followers to wage war on the British as part of the *khilafat* movement, a campaign by Indian Muslims to persuade the British government to maintain the authority of the Ottoman emperor as the Caliph of Islam after the war. Thousands of Shah's followers converged on Hyderabad in protest against his incarceration. He then went on hunger strike for release, having heard that Irish political prisoners had been released after just seven days' fast. Local officials panicked when an outside official suggested in an open telegram that they might feed Shah by enema—an open telegram being accessible to Indian staff and thus a potential source of dangerous rumor. The British commissioner informed the central government that forcibly feeding Shah would be "very unwise. . . . He is practically worshipped by his *murids* [followers], and any violence done to his person (as would be inevitable) would very probably lead to outbreak of violence or outrage." The government promptly released Shah on a pretense.[56]

Medical officers in India, like their counterparts in Britain and Ireland, found hunger strikes to be onerous forms of protest, especially when forcible feeding was involved.[57] Neither laws nor prison rules provided satisfactory guidance or options. Section 52 of the 1894 Prisons (India) Act enabled superintendents to prosecute prisoners for the offense of refusing to eat the food prescribed by the prison dietary scale.[58] While the threat of an extended sentence might have deterred hunger strikers of limited resolve, this did not concern determined strikers prepared to die for a cause. As provincial prison rules on hunger striking were generally inadequate and belated, prison officials were often left to determine where the hunger strike should fall in the scale of prison offenses. Their perception of the threat posed by the hunger strike was clearly conveyed in their occasional choice of punishment: whipping.

In 1919 the Indian Jails Committee opened a broad discussion about whipping as a punishment for prison offenses. Most provincial government officials, and all prison officials, wanted to retain whipping as a punishment for the most serious acts of mutiny, as stipulated under the Whipping Act, 1909.[59] These discussions formed the basis of the Indian Criminal Law Amendment Act of 1923, which reaffirmed the 1909 statute.[60] Remarkably, both before and after the amendment act, prison officials used whipping to punish hunger strikers, whose acts of self-starvation were thus equated with the most dangerous threats to prison discipline. At the same time, prison medical officers in India worried about their liability should a hunger striker die in their care.[61] The practice of whipping and the fears of medical officers came together in an influential case of hunger striking and punishment in the Madras Presidency.

MUTINY, WHIPPING, AND CIVILIZATION

In August 1921 the government of India transferred forty-seven prisoners to Madras from Hazaribagh Jail, probably to counter prison unrest. These prisoners included Sikhs who had been imprisoned for their roles in the *Ghadar* in 1915. Five of these Sikhs, imprisoned in the Central Jail at Coimbatore, began a hunger strike in October after the superintendent refused their request for a Punjabi diet.[62] The superintendent then placed the prisoners in handcuffs and solitary confinement. He attempted to bargain with them, and when this failed he gave the leader, Jawala Singh, a flogging of thirty stripes.[63] The prisoners remained defiant, so the medical officer commenced to forcibly feed them by rectum.[64] To the doctor's dismay, the prisoners informed him on the following day that they desired to be fed again by rectum, and they furthermore increased the specificity of their dietary demands and insisted that they should be allowed to send letters to their friends and to be relieved of half of their work duties in order to devote more time to prayer.[65] Given that these prisoners were serving terms of years, the medical officer requested that the superintendent seek formal instructions from the government of Madras. The medical officer asked: "As [the prisoners] are now weak (1) are they to be released or (2) are they to be forcibly fed as we are now doing; (3) or are they to be left like the late Mayor of Cork, Mr. McSweney [sic], whom last year the British Government allowed to hunger strike till he died. Personally I favour the McSweney [sic] procedure, but we will feed them forcibly till we hear from Government."[66] The government of Madras declined to rule on this matter, despite its authority to do so. Instead, it forwarded the inspector's report to the Home Department of the government of India, seeking instructions.[67] The Home Department then passed the decision to the secretary of state for India in London.

In mid-December a report on the hunger strike at Coimbatore reached the desk of the undersecretary, Lord Lytton, who had already given serious thought to hunger strikes and forcible feeding on a different front. He was the brother of Lady Constance Lytton, the well-known suffragette who had been forcibly fed while on hunger strike in a British prison.[68] Supportive of his sister's cause, Lord Lytton had joined the Men's League for Women's Suffrage, and he had drafted the Parliamentary Franchise (Women) Bill in 1910. Although his progressive politics did not extend to Indian rebels, he was appalled by the news that an Indian prisoner on hunger strike had been flogged.[69] "I am amazed that the Madras Government should apparently support the action that was taken," he declared. "If these things are done and receive official approval is it surprising that non-co-operators believe us to be capable of any brutality?"[70] Lytton's phrasing leaves one to question whether he mistakenly assumed that the Sikhs at Coimbatore were members of Gandhi's noncooperation movement, or whether he simply feared the moral authority that noncooperators might wield in view of further government brutalities. Either way, Lytton ordered the Public and Judicial Department of the India Office to formulate recommendations on the treatment of hunger strikers in Indian prisons.

The officials charged with this task addressed not whipping but the issue of central concern to the medical officer—that is, whether he would be prosecuted for murder if a hunger striker died on his watch. He had referred to MacSwiney's case because he feared prosecution in India's high courts under British common law. The medical officer may or may not have known whether his counterpart at Brixton Prison had been prosecuted for MacSwiney's death—which he was not. Yet the officer apparently understood that under common law MacSwiney's case offered him a legal precedent.

Events in Coimbatore outpaced government correspondence when, on 11 January 1922, the five prisoners called off their strike after three months on the advice of the Executive Council of the Sikh League.[71] Officials in London nevertheless continued to pursue their research on hunger strikes by contacting the Home Office. Sir Ernley Blackwell, the legal assistant undersecretary at the Home Office, explained that in dealing with hunger strikers British officials made "political decisions" between three options: forcible feeding, temporary release, or "[letting] the prisoner take his own course," while providing food within easy reach. In the case of MacSwiney, the cabinet had chosen, and prison authorities had then followed, the third course.[72] Officials in London next inquired about relevant legal opinions and case law, which, it became clear, focused upon the duty of prison officials to forcibly feed hunger strikers.[73] Just as some militant Indian strikers had followed the precedents of Irish republican and, perhaps, suffragette hunger strikers, the India Office looked to opinions by the Law Officers of the Crown regarding Irish strikes in 1920 and British suffragette strikes in 1913. In crafting both of these opinions, the crown lawyers had themselves looked to the case of *Leigh v. Gladstone* in 1909 and determined that if a government decided not to release a prisoner on hunger strike, the decision to forcibly feed should be left to the medical officer.[74] The crown lawyers determined that "it [was] legally incumbent on the Medical Officer to feed forcibly" unless it was his medical opinion that the process would put the prisoner's life in jeopardy. In the event that the medical officer, or superior prison officers, did not forcibly feed a hunger striker who was deemed fit, they would "be open to an indictment for manslaughter."[75]

Having consulted legal opinions established in response to the forcible feeding of British suffragettes and Irish republicans, the India Office issued recommendations on forcible feeding that the government of India distributed as a policy statement to local governments in October 1922. This statement cited *Leigh v.*

Gladstone and explained that this case had established that prison officials "[who resorted] to forcible feeding [would] be immune, both criminally and civilly, provided that neither negligence or unnecessary violence occurs and that the case is a suitable one having regard to the physical condition of the patient." The government then left officials to make "political decisions" about whether strikers should be released, forcibly fed, or left to starve. When, for instance, the secretary of state expressed concern in 1935 that officials might forcibly feed Gandhi during one of his public fasts, the viceroy assured him that no such action would be considered in view of "popular attention."[76] Remarkably, the 1922 policy statement did not address whipping, although it was this punishment that had prompted Lytton to order an inquiry into prison policy in the first place. It would come up again, however, several years later, in the second period of mass nationalist protest, when the prison system found itself overwhelmed by a combination of militants and satyagrahis.

After 1929 the British regime became increasingly concerned that the hunger strike might break down discipline across the prison system and demoralize the police and army. In this year the power of the hunger strike was demonstrated by members of the Hindustan Socialist Republican Association before and during their trial in the second Lahore conspiracy case.[77] This case was widely publicized because several of the defendants had been involved either in the assassination of a police official and a head constable or in the bombing of the Central Legislative Assembly in Delhi. Bhagat Singh, the charismatic leader of the group, had participated in both actions.

Singh and other defendants conducted a hunger strike for political status during their trial, asserting that all Indian political prisoners should receive the same privileges as any European prisoner. From Mianwali Jail, Singh wrote to the inspector general of prisons in Punjab, Lieutenant Colonel Frederick A. Barker:

> I have been sentenced to life transportation in connection with the Assembly Bomb case, Delhi; and am obviously a political prisoner. We got special diet in Delhi Jail, but since my arrival here I am being treated as an ordinary criminal. Therefore, I have gone on hunger strike. . . .
>
> I wish to bring to your kind attention that I must get special treatment as a political prisoner. My demands being: (1) Special diet (including milk and ghee, rice and curd, etc.). (2) No forcible labour. (3) Toilet (soap, oil, shaving, etc.). (4) Literature of all kinds (History, Economics, Political Science, Poetry, Drama or Fiction), newspapers.[78]

As these prisoners were on trial in a public court, their deteriorating condition received intense media coverage. On the strength of Singh's compelling rhetoric, these young, undoubtedly brave opponents of the British regime became symbolic figures, like their Irish idol, MacSwiney.[79] Their demands for privileged treatment, and their explicit equation of such treatment with political status, rendered their protest a crisis for the government, which once more consulted the Home Office regarding the precedents of suffragette and Irish republican hunger strikes.[80] On the basis of the 1922 policy statement, the government made a political decision to forcibly feed these strikers, because it wished to keep them fit for trial and to put off the grim consequences of either martyrdom or release. The viceroy observed to the secretary of state, "Failure to bring accused to justice will have a very bad effect on the Services." He further commented, "Method of hunger strike is already proving infectious. . . . Unless a remedy is found, tactics are likely to be adopted in every large conspiracy case. . . . Moreover, methods are such as are likely to commend themselves to gangs of criminals in ordinary cases."[81] One of the strikers, Jatin Das, died in September and was hailed as the "Indian Terence MacSwiney." The government subsequently agreed to the strikers' demands for prison reforms, so the remaining strikers ended their protest. Thirteen of the accused were eventually sentenced to prison. Singh, Shivram Rajguru, and Sukhdev were subsequently hanged in March 1931 for the murder of a police official. Prior to his execution, Singh quoted MacSwiney: "I am confident that my death will do more to smash the British Empire than my release."

This hunger strike exerted considerable influence upon both future nationalist protests and the management of Indian prisons.[82] The Punjab government appointed a committee of enquiry, with Barker as chair, to review this politically damaging prison protest and make policy recommendations. The committee rejected the classification of prisoners established in 1922 and proposed the creation of three classes, A, B, and C, on the model of the United Kingdom. No attempt was made to define what Barker dismissed as "the vague term 'political prisoner.'" Classification would henceforth depend, in Barker's words, "not on such a term but on the character, status and mode of life of the accused and on the nature of the crime itself without taking into consideration its motive."[83] This proposal was instituted in Punjab and adopted widely in other provinces after 1930. Barker presumed that the elimination of motive from the classification of prisoners would undermine prisoner protests for political status. However, as in Britain and Ireland, most prisoners in India did not hunger strike to establish "political status" only under law or in prison rule books. Instead, they represented privileged treatment as *de facto* political status. After 1930 they simply equated political status with an improvement in their prison classification or conditions, as the suffragettes and Irish republicans had done before them.

The potential for mass hunger strikes was realized in 1932 and 1933, when political prisoners, especially Bengali militants, staged hunger strikes in the Detention Camp at Deoli, Rajasthan, and in the Cellular Jail at Port Blair. These prisoners complained that they had been classified as C- or, in fewer cases, B-class prisoners and thus reduced to the status of ordinary criminals. They starved for weeks in order to achieve new classifications and improved conditions; in the Cellular Jail, three men died.[84] Both strikes received significant publicity, and in both cases, in the face of public criticism, prison officials gave in to the strikers' demands. Predictably, these strikes became a central subject of discussion during the All-India Conference of Inspectors-General of Prisons, convened in New Delhi in January 1934.

The inspectors general addressed the great difficulties posed by "Civil Disobedience prisoners," a category that appears to have encompassed satyagrahis and revolutionaries. They recommended that additional staff should be provided to deal with this group, that the leaders of these prisoners should be segregated, and that recalcitrant prisoners should be transferred. They further observed that whipping was a useful means of maintaining discipline among these prisoners. Whipping should be used rarely, they noted, but the process of authorizing the whipping of A and B prisoners should be streamlined so that whipping could be inflicted more quickly when necessary.[85]

The inspectors general regarded the hunger strike, of all forms of prison protest that they discussed, as the greatest threat to prison discipline. They unanimously recommended that medical officers should not be liable to prosecution for "commencing artificial feeding either too soon or too late." They agreed that strikers should be immediately segregated and inquiries conducted to evaluate the validity of the strikers' complaints.[86] If the complaints were found to be groundless, then after twenty-four hours the superintendent should warn the strikers that they would be whipped or tried under section 52 of the Prisons Act if they did not desist. The proceedings then indicate: "Evidence was produced at the Conference showing that one early flogging often proves most successful in aborting hunger strikes. . . . Any order forbidding flogging for hunger striking, which is mutinous conduct in a jail sense, is strongly deprecated by the Conference."[87]

In May the Home Department surveyed provincial governments to evaluate their policies on hunger strikes. It found that all of the governments, in practice, made political decisions between three options in punishing strikers: prosecution under section 52, isolation, and whipping. The governor of the United Provinces was "strongly of the opinion" that a mass hunger strike could be broken most effectively by whipping a few selected ringleaders.[88] The government of Bombay observed, "Whipping after due warning, if the prisoner was medically fit to receive it, has been found to have very satisfactory results and has aborted hunger strikes most successfully."[89] The strongest argument against whipping was made by the governor of Bengal, John Anderson. This is noteworthy because during the Anglo-Irish War Anderson, then the undersecretary in the Castle, had played an important role in combating Irish republican guerrilla warfare and responding to hunger strikes. Possibly, in the light of his previous experience, he appreciated that the abuse of strikers could incite the public and aggravate a government's problems. In the midst of rebellion in Bengal, Anderson explained that whipping was an "obviously unsuitable punishment" for mass hunger strikes due to public condemnation of this practice. He asserted that prosecution under section 52 was an effective alternative, but he acknowledged that whipping might be necessary in "exceptional circumstances."[90]

In the end the Home Department deferred to the majority of provincial governments and declared "that it would be inadvisable to issue any orders prohibiting the infliction of whipping as a jail punishment in these cases."[91] It further offered several recommendations for the treatment of prisoners on hunger strike. Its most important recommendation, augmenting previous official policy, was that prison officials should isolate individual hunger strikers in order to break both morale and the coordination of prison protests. It should then inform these prisoners that hunger striking was a major jail offense and that mass hunger striking amounted to mutiny. Punishments for hunger striking could include extended sentences and whipping, and there would be no redress of grievances as long as a strike continued. The Home Department additionally instructed, "As little publicity as possible should be given to the hunger-strike." Turning finally to the liability of medical officers, it stated, "No criminal prosecution or civil action would be sustainable . . . provided the medical officer is of the honest opinion, reached with due care and attention, that the treatment given is in the best interest of the prisoner's health."[92]

The Home Department worried that the whipping of civil-disobedience prisoners, and particularly hunger strikers, might undermine the government of India's moral authority as the arbiter of a civilized rule of law.[93] In 1932 members of the British Parliament began asking pointed questions about the whipping of civil-disobedience prisoners, a fact that Jawarhalal Nehru exploited in 1934 in condemning the government's treatment of "political prisoners." In an article entitled "Prison-land," Nehru observed, "It has been stated on behalf of Sir Samuel Hoare in the House of Commons that 'over 500 persons in India were whipped during 1932 for offenses in connection with the civil disobedience movement.' The existence or otherwise of whipping is often considered a test of the degree of civilization in a State."[94] In a subsequent article, "The Mind of a Judge," published in 1935, Nehru charged that whipping was "widely prevalent in India." In a strong rhetorical gesture, he observed, "The official defence for the punishment of whipping is that it is meant for horrible crimes, like rape with violence." However, political prisoners who were not guilty of violence were also being whipped. "It has now been laid down officially," Nehru charged, "that in serious cases of hunger-strike in gaol whipping may be resorted to. We thus have it that in the opinion of the British Government in India a hunger-strike or breaches of gaol discipline stand on the same level as rape with violence."[95]

Nehru drew a distinction between whippings assigned by the court to a convict as a punishment for his crime and whippings assigned by prison officials as a punishment for offenses against prison rules. In the years in which he wrote these articles, 1934 and 1935, the government reported that the total numbers of prisoners sentenced to whipping in British India were 6,709 and 5,726 respectively. The latter number did not include figures for Bengal, Madras, and Bihar and Orissa; the number would have probably been over 6,000 had it done so, judging conservatively from numbers for the previous two years. The reported numbers of whippings inflicted on prisoners for offenses against prison rules in 1934 and 1935 were 167 and 108 respectively. The inspectors general of prisons of the Bombay Presidency and Burma reported the most whippings for jail offenses. The former reported 51 in 1934 and 44 in 1935. The latter reported 30 in 1934 and 27 in 1935. The inspectors general of the Central Provinces and Assam reported the fewest whippings in this two-year period; the former reported 1 and the latter a total of 3.[96] Unfortunately, the annual provincial prison reports do not provide complete statistical breakdowns of the major offenses for which whippings were inflicted. It appears from the narrative summaries of disciplinary problems that hunger strikes were generally handled with isolation, forcible feeding, or prosecution under section 52, and that the great majority of whippings were inflicted for assaults against prison staff or refusal to work. The annual provincial prison reports do not refer specifically to a hunger striker being whipped after 1922, but these records, given their structure and content, do not enable us to rule out this possibility. Still, bearing in mind that provincial prison populations numbered from the thousands to the tens of thousands in the mid-1930s, one might conclude that whippings for hunger striking were, in fact, rare.

Nehru probably emphasized and condemned whipping because a public scandal was then surging around the whippings of thousands of his fellow nationalists under court orders. Nehru had not witnessed the whipping of a hunger striker, but he claimed to have heard about such acts. It was a potent symbol of the savagery that underlay the government's claim to political legitimacy and its refusal to acknowledge the political status of nationalist prisoners. Symbolism aside, the insistence of the inspectors general of prisons on retaining the option of whipping hunger strikers in 1934 is remarkable for the apparent infrequency of this practice, at least as recorded in their own provincial reports. Of course, the whipping of hunger strikers may have been more prevalent than the reports indicated. This explanation is supported by the observations of inspectors general that whipping was a proven deterrent to hunger strikers. This explanation is arguably weakened, however, by two facts. First, whipping was legal, and, second, there were prison rules for authorizing and documenting whippings that involved multiple officials inside and outside the prison service. Prison officials had no legal incentive to conceal whippings, but they had a professional incentive to avoid censure for concealing whippings. There is another, more mundane explanation for the desire of the inspectors general to retain whipping as a punishment for hunger strikers.

Perhaps these officials of a state in crisis wished to keep all of their options open, recognizing that the political concerns of their superiors sometimes tied their hands. As they managed a prison system in crisis, they anticipated that civilization might require more than a little savagery to sustain it.

Both moderate and radical Indian nationalists had asserted that, in and out of crises, racism defined the state's coercive power.[97] The British were especially sensitive to the charge of differential policies on corporal punishment in British and Indian prisons. In 1922 and 1923 several provincial legislative councils debated the law on whipping. According to an India Office report, legislators suggested that "there was something exceptional in prescribing in the case of India the punishment of whipping in jails."[98] There were indeed more whippings for jail offenses in India than in Britain, but then, one might argue, the Indian prison population was disproportionately larger, and only a miniscule percentage of this population was subjected to whipping.[99] What is more suggestive of the role of race is the differential application of whipping to hunger strikers. In late November 1933, John Fury, a prisoner in H. M. Prison Liverpool, with a full record of convictions for burglary and larceny since 1925, made his third assault on a prison officer in that year. The Visiting Committee recommended thirty-six lashes with the cat, the maximum sentence under prison rules. The secretary of state approved a reduced sentence of twenty-four lashes and simultaneously postponed the punishment because Fury had gone on hunger strike after the assault and was therefore deemed "physically unfit" for whipping. Only after Fury ended his strike in mid-December was his punishment finally inflicted on 3 January 1934.[100] The inspectors general in India surely did not know about Fury, but they took seriously Indians' critical assessment of whipping as a racist act. This issue became all the more problematic in 1937, when, under the terms of the Government of India Act, 1935, Indian provincial ministries took office and assumed a large measure of authority over prisons. Under Indian administration, the whipping of a hunger striker was inconceivable. The report of the Inspectors-General of Prisons All-India Conference in 1939 reaffirmed the recommendations on the treatment of hunger strikers in 1934, but made no reference to whipping.

In 1940 the office of the governor general undertook another review of the government's policy on hunger strikes due to escalating civil disobedience and the possible return to hunger striking by large numbers of prisoners. The government determined, "The 1934–35 instructions . . . may be accepted as a guide in dealing with 'political' hunger-strikers of ordinary standing."[101] Remarkably, this general determination made little of a major change in policy on forcible feeding and the responsibility of the medical officer. For reasons that are not clear, the government also declared that "no duty to feed forcibly comes into existence so long as the prisoner is conscious and able to feed himself." It added that prison medical officers who violated this principle would be held liable in the event of a striker's death.

These recommendations regarding hunger strikes were distributed to the provincial governments in July 1940, providing little benefit to increasingly desperate British officials over the next several years.

The governor general greatly expanded the use of whipping as a punishment for rioting, crimes of bodily violence, arson, or sabotage under the Penalties (Enhancement) Ordinance, 1942. Yet there was no reported return to whipping hunger strikers. The regime probably gave up whipping strikers because the symbolism of this act exceeded the broadest conceptions of civilized violence, if only in the eyes of liberal critics at home and an essential ally, the United States. The US had come to the aid of Britain under the principles of the Atlantic Charter and was decidedly unsupportive of Prime Minister Winston Churchill's desire to maintain its empire during and after the war.[102] The British were aware of sympathetic support in the United States for Gandhi's fasts and critical US media coverage of the whipping of Indians during the civil disobedience movement.[103] When informed of the proposed ordinance on whipping, the cabinet had expressed grave misgivings about the political ramifications, but it had nonetheless sanctioned the measure and instructed the secretary of state "to consider whether some statement could not be issued for the guidance of the Press in this country and the United States, indicating the limited extent to which the courts would, in fact, impose sentences of corporal punishment in these cases."[104] The cabinet was concerned that in view of an increase in whippings the US might think their British allies capable of any brutality.

THE POLITICAL CALCULUS OF LIFE AND DEATH

Government officials in Britain, Ireland, and India regarded the management of hunger strikes as a juggling act with three objects in mind. First, they attempted to maintain stability in the prison system and the confidence of the police and military. Second, they attempted to project legitimate authority on the basis of the government's duty to enforce the rule of law. Finally, they wished to avoid rebellion. The first factor was the most critical, for without the commitment of prison staff, the police, and the army, the government would be unable to achieve either of its other two goals. For all the fears of government officials, hunger strikes seldom threatened actually to destabilize a government's political authority, let alone inspire a civil society to rebellion. Only the strikes by Ashe in 1917, republican prisoners in Mountjoy in April 1920, and MacSwiney later in 1920 arguably had this effect, the first because it triggered the public mobilization of republican forces and the latter two because they exacerbated a rebellion already underway.[105]

It was not uncommon for determined hunger strikers to gain concessions of special privileges, de facto political status, and, in particular periods, even release. Most, if not all, successful hunger strikes had five characteristics: The strikers attacked the structure of the prison system in groups; officials believed that a critical number of the strikers were prepared to die; the strikers' actions exceeded the system's practical capacities to respond; the strikers enjoyed publicity, whether through the media or word of mouth; and public support for the strikers was greater than the support that the government believed it could afford to lose at that specific time.

Prison officials wished to establish uniform policies in response to hunger strikes, but this proved difficult in changing circumstances. In the case of Mac-Swiney, in the context of the Anglo-Irish War in 1920, the British opted for the versatility of a political decision that took into account particular exigencies and objectives. In India the government augmented this political policy after 1934 by systematically isolating hunger strikers whenever possible. This isolation served to undermine the strikers' esprit de corps, and it concealed from the public the strikers' physical deterioration. Isolation also concealed from public view the government's inconsistent responses to hunger strikes that apparently contradicted the uniform rule of law. Lloyd George could declare, "A law which is a respecter of persons is no law." Yet even when the government publicly refused to make any concessions to strikers, there were exceptions. Negotiations were always underway, whether at the level of official policy or at the level of the prison wards. Regardless of the ideological convictions of officials in the halls of power, hunger strikes exerted pressure upon the daily operations of prison systems. This pressure, if sustained, could compel prison officials to respond with compromise and differential treatment, which prisoners then equated with political status. Through the policy of isolation the government of India hoped to conceal the rule of exceptions that actually dictated its responses to the instrumental and occasionally symbolic power of hunger strikes. Yet strikers themselves recognized the rule of exceptions, so they persisted.

The cases of the Irish Free State after 1922 and the Indian provincial ministries in 1937–38 suggest that a state's response to the hunger strike may be determined not by ideological distinctions, but by the simple recognition among ruling parties that the preservation of the state is imperative for the realization of their political visions in a given civil society. In conceding to the hunger strike, the state concedes in the starkest terms the power of coercion upon which its rule of law depends. In 1931 a British intelligence officer in Bengal commented, "The Irish Free State Government is composed of persons who themselves were terrorists and presumably know the best methods of dealing with terrorism."[106] Alternatively, one might conclude that the Irish government, like the Indian provincial governments, like the British governments in London and Delhi, was a state like any other. In its particular circumstances, it calculated that it might survive the deaths of hunger strikers, but that it would never survive the consistent, ongoing surrender of its arms to starvation. In early May 1946, IRA prisoner Seán McCaughey neared death on a hunger and thirst strike for political status in Portlaoise Prison, County Laois, in the Irish Free State. As de Valera was well aware, another IRA striker, David Fleming, was in a weakened condition in Belfast Jail in Northern Ireland, where he was also starving for political status. It was difficult to miss the parallel between the Irish Free State and British government's rejections of the hunger strikers' demands for political status and their refusals to release the two men.

In the wake of McCaughey's death by starvation later in May, de Valera met informally with the United Kingdom representative in Dublin, Sir John Maffey. De Valera wanted to insure that Maffey appreciated the "tragic difficulty" in which de Valera was placed by hunger strikers. He reflected that if he were then a young man in Northern Ireland, he would probably give his life to fight the current order of things. Yet as an older man and the leader of the Irish Free State, he appreciated the historical complexities of Anglo-Irish relations and the present dangers before his nation. So he had faced McCaughey's death and confronted charges of collusion with the British. The impression that he had done Britain's dirty work was enforced when McCaughey's remains were transported to Northern Ireland for burial in a family grave in Milltown Cemetery, West Belfast, in a ceremony attended by thousands. One infers that de Valera wished to convey to Maffey that it was now the British government's turn to resist concessions to Fleming. He apparently could not resign himself to Britain's possible release of Fleming and the inevitable charge that his government was, in fact, more brutal in its betrayal of a united Ireland than the British were in their continuing occupation of six counties in Ulster. Ironically, de Valera and his erstwhile republican comrades had once leveled precisely this charge against Cosgrave's first Free State government for its treatment of hunger strikers during the civil war.

In a report to the secretary of state for dominion affairs, Maffey recounted his response to de Valera: "I said that clearly there was no alternative since no Government could be stampeded by law-breakers on hunger strike. I felt that the firm line taken in the case of McCaughey would deter others from following his example and that in this way hunger striking would cease to be a problem." De Valera appeared to be satisfied with this response. Toward the end of this meeting characterized by mutual understanding and notes of empathy, the men agreed that someday there might be a unified Ireland, and that unity could only develop over a long course of peaceful working relationships. Maffey observed of de Valera, "It certainly seems to do him good to give vent to his feelings. It is to be hoped that the 'martyrdom' tactics do not catch on. Mr. de Valera's Government have been sane and sound on this issue up to date. But the blood-sacrifice tradition in Ireland is strong. I can understand Mr. de Valera's anxieties."[107]

Less than two weeks later, the British government released Fleming.

Epilogue

John Stuart Mill had a perfunctory way with violence. A philosopher of liberalism and a longtime servant of the East India Company, Mill published *On Liberty* in 1859, a year after the dissolution of the company following an Indian rebellion and terrible British reprisals. In this treatise, Mill observed, "Despotism is a legitimate mode of government in dealing with barbarians, provided the end be their improvement, and the means justified by actually effecting that end."[1] Forty years later, many liberals no longer had the stomach for this hard paternalism. Rudyard Kipling still did. He echoed Mill in "The White Man's Burden," his elegy to the moral necessity of the empire's "savage wars of peace." Contrary to Kipling's cold-eyed perspective on dutiful violence, his contemporary, Gandhi, saw vulnerability at the brutal heart of the British Empire. The morality of British violence depended upon building, not destroying; upon elevating, not debasing.

The problem was the prospect of equality. Liberal principles pointed in this direction, but many in Britain, and in the British government, struggled to accept this principled end game of their own making. The hunger strike and fast demonstrated not only that equality did not exist, but that it was being purposefully, violently postponed. A subject of the crown, whether a British or Irish suffragette or an Irish or Indian nationalist, who chose death over life under British governance might be discounted as a rebel. However, that subject's death, in some small or large way, affected the balance of the government's moral authority as an ostensibly liberal power. In 1921 Gandhi commented on the treaty that ended the Anglo-Irish War: "It is not the fear of losing more lives that has compelled a reluctant offer from England, but it is the shame of any further imposition of agony upon a people that loves its liberty above everything else. It is the magnitude of the Irish sacrifice which has been the deciding factor. . . . And England has yielded when she is able no longer to bear the sight of blood pouring out of thousands of Irish arteries."[2] Off the battlefield, hunger strikes and fasts were also difficult to bear. British officials confronted women and men wielding their last weapon, the ability to starve against a government that was expected not only to protect but to nourish its civil society. Their wasting embodied the emptiness of the government's moral claim to power.

Their wasting also filled their campaigns with inspired meaning, shared resolve, or debilitating uncertainty and distrust. The women and men discussed in this book, from Kara to Cork, from London to Lahore, testified to the patent truth that hunger means something to everyone, and that it means different things to different people, especially when one chooses to hunger to the last. Hunger is a most visceral form of protest, communicative even when inarticulate. One biographer of the hunger striker Jatin Das observed, "Hunger strike has no tongue: it speaks for itself."[3] This calls to mind refugees who now sew their lips shut. In doing so, they display a silence imposed upon them, and they bear mute testimony to the transcendent language of their starvation. Russian, British, Irish, and Indian women and men had different goals, and their protests reflected different cultures; yet they all found in hunger an adaptable tool of protest and, in some cases, symbolic expression. For all the differences between the protests addressed in this book, it is noteworthy that more often than not their disparate tools and symbols were shaped by beliefs in spirituality, religion, and prescriptive gender roles bent against political subjugation. Those beliefs were affirmed through hunger strikes and fasts as sacrificial acts resonant with an old, fearless piety, that of earlier martyrs and *shahids* who went singing to the arena to die. Only the most foolish saints would choose, after all, to embody injustice in living death. At the same time, beliefs were put at great risk when the will to sacrifice failed, whether after hours or days, or after weeks or months. The risk ennobled the reward, inspiring women and men to starve.

The second half of the twentieth century witnessed the further international adaptation and proliferation of hunger in protest. Prisoners starved in support of militant campaigns, as in the case of hunger strikes by the Red Army Faction in Germany in the 1970s.[4] They also starved in support of nonviolent campaigns, as in the case of hunger strikes by Chicana/o students on US university campuses in the 1980s and 1990s.[5] In some instances, the inspiration and model for self-starvation were clear, as when Irish militant republican hunger strikers in the 1970s and 1980s invoked the republican tradition of "biting at the grave,"[6] or when the US civil rights activist Cesar Chavez, the so-called Latino Gandhi, combined satyagraha and his own Catholic faith in undertaking several "spiritual fasts" for a variety of causes between 1968 and 1988. Yet even when we have evidence of the origin of an act of hunger in protest, the lines between violence and nonviolence commonly blur or even disappear. In South Africa, militant and nonviolent prisoners began hunger striking in the 1960s, both having apparently adapted the tactic from Gandhi.[7] By the 1980s, many thousands of imprisoned antiapartheid activists, militant and nonviolent alike, continued hunger striking across the country, further inspired by the Irish republican hunger strike that left ten men dead in 1981.[8]

It is most often difficult, if not impossible, to discern how latter-day protests connect to the trajectories of hunger strikes and fasts traced in this book. One might speculate that Irish republicans and Gandhi have been the main global models of hunger in protest, but such speculation falters before the vast miscellany of hunger strikes and fasts since the mid-twentieth century. In 1951 twenty-nine prisoners in the county jail in Mobile, Alabama, went on hunger strike because their meals were served by "Negro orderlies."[9] In 1970, in a prison in Beirut, Lebanon, Christian Below, a Frenchman who had hijacked a plane, went on hunger strike to protest his continued detention.[10] In 1983 Bishop Abel Muzorewa, the first prime minister of Zimbabwe, went on hunger strike to protest his detention by his successor to power, Robert Mugabe.[11] In 1999 Ahmad Ajaj, a Palestinian serving a 240-year sentence in the US for his role in the 1983 bombing of the World Trade Center in New York, went on hunger strike to protest against his mistreatment by prison guards.[12] We do not know precisely where these and innumerable other prisoners found their inspirations to starve, but the answer is surely broader than the framework of this book. Reflecting on the many cases of hunger in protest in the early twenty-first century in Turkey and elsewhere in the world, Banu Bargu observes, "The very synchronicity of these multiple struggles and their wide-ranging geographical distribution suggest that we are faced with a global political phenomenon. This does not mean that these struggles are organically connected, nor that the individuals who resort to these tactics fight for the same cause. . . . Each struggle has its own specificity, complex set of determinations, particular trajectory, distinct discourses, and, of course, divergent effects and reverberations."[13] This is to agree with Ahmed Kathrada: Starvation is "a universal form of prison protest."

This book has spent substantial time drawing transimperial connections and observing where connections cannot be drawn between acts of protest. I have addressed connections in terms of who knew whom, who read what, who wrote what, and who said what. The point is that hunger in protest as a global political phenomenon developed within and from an imperial world. That is all well and good. What is all the more interesting is the challenge of understanding hunger strikes and fasts not as connected or synchronistic, but as a syncretic process, local and global. Whether or not we can historically trace direct connections, we know commonsensically that those who hunger in protest, as well as their followers, are aware of various others who have hungered in protest. The knowledge of other protests inflects, at the very least, what the starving subject thinks about what she or he is doing and what it means. Likewise for those who follow hunger by sight, in print, or by word of mouth. The refraction of hunger in protest, regardless of its provable, primary cause or source, creates something distinctive and yet resonant of what came before. One sees this in the difficulty of British officials and Indian nationalists alike in establishing who among fasting Indian prisoners were satya-grahis. The fasting prisoner's message, without a tongue, is mixed, versatile, and thus more powerful. Mary Bosworth observes the intractable resonance of previ-ous hunger strikes in contemporary hunger strikes in British Immigrant Removal Centers. These hunger strikes are carefully monitored and identified officially as "food refusal," "a phrase," she observes, "that neutralizes their historical and ideo-logical associations with political prisoners."[14] In a related vein an anonymous official at the prison at Guantanamo Bay explained in 2006 that they were force feeding prisoners because, "We don't want a Bobby Sands."[15]

It strikes me that the main subjects of this book lived in a slower-moving world. I appreciate that this impression is problematic, but bear with me. It was a world in which the historian can follow with relative ease a significant fraction of the hun-ger strikes and fasts across cultural and political boundaries. This is made possible by both the structure of the imperial archive, representing and preserving as it does a particular, global web of information, and by my historical subjects' use of paper, especially their writings and publications that have found their ways into archives and libraries. Of course, this transimperial world was exclusive, and the historian's perspective on it is necessarily limited. Still, within the imperial archive, the historian can move methodically and pause to reflect.

In contrast, following the global practice of hunger in protest today is like fol-lowing smoke. There are certainly more hunger strikes and fasts, but the new global web of digital communication renders hunger in protest bewildering in nuance and scope. Scholars using the tools of oral history and ethnography stand a chance, but even they require protests that are sustained over a critical period and memorialized formally or informally by an identifiable community.[16] Most protests do not fit this bill. Most are brief, even fleeting, as before. It is now harder to distinguish and compare the substance and scale of starving subjects, then to pursue them, as the information conveyed through social media swells dramati-cally then dissipates into a new welter of posts and images. The refraction of a hunger strike or fast no longer appears to develop over time, but to flash once or intermittently. I am not complaining. Rather, I want to acknowledge the limita-tions of my sources and methodology. They are dated. If other scholars wish to follow the proliferation of hunger in protest in more recent decades, they will have to choose different methodologies, or create new ones, and these must work at great historical speed.

Starvation, meanwhile, remains a slow, deathly tedium. Many have attempted to turn starvation into a spectacle, but the actual process of starving, stretching out over many weeks, is not spectacular. So the hunger artist in Kafka's story is forgotten in his cage and dies. It is fascinating that such an unspectacular act should spread internationally as a tactic of protest; that peace activists and terrorists should implode in slow motion even as the terrorists' brethren explode in car bombs and bomb vests. There are advantages to starvation. Terrorists in bomb vests may be killed in an instant by those with law on their side. Yet modern states—hulking institutions armed to the teeth, whether liberal or despotic—are unsettled by a person too weak to roll over, let alone stand. Since the late nineteenth century, hunger strikes and fasts have been more than weapons to be countered and dispatched with stomach tubes or whips. They have been measures of the captor's humanity, which no amount of forcible feeding could or can prove. Of course, the effect of starvation largely depends on the perceived justice of the prisoner's cause. While the prisoner's starvation may increase the captor's burden of work, it will not burden the conscience of the captor or the public if the prisoner was once a tyrant. Such cases are rare, however. Most prisoners aspire to power having not fallen from it. In starving to demonstrate that the captor has failed in duty and strength, the prisoner claims power and a higher justice. With the last weapon, the prisoner attempts to untether the captor from law, leaving the captor, lawless, to share in the performance of death.

NOTES

INTRODUCTION

1. See, for example, CNN coverage, " 'Iron Lady of Manipur': World's Longest Hunger Strike Ends," 9 August 2016, https://www.cnn.com/2016/08/09/asia/longest-hunger-strike-ends/index.html (accessed 15 February 2018) and BBC coverage, "Irom Sharmila: India activist to end 16-year hunger strike," 9 August 2016, http://www.bbc.com/news/av/world-asia-india-37017707/irom-sharmila-india-activist-to-end-16-year-hunger-strike (accessed 15 February 2018).

2. Stephen J. Scanlan, Laurie Cooper Stoll, and Kimberly Lumm, "Starving for Change: The Hunger Strike and Nonviolent Action, 1906–2004," *Research in Social Movements, Conflicts, and Change*, vol. 28, ed. Patrick G. Coy (Bingley: Emerald Publishing Group, 2008), 275–323.

3. Matthew Taylor and Saeed Kamali Dehghan, "Iranian Hunger Strikers Sew Their Lips Together in Protest at UK Deportation," *The Guardian,* 21 April 2011, https://www.theguardian.com/world/2011/apr/21/iranian-hunger-stikers-sew-lips-uk-deportation (accessed 15 February 2018).

4. Kunal Dutta, "Asylum Detainees Stage Hunger Strike over Poor Treatment," *The Independent,* 4 May 2014, http://www.independent.co.uk/news/uk/home-news/asylum-detainees-stage-hunger-strike-over-poor-treatment-9322812.html (accessed 16 February 2018).

5. UNHCR London, "Briefing Note: Committee in advance of the visit by the European Committee for the Prevention of Torture and Inhuman or Degrading Treatment or Punishment (CPT), Visit the United Kingdom, 2012," http://www.unhcr.org/en-au/5756ec877.pdf (accessed 20 February 2018).

6. Mary Bosworth, *Inside Immigration Detention* (Oxford: Oxford University Press, 2014), 43.

7. Deirdre Conlon, "Hunger for Freedom: Asylum Seekers' Hunger Strikes—Rethinking Resistance as Counter-Conduct," in *Carceral Spaces: Mobility and Agency in Imprisonment*

and Migrant Detention, ed. Dominique Moran, Nick Gill, and Deirdre Conlon (Farnham: Ashgate, 2013), 135.

8. W. T. Stead, synopsis of the article "The Revolution of the Twentieth Century," which originally appeared in *The Independent Review, The Review of Reviews,* 33:194 (February 1906), 163.

9. Padraic Kenney, *Dance in Chains: Political Imprisonment in the Modern World* (Oxford: Oxford University Press, 2017).

10. Barton L. Ingraham, *Political Crime in Europe: A Comparative Study of France, Germany, and England* (Berkeley: University of California Press, 1979).

11. Banu Bargu, "The Silent Exception: Hunger Striking and Lip-Sewing," *Law, Culture and the Humanities,* 2017, DOI: 10.1177/1743872117709684, 11.

12. Thank you to Shoshana Keller for informing me that this passage from Isaiah is used as the Haftorah portion of the morning Yom Kippur service.

13. For Christian practices of corporate fasting, see Caroline Bynum, *Holy Feast and Holy Fast* (Berkeley: University of California Press, 1987), 31–69; A. J. Maclean, "Fasting (Christian)," in *Encyclopedia of Religion and Ethics,* vol. 5, ed. James Hastings (Edinburgh: T&T Clark, 1912), 765–71.

14. J. A. MacCullough, "Fasting (Introductory and Non-Christian)," in *Encyclopedia of Religion and Ethics,* vol. 5, ed. James Hastings (Edinburgh: T&T Clark, 1912), 759–65, cited in Bynum, *Holy Feast,* 321, note 11.

15. See, for example, "Succi's Forty Days' Fast," *The Times,* 28 April 1890, 6.

16. Richard English, *Ernie O'Malley: IRA Intellectual* (Oxford: Oxford University Press, 1998), 25.

17. Joseph Alter, *Gandhi's Body: Sex, Diet, and the Politics of Nationalism* (Philadelphia: University of Pennsylvania Press, 2000), 38–39.

18. M. K. Gandhi, *Satyagraha in South Africa* (Ahmedabad: Navajivan Publishing House, 2003), 206–07.

19. See Neeti Nair, "Bhagat Singh as Satyagrahi: The Limits of Non-Violence in Late Colonial India," *Modern Asian Studies,* 43:3 (May 2009), 649–81.

20. For examples of studies of hunger in protest in exclusive national contexts, see Ralph Armbruster-Sandoval, *Starving for Justice: Hunger Strikes, Spectacular Speech, and the Struggle for Dignity* (Tucson: University of Arizona Press, 2017); Pramod Kumar, *Hunger-strike in Andamans: Repression and Resistance of Transported Prisoners in Cellular Jail, 12 May–26 June 1933* (Lucknow: Martyrs Memorial and Freedom Struggle Research Centre, 2004); Francis Costello, *Enduring the Most: The Life and Death of Terence MacSwiney* (Dingle: Brandon, 1995); Dennis Dalton, *Mahatma Gandhi: Nonviolent Power in Action* (New York: Columbia University Press, 1993); Lisa Tickner, *The Spectacle of Women: Imagery of the Suffrage Campaign, 1907–1914* (Chicago: University of Chicago Press, 1988).

21. For general, relevant studies of transnationalism and empire, see Michael Silvestri, *Ireland and India: Nationalism, Empire and Memory* (New York: Palgrave Macmillan, 2009); Kevin Grant, Philippa Levine, and Frank Trentmann, eds., *Beyond Sovereignty: Britain, Empire and Transnationalism, c. 1880–1950* (New York: Palgrave Macmillan, 2007); Peter Hart, "A New Revolutionary History," in Peter Hart, *The I.R.A. at War, 1916–1923* (Oxford: Oxford University Press, 2003), 3–29.

22. See, for example, "The Ancient Hunger Strike," *The Nation,*, 27 October 1920, 469; Padraig O'Malley, *Biting at the Grave* (Boston: Beacon Press, 1990), 25–26; David Beresford, *Ten Men Dead* (London: Harper Collins, 1987), 14–16. For an intellectual history of nineteenth-century scholarship that compared ancient Irish and Indian practices of fasting, see Joseph Lennon, *Irish Orientalism: A Literary and Intellectual History* (Syracuse: Syracuse University Press, 2004), 196–203.

23. For use of the preceding quotation, see O'Malley, *Biting at the Grave*, 1; Beresford, *Ten Men Dead*, 9.

24. Hanna Sheehy Skeffington, "Reminiscences of an Irish Suffragette" (1941), in *Votes for Women,* ed. Andrée Sheehy Skeffington and Rosemary Owens (Dublin: E. and T. O'Brien, Ltd., 1975), 23.

25. Gandhi, *Satyagraha in South Africa*, 207.

26. Howard Spodek, "On the Origins of Gandhi's Political Methodology: The Heritage of Kathiawad and Gujarat," *Journal of Asian Studies,* 30:2 (1971), 361–72.

27. Mohandas Gandhi, "London: Suffragettes," 30 July 1909, *Collected Works of Mahatma Gandhi*, vol. 9 (Delhi: Government of India, 1983), 325.

28. Mohandas Gandhi, "Was it Coercive?" *Harijan*, 9 September 1933, *Collected Works of Mahatma Gandhi*, vol. 55 (Delhi: Government of India, 1983), 412.

29. Declan Kiely, ed., *The King's Threshold: Manuscript Materials by W. B. Yeats* (Ithaca: Cornell University Press, 2005), liii.

30. Durba Ghosh, *Gentlemanly Terrorists: Political Violence and the Colonial State in India, 1919–1947* (Cambridge: Cambridge University Press, 2017).

31. Joseph Lennon, "'Dreams that hunger makes': Memories of Hunger in Yeats, Mangan, Speranza, and Irish Folklore," *Irish University Review,* 47:1 (2017), 62–81; Margaret Kelleher, *The Feminization of Famine: Expressions of the Inexpressible?* (Durham: Duke University Press, 1997); Bankimcandra Chatterji, *Anandamath, or The Sacred Brotherhood*, translated and edited by Julius J. Lipner (Oxford: Oxford University Press, 2005).

32. For an intriguing argument that famine memory resonated in the hunger strike of Terence MacSwiney, see Joseph Lennon, "The Starvation of a Man: Terence MacSwiney and Famine Memory," in *Memory Ireland*, vol. 3, *The Famine and the Troubles*, ed. Oona Frawley (Syracuse: Syracuse University Press, 2014), 62–64.

33. Cormac O'Grada, *Black '47 and Beyond* (Princeton: Princeton University Press, 1999), 212.

34. Amartya Sen, *Poverty and Famines* (New Delhi: Oxford University Press, 1981), 1.

35. Mike Davis, *Late Victorian Holocausts: El Niño Famines and the Making of the Third World* (London: Verso, 2001), 11.

36. Ibid.; Janam Mukherjee, *Hungry Bengal: War, Famine and the End of Empire* (Oxford: Oxford University Press, 2015).

37. Zahid R. Chaudhary, *Afterimage of Empire: Photography in Nineteenth-Century India* (Minneapolis: University of Minnesota Press, 2012), 171–72.

38. Damien Cave, "As a Tactic, Starving Is Found Wanting," *New York Times*, 30 July 2006; Philip J. Cunningham, *Tiananmen Moon: Inside the Chinese Student Uprising of 1989* (New York: Rowman and Littlefield, 2014); Scott Anderson, "The Hunger Warriors," *New York Times Magazine*, 21 October 2001, 43–47, 74, 124–25.

39. Scanlan, Stoll, and Lumm find significant evidence of success in their international survey of hunger strikes. See Scalan et al., *Starving for Change*, 299.

40. Moralistic perceptions of the hungry poor were influenced at this time by Thomas Malthus's *Essay on the Principle of Population* (1798). See James Vernon, *Hunger: A Modern History* (Cambridge: Harvard University Press, 2007), 40.

41. Cormac Ó Gráda, *Black '47*; Peter Gray, *Famine, Land and Politics: British Government and Irish Society, 1843–50* (Dublin: Irish Academic Press, 1999); David Hall-Matthews, "Inaccurate Conceptions: Disputed Measures of Nutritional Needs and Famine Deaths in Colonial India," *Modern Asian Studies*, 42:6 (2008), 1189–212.

42. Vernon, *Hunger*.

43. Robert William Fogel, *The Escape from Hunger and Premature Death, 1700–2100* (Cambridge: Cambridge University Press, 2004), 42.

44. Mary Carpenter, *Reformatory Schools for Children of the Dangerous and Perishing Classes, and for Juvenile Offenders* (Cambridge: Cambridge University Press, 2013).

45. Boyd Hilton, *The Age of Atonement: The Influence of Evangelicalism on Social and Economic Thought, 1785–1865* (Oxford: Clarendon Press, 1988).

46. Vernon, *Hunger*, 273.

47. Gerard Moran, "Near Famine: The Crisis in the West of Ireland, 1879–82," *Irish Studies Review*, 18 (Spring 1997), 14–21.

48. Peter Gray, "Famine and Land in Ireland and India, 1845–1880: James Caird and the Political Economy of Hunger," *Historical Journal* 49:1 (March 2006), 203.

49. D. A. Barker, "Famine Relief in India," *Economic Review*, July 1913, 245–62.

50. Gray, "Famine and Land," 206. Also see Cormac Ó Gráda, *Famine: A Short History* (Princeton: Princeton University Press, 2009), 204–8.

51. Niall Whelehan, *The Dynamiters: Irish Nationalists and Political Violence in the Wider World, 1867–1900* (Cambridge: Cambridge University Press, 2012), 211–16.

52. Maude Gonne, "The Famine Queen," in *Irish Writing: An Anthology of Irish Literature in English, 1789–1939*, ed. Stephen Regan (Oxford: Oxford University Press, 2004), 184.

53. Gonne published this essay on the same day, 7 April, that the queen hosted a "patriotic children's treat," in which tens of thousands of children enjoyed a picnic in Phoenix Park. She undoubtedly conceived this essay in view of her recent experience in relief work during a famine in North Mayo in 1898.

54. Sumit Sarkar, *Modern India: 1885–1947* (Madras: Macmillan India, Ltd., 1983), 169, 171.

55. Ibid., 176.

56. Vernon, *Hunger*, 42.

57. Mohandas Gandhi to Lord Irwin, 2 March 1930, *Collected Works of Mahatma Gandhi*, vol. 43 (Delhi: Government of India, 1983), 5–6.

58. This followed the Congress's momentous *purna swaraj* (independence) resolution on 19 December 1929 in its annual meeting at Lahore.

59. B. D. Chattopadhyaya, *The Concept of Bharatavarsha* (Ranikhet: Permanent Black, 2017).

60. Also noteworthy is a short poem about hunger under the title of the picture and, above the picture, the declaration *Bande Mataram* (Hail the Mother), to which we will return in chapter 4.

61. For clear illustrations of these points, see Joseph Lennon and Michael F. Johnson, "A Digital Exploration of Hunger Strikes in British Prisons, 1913–1940," in *The Digital Arts and Humanities*, ed. C. Travis and A. von Lünen (New York: Spring Publishing Co., 2016), 77–93.

62. Constance Lytton and Jane Wharton, *Prisons and Prisoners: Some Personal Experiences* (London: Heinemann, 1914).

CHAPTER 1. KNOWING STARVATION:
SCIENCE AND STRANGE STORIES

1. *-ji* is a nominal, honorific suffix.

2. Pyarelal, *The Epic Fast* (Ahmedabad: Navajivan Publishing House, 2007), 40.

3. Ian Miller observes that in the early twentieth century there was a prevailing belief among medical professionals that physiological studies had little clinical value. See Ian Miller, *A History of Force Feeding: Hunger Strikes, Prisons and Medical Ethics, 1909–1974* (London: Palgrave Macmillan, 2016), 103.

4. Bombay Legislative Council Debates, 26 September 1932, Oriental and India Office Collection, British Library (hereafter OIOC), L/PJ/7/423.

5. Nick Cullather, "The Foreign Policy of the Calorie," *American Historical Review* 112:2 (April 2007), 337–64.

6. James Vernon, *Hunger: A Modern History* (Cambridge: Harvard University Press, 2007), especially chapters 4–7.

7. Francis Benedict, *The Influence of Inanition on Metabolism* (Washington, DC: Carnegie Institution of Washington, 1907), 5.

8. It is noteworthy that the concept of "holy foolishness" is to be found in Catholicism, Protestantism, Eastern Orthodoxy, Hinduism, Sufism, and Islam, among other faiths.

9. Benedict, *The Influence of Inanition*, 5–6; Francis Benedict, *A Study of Prolonged Fasting* (Washington, DC: Carnegie Institution of Washington, 1915), 13–18.

10. Benedict, *A Study of Prolonged Fasting*, 71; Agustí Nieto-Galan, "Mr Giovanni Succi Meets Dr. Luigi Luciani in Florence: Hunger Artists and Experimental Physiology in the Late Nineteenth Century," *Social History of Medicine* 28:1 (2014), 64–81.

11. David Hall-Matthews, "Inaccurate Conceptions: Disputed Measures of Nutritional Needs and Famine Deaths in Colonial India," *Modern Asian Studies* 42:6 (2008), 1189–1212; Kenneth J. Carpenter, "Nutritional Studies in Victorian Prisons," *Journal of Nutrition,* 136 (2006), 1–8; Kenneth J. Carpenter, *Protein and Energy: A Study of Changing Ideas in Nutrition* (Cambridge: Cambridge University Press, 1994), 60–64; David Arnold, *Colonizing the Body* (Berkeley: University of California, 1993), 110–13.

12. On the intersection of nutritional science, social science, and public policy in Britain in this era, see Vernon, *Hunger*, 81–117.

13. Kenneth J. Carpenter, "A Short History of Nutritional Science: Part 1 (1785–1885)," *Journal of Nutrition*, 133 (2003), 641.

14. Carpenter, "Nutritional Science in Victorian Prisons," 2.

15. Ibid., 5; Kenneth J. Carpenter, "A Short History of Nutritional Science: Part 2 (1885–1912)," in *Journal of Nutrition*, 133 (2003), 975; Graham Lusk, *The Elements of the Science of Nutrition* (Philadelphia: W. B. Saunders Co., 1928), 82–83.

16. Carl von Noorden, *Metabolism and practical medicine* (Chicago: W. T. Keener and Co., 1907), 14; Carpenter, "Nutritional Science in Victorian Prisons," 3.

17. Robert Hutchison, *Food and the Principles of Dietetics,* 3rd ed. (New York: William Wood and Company, 1911), 2.

18. Ibid., 2–3.

19. Ibid., 3.

20. Benedict, *A Study of Prolonged Fasting,* 402–3, 407.

21. Von Noorden, *Metabolism,* 47–49.

22. Carpenter, "Nutritional Science in Victorian Prisons," 4.

23. Graham Lusk, *The Elements of the Science of Nutrition* (Philadelphia: W. B. Saunders Co., 1906), 61.

24. Van Noorden, *Metabolism,* 5, 11–14, 17–18; Benedict, *A Study of Prolonged Fasting,* 403.

25. Lusk, *Elements* (1906), 67–68.

26. Benedict, *A Study of Prolonged Fasting,* 117–18, 123; Miller, *A History of Force Feeding,* 104.

27. Benedict, *A Study of Prolonged Fasting,* 14–15.

28. Von Noorden, *Metabolism,* 9.

29. Benedict, *A Study of Prolonged Fasting,* 221.

30. Ibid., 51.

31. Hyder E. Rollins, "Notes on Some English Accounts of Miraculous Fasts," *Journal of American Folklore,* 34 (1921), 357–76.

32. For a summary of the case of Sarah Jacobs, see "The Welsh Fasting Girl," *British Medical Journal,* 2:469 (25 December 1869), 685–88.

33. "Succi's Forty Days' Fast," *The Times,* 28 April 1890, 6.

34. Walter Vandereycken and Ron Van Deth, *From Fasting Saints to Anorexic Girls: The History of Self-Starvation* (New York: New York University Press, 1994), 74–90.

35. Ina Zweiniger-Bargielowska, *Managing the Body: Beauty, Health, and Fitness in Britain, 1880–1939* (Oxford: Oxford University Press, 2010), 142.

36. Upton Sinclair, *The Fasting Cure* (London: William Heinemann, 1911), 43.

37. Ibid., 79.

38. Ibid., 46.

39. Ibid., 44–45.

40. Ibid., 44–49.

41. Ibid., 48.

42. As quoted in Zweiniger-Bargielowska, *Managing the Body,* 146.

43. "The Fasting Cure," *British Medical Journal,* 1:2632 (10 June 1911), 1379–80.

44. Benedict, *A Study of Prolonged Fasting,* 76.

45. Ibid., 2–3; Robson Roose, "Fasting and Its Physiology," *New Review* (May 1890), 411–12.

46. Benedict, *A Study of Prolonged Fasting,* 5.

47. Ibid., 9.

48. Roose, 417; Lusk (1906), 74.

49. David Arnold, "British India and the Beriberi Problem, 1798–1942," *Medical History,* 54:3 (July 2010), 295–314.

50. Hall-Matthews, "Inaccurate Conceptions."

51. Arnold, *Colonizing the Body*, 112.

52. Hutchison (1911), 293.

53. Bart Kennedy, *The Hunger Line* (London: T. Werner Laurie, 1908), 10, 28.

54. Vaughn Nash, *The Great Famine and Its Causes* (London: Longmans, Green, and Co., 1900), 86.

55. Reverend J. E. Scott, *In Famine Land: Observations and Experiences in India during the Great Drought of 1899–1900* (New York: Harper and Brothers Publishers, 1904), 105.

56. Ibid., 36.

57. Mark Sturgis, diary entry 24 August 1920, *The Last Days of Dublin Castle: The Mark Sturgis Diaries*, ed. Michael Hopkinson (Dublin: Irish Academic Press, 1999), 27.

58. Ibid., diary entry 2 September 1920, 33.

59. Notes by Dr. G. B. Griffiths on his consultation with Dr. Beddard, 4 October 1920, British National Archives, Kew (hereafter cited as BNA), HO144/10308.

60. Ian Miller, "Food, Medicine and Institutional Life in the British Isles, c. 1790–1900," in *The Routledge History of Food,* ed. Carol Helstosky (New York: Routledge, 2015), 202–7.

61. Hutchison (1911), 570–76.

62. George Laval Chesterton, *Revelations of Prison Life*, vol. 2 (New York: Garland Publishing, 1984), 100–104.

63. Major Arthur Griffiths, *Fifty Years of Public Service* (London: Cassell and Company, 1904), 223.

64. Memorandum on Hunger Strikes, 12 October 1909, BNA, HO144/1042/183256.

65. William Murphy, *Political Imprisonment and the Irish, 1912–1921* (Oxford: Oxford University Press, 2014), 83.

66. See chapter 5.

67. Records on the hunger strikes of Harriet Kerr in 1913–14, BNA, HO144/1275/239581.

68. Governor of Mountjoy Prison to the General Prisons Board, 6 November 1919, National Archives of Ireland, GPB, Hunger Strikers, 1919, 7916–90.

69. Hutchison (1911), 350–51.

70. Ibid., 358, 395.

71. Records on the hunger strikes of Harriet Kerr in 1913–14, BNA, HO144/1275/239581.

72. Ujjwal Kumar Singh, *Political Prisoners in India* (Delhi: Oxford University Press, 1998), 126.

73. Manmathnath Gupta, *They Lived Dangerously: Reminiscences of a Revolutionary* (Delhi: People's Publishing House, 1969), 200–201.

74. Robert Hutchison, *Food and the Principles of Dietetics*, revised by V. H. Mottram and George Graham (London: Edward Arnold and Co., 1948), xxvi.

75. H. Basil Rosair, "Nineteen Months' Hunger Strike," *The Lancet*, 227 (4 April 1936), 778–79.

76. Richard English and Cormac O'Malley, *Prisoners: The Civil War Letters of Ernie O'Malley* (Dublin: Poolbeg, 1991), 41.

77. Ibid., 42.

78. Ibid., 51–52.

79. Miller, *A History of Force Feeding*, 105.

80. See chapter 3.

81. Miller, *A History of Force Feeding*, 111.

82. See, for example, the letter from Violet Crichton to Hanna Sheehy-Skeffington, 5 July 1915, ms. 33,604 (9), Sheehy Skeffington Collection, National Library of Ireland.

83. Miller, *A History of Force Feeding*, 52–53, 106.

84. Uinseann MacEoin, ed., *Survivors* (Dublin: Argenta Publications, 1980), 194.

85. Joseph Campbell, *"As I Was among the Captives": Joseph Campbell's Prison Diary, 1922–1923* (Cork: Cork University Press, 2001), 106–8.

86. Margaret Buckley, *The Jangle of the Keys* (Dublin: James Duffy and Co., 1938), 106–7.

87. English and O'Malley, *Prisoners*, 49, 58.

88. Higson memorandum, 23 October 1920, BNA, HO144/10308.

89. Tim Pat Coogan, *The I.R.A.* (New York: Palgrave, 2000), 144.

90. English and O'Malley, *Prisoners*, 45.

91. Memorandum by G.B. Griffiths, senior medical officer, on Terence MacSwiney, 11 September 1920, BNA, HO144/10308; English and O'Malley, *Prisoners*, 46.

92. C.S. Andrews, *Dublin Made Me* (Dublin: The Lilliput Press, 2008), 150.

93. Miller, *A History of Force Feeding*, 109–11.

94. Sohan Singh Josh, *My Tryst with Secularism: An Autobiography* (New Delhi: Patriot Publishers, 1991), 48.

95. Frank Gallagher, *Days of Fear* (New York: Harper Brothers, 1929), 25.

96. R.C. Majumdar, *Penal Settlement in Andamans* (New Delhi: Government of India, 1975), 217.

97. MacEoin, *Survivors*, 347.

98. See, for example, the recollections of the Irish republicans Billy Mullins and Dinny Daly in Ernie O'Malley, *The Men Will Talk to Me: Kerry Interviews* (Cork: Mercier Press, 2012), 77, 330.

99. MacEoin, *Survivors*, 145.

100. Gupta, *They Lived Dangerously*, 191.

101. Ancel Keys, "Human Starvation and Its Consequences," *Journal of the American Dietetic Association*, 22 (July 1946), 582.

102. Dana Simmons, "Starvation Science: From Colonies to Metropole," in *Food and Globalization: Consumption, Markets and Politics in the Modern World*, ed. Alexander Nützenadel and Frank Trentmann (Oxford: Berg, 2008), 179–87.

103. Myron Winick, *Hunger Disease: Studies by the Jewish Physicians in the Warsaw Ghetto* (Chichester: John Wiley, 1979).

104. Todd Tucker, *The Great Starvation Experiment: Ancel Keys and the Men Who Starved for Science* (Minneapolis: University of Minnesota Press, 2008).

105. Keys, "Human Starvation and Its Consequences," 586.

106. Ancel Keys, *The Biology of Human Starvation*, 2 vols. (Minneapolis: University of Minnesota, 1950).

107. Vernon, *Hunger*, 159–235.

108. Coogan, *The I.R.A.*, 144.

109. "Fleming Is 'Distinctly Weaker,'" *New York Times*, 26 May 1946, 12.

110. "Irish Hunger Striker Ends Fast That Began March 20," *New York Times*, 9 June 1946, 27.

111. "Fleming Ends Hunger Strike," *Irish Independent*, 9 June 1946, 6.

112. Copy of a personal telegram from the viceroy to governors of provinces, no. 368-S.C., 30 September 1942, enclosed in secret correspondence from Sir G. Laithwaite to the secretaries to all provincial governors, 30 September 1942, in *The Transfer of Power, 1942–7*, vol. 3, ed. Nicholas Mansergh (London: Her Majesty's Stationery Office, 1971), 64–65.

113. Home Department telegram 44-G of 14 February 1943, ibid., 668, footnote 1.

114. Telegram from Sir R. Lumley (Bombay) to the Marquess of Linlithgow, 16 February 1943, ibid., 671.

115. The Marquess of Linlithgow to Mr. Amery, 16 February 1943, ibid., 675.

116. Mr. Amery to Viscount Simon, 20 February 1943, ibid., 707.

117. The Marquess of Linlithgow to Sir R. Lumley (Bombay), 11 March 1943, ibid., 787–88.

118. Major General R. H. Candy, surgeon general of Bombay presidency, note on Mr. Gandhi's fast, February 10 to March 3, 5 March 1943, ibid., 771.

119. Bulletin signed by Gandhi's six doctors, 22 February 1943, ibid., 719, footnote 1.

120. Telegram from Mr. Churchill to the marquess of Linlithgow, 25 February 1943, ibid., 730.

121. Telegram from the marquess of Linlithgow to Mr. Churchill, 26 February 1943, ibid., 737.

122. Major General R. H. Candy, surgeon general of Bombay presidency, note on Mr. Gandhi's fast, February 10 to March 3, 5 March 1943, ibid., 769.

123. Miller, *A History of Force Feeding*, 227.

CHAPTER 2. BRITISH SUFFRAGETTES AND THE RUSSIAN METHOD OF HUNGER STRIKE, 1890–1914

1. The preceding account is drawn from *The Anglo-Russian* 11, 12 (June 1907), 1116; Leo Deutsch, *Sixteen Years in Siberia* (New York: Dutton, 1903), 263–64; Jonathan W. Daly, *Autocracy under Siege: Security Police and Opposition in Russia, 1866–1905* (DeKalb: Northern Illinois University Press, 1998), 4, 22–23; Charles Ruud and Sergei Stepanov, *Fontanka 16: The Tsars' Secret Police* (Montreal and Kingston: McGill-Queen's University Press, 1999), 40–44; Hugh Seton-Watson, *The Decline of Imperial Russia, 1855–1914* (London: Methuen and Co., 1952), 68–69.

2. Regarding the specific privileges and conditions of the three prison divisions, see Stephen Hobhouse and A. Fenner Brockway, *English Prisons To-Day* (London: Longmans and Co., 1922), 214–29, and Leon Radzinowicz and Roger Hood, "The Status of Political Prisoner in England: The Struggle for Recognition," *Virginia Law Review*, 65:8 (December 1979), 1458–59.

3. Joseph Lennon, "Fasting for the Public: Irish and Indian Sources of Marion Wallace Dunlop's 1909 Hunger Strike," in *Enemies of Empire*, ed. Eóin Flannery and Angus Mitchell (Dublin: Four Courts Press, 2007), 19–39.

4. F. W. Pethick-Lawrence, "The Treatment of Suffragettes in Prison," WSPU leaflet no. 59, WSPU Collection, Museum of London.

5. Michael Hughes, *Diplomacy before the Russian Revolution: Britain, Russia, and the Old Diplomacy, 1894–1917* (New York: St. Martin's Press, 2000); Martin Malia, *Russia under Western Eyes* (Cambridge: Belknap Press of Harvard University Press, 1999), 179–82.

6. Malia, *Russia under Western Eyes*, 163, 167.

7. Ibid., 8–9, 175.

8. For references to women's hunger strikes, see Barbara Clements, *Bolshevik Women* (Cambridge: Cambridge University Press, 1997); Barbara Alpern Engel and Clifford N. Rosenthal, *Five Sisters: Women against the Tsar* (New York: Routledge, 1992).

9. Abby Schrader, *Languages of the Lash: Corporal Punishment and Identity in Imperial Russia* (DeKalb: Northern Illinois University Press, 2002); Volker Rabe, *Der Widerspruch von Rechtsstaatlichkeit und strafender Verwaltung in Russland, 1881–1917* (Karlsruhe: Verlag M. Wahl, 1985); Jonathan Daly, "Political Crime in Late Imperial Russia," *Journal of Modern History*, 74 (March 2002), 62–100.

10. Rebecca Beasley and Philip Ross, eds., *Russia in Britain, 1880–1940: From Melodrama to Modernism* (Oxford: Oxford University Press, 2013); John Slatter, ed., *From the other Shore: Russian Political Emigrants in Britain, 1880–1917* (London: Frank Cass, 1984); Barry Hollingsworth, "The Society of Friends of Russian Freedom: English Liberals and Russian Socialists, 1890–1917," *Oxford Slavonic Papers*, vol. 3 (Oxford: Clarendon Press, 1970), 45–64.

11. Lisa Tickner, *The Spectacle of Women: Imagery of the Suffrage Campaign, 1907–1914* (Chicago: University of Chicago Press, 1988); Barbara Green, *Spectacular Confessions: Autobiography, Performative Activism, and the Sites of Suffrage, 1905–1938* (New York: St. Martin's Press, 1997).

12. Regarding hunger strikes as rejections of maternalism, see Mary Jean Corbett, *Representing Femininity: Middle-Class Subjectivity in Victorian and Edwardian Women's Autobiographies* (New York: Oxford University Press, 1992), 163. For hunger strikes as embodiments of maternalism, see James Vernon, *Hunger: A Modern History* (Cambridge: Harvard University Press, 2007), 72–73.

13. Vernon, *Hunger*, 44, 61, 64.

14. Lennon, "Fasting for the Public."

15. Laura E. Nym Mayhall, *The Militant Suffrage Movement* (Oxford: Oxford University Press, 2003), 3; Vernon, *Hunger*, 64.

16. "Forcible Feeding. A Letter to a Liberal Member of Parliament," leaflet, WSPU Collection, Museum of London.

17. Sergius Stepniak, *Russia under the Tzars*, vol. 1 (London: Ward and Downey, 1885), 185; Rabe, *Der Widerspruch*, 280.

18. George Kennan, *Siberia and the Exile System*, vol. 2 (New York: The Century Co., 1891), 238. Kennan spelled the word *golodófka*, but I have modified this in accordance with current transliteration.

19. I thank Shoshana Keller for consulting the Russian explanatory dictionaries and providing me with the following information on golodovka.

20. Vladimir Ivanovich Dal', *Tolkovyi slovar' zhivogo velikorusskogo iazyka* (188–82; repr., Moscow: Gosizdat, 1955)

21. Stepniak, *Russia under the Tzars*, 185; Prince Kropotkin, *The Terror in Russia: An Appeal to the British Nation* (London: Methuen and Co., 1909), 18.

22. D. N. Ushakov, *Tolkovyi slovar' russkogo iazyka* (Moscow: Gosizdat, 1935–40).

23. Niall Whelehan, *The Dynamiters: Irish Nationalism and Political Violence in the Wider World, 1867–1900* (Cambridge: Cambridge University Press, 2012).

24. Ben Phillips, "Political Exile and the Image of Siberia in Anglo-Russian Contacts Prior to 1917" (PhD diss., University College London, 2016), chapters 4–6; Jane E. Good, "America and the Russian Revolutionary Movement, 1888–1905," *Russian Review*, 41, 3 (July 1982), 279–80.

25. Ibid., 274; Donald Senese, "Felix Volkhovsky in London, 1890–1914," in Slatter, ed., *From the Other Shore*, 73.

26. June Purvis, *Emmeline Pankhurst: A Biography* (London: Routledge, 2002), 28.

27. Daly, "Political Crime," 88.

28. Rabe, *Der Widerspruch*, 167–70.

29. Daly, "Political Crime," 91.

30. Ibid., 88, 92.

31. Rabe, *Der Widerspruch*, 198, 242–54.

32. Schrader, *Languages of the Lash*, 168–75.

33. Daly, "Political Crime," 89, 91.

34. Sarah Badcock, *A Prison without Walls? Eastern Siberian Exile in the Last Years of Tsarism* (Oxford: Oxford University Press, 2016), 3, 30, 47–53.

35. Deutsch, *Sixteen Years*, v.

36. Ibid., 263–64.

37. Kennan, *Siberia*, vol. 1, 52, 81; Rabe, *Der Widerspruch*, 177.

38. Katerina Breshkovskaia, *Hidden Springs of the Russian Revolution*, ed. Lincoln Hutschinson (Stanford: Stanford University Press, 1931), 191.

39. Kennan, *Siberia*, vol. 2, 260–70; Deutsch, *Sixteen Years*, 271–94.

40. Kennan, *Siberia*, vol. 2, 260; Deutsch, *Sixteen Years*, 271. For more on Kovalskaya, see Engel and Rosenthal, *Five Sisters*, 202–49.

41. Deutsch, *Sixteen Years*, 272.

42. Ibid., 273.

43. Ibid.

44. George Kennan, "Exiles at Irkutsk," *The Century* 37, 15 (1889), 502–11.

45. Deutsch, *Sixteen Years*, 273.

46. Ibid.

47. Ibid., 277–78.

48. Ibid., 278.

49. Ibid., 280–81.

50. Ibid., 91.

51. Ibid., 288.

52. Ibid., 290.

53. Ibid., 294.

54. Richard Stites, *The Women's Liberation Movement in Russia: Feminism, Nihilism, and Bolshevism, 1860–1930* (Princeton: Princeton University Press, 1978), 149.

55. Ibid., 19, 100, 113.

56. Ibid., 19, 233–39.

57. Ibid., 126–28, 153.

58. Amy Knight, "Female Terrorists in the Russian Socialist Revolutionary Party," *Russian Review*, 38, 2 (April 1979), 139–59.

59. Stites, *Women's Liberation*, 229, 272; Daly, "Political Crime," 99; Mayhall, *Militant Suffrage Movement*, 38.

60. E. Sylvia Pankhurst, *The Suffragette* (New York: Sturgis and Walton, Co., 1911), 91. The Russian suffragists who were more like British suffragettes made up a small, middle-class pressure group that advocated constitutional reforms through constitutional means and never set foot in prison. See Stites, *Women's Liberation*, 191–230.

61. For examples of other accounts of Russian hunger strikes, see Stepniak, *Russia under the Tzars*, 185, 248–49; Ernest Poole, "Katharine Bereshkovsky: A Russian Revolutionist," *The Outlook*, 79 (Jan.–Apr. 1905), 85; Kropotkin, *Terror in Russia*, 18; and various references in *Free Russia* (1890–1915) and *The Anglo-Russian* (1897–1914).

62. For "customary," see "Prison Strikers," *Manchester Guardian*, 29 March 1912. For "traditional," see *Free Russia*, 1 November 1904, 89.

63. Tatjana Voronina, "Fasting in the Life of Russians (19th–20th Centuries)," *Acta Ethnographica Hungarica*, 51, 3–4 (2006): 235–55.

64. *Ibid.*, 244

65. If there is a connection between fasting by peasants and hunger strikes by politicals, it might come to light in new scholarship that rejects the binary opposition of "popular" and "elite" faiths and challenges the concept of *dvoeverie*. See Christine Worobec, "Lived Orthodoxy in Imperial Russia," *Kritika*, 7, 2 (Spring 2006), 329–50.

66. Malia, *Russia under Western Eyes*, 171.

67. Deutsch, *Sixteen Years*, 189.

68. "Prison Strikers," *Manchester Guardian*, 29 March 1912; Vera Figner, *Memoirs of a Revolutionist* (DeKalb: Northern Illinois University Press, 1991), 223–25.

69. For similar goals, see the hunger strike of 1878, in Stepniak, *Russia under the Tzars*, 185.

70. Hanna Sheehy Skeffington, "Reminiscences of an Irish Suffragette" (1941), in *Votes for Women,* ed. Andrée Sheehy Skeffington and Rosemary Owens (Dublin: E. and T. O'Brien, Ltd., 1975), 23.

71. For example, *The Times* featured three critical articles about the Kara Tragedy in February and March of 1890. See "Flogging and Suicide of Female Political Prisoners in Siberia," *The Times*, 11 February 1890, 4; "The Siberian Suicides and Hunger Strikes," *The Times*, 28 February 1890, 13; "Russian Conservative View of the Siberian Atrocities," *The Times*, 14 March 1890, 13.

72. Nicholas Riasanovsky and Mark D. Steinberg, *A History of Russia*, 7th ed. (Oxford: Oxford University Press, 2005), 378–91.

73. A. J. Anthony Morris, *Radicalism against War, 1906–1914* (Totowa, NJ: Rowman and Littlefield, 1972), 52–70.

74. John A. Murray, "Sir Edward Grey and His Critics, 1911–1912," in *Power, Public Opinion, and Diplomacy,* ed. Lillian Parker Wallace and William Askew (Durham: Duke University Press, 1959), 142.

75. Hughes, *Diplomacy*; Fiona Tomaszewski, "The Tsarist Regime's Manipulation of Public Opinion in Great Britain and France, 1906–1914," *Russian History*, 24, 3 (Fall 1997), 279–92.

76. Hollingsworth, "Society of Friends," 47–51.

77. *Ibid.*, 50–51.

78. John Slatter, "Among British Liberals: Jaakoff Prelooker and *The Anglo-Russian*," in J. Slatter, ed., *From the Other Shore*, 53.

79. *The Anglo-Russian,* 12, 5 (November 1908), 1215.

80. Martin Pugh, *The March of the Women* (Oxford: Oxford University Press, 2000), 189.

81. *The Anglo-Russian*, 12, 5 (November 1908), 1215.

82. Slatter, "Among British Liberals," 57.

83. *The Anglo-Russian*, 11, 10 (April 1908): 1176–78.

84. Henry Nevinson, *The Dawn in Russia* (London: Harper and Bros., 1906).

85. For example, "Medieval Prisons," *Free Russia,* January 1909, 2–3. See the Labour Party resolution in the *Daily News,* 29 June 1909.

86. A. J. P. Taylor, *The Troublemakers* (London: Pimlico, 1993), 95–131.

87. J. A. Hobson, *Imperialism: A Study* (1902; repr., Ann Arbor: University of Michigan Press, 1965), 56, 61.

88. Emily Hobhouse, *Report of a Visit to the Camps of Women and Children in the Cape and Orange River Colonies* (London: Friars Printing Association, Ltd., 1901); E. D. Morel, *King Leopold's Rule in Africa* (London: Heinemann, 1904).

89. See Kevin Grant, *A Civilised Savagery: Britain and the New Slaveries in Africa, 1884–1926* (New York: Routledge, 2005).

90. Lynne Ann Hartnett, "Perpetual Exile: The Dynamics of Gender, Protest, and Violence in the Revolutionary Life of Vera Figner (1852–1917)" (PhD diss., Boston College, 2000), 755–56.

91. Ibid., 763.

92. Repr. in *Free Russia*, July 1909, 2.

93. For Figner's political views, see Lynne Ann Hartnett, *The Defiant Life of Vera Figner: Surviving the Russian Revolution* (Bloomington: Indiana University Press, 2014).

94. Ibid., 163.

95. *Free Russia,* July 1909, 7.

96. "The Women's Movement in Russia," *The Review of Reviews,* July 1909, 73.

97. Pankhurst, *The Suffragette*, 436.

98. Andrew Rosen, *Rise Up, Women!* (London: Routledge and Kegan Paul, 1974), 86–94.

99. Thank you to John Bartle for translating this information from Figner's memoir for me. See Vera Figner, *Polnoe sobranie sochinenii v semi tomakh*, vol. 3 (Moscow: Izd-vo Vses. ob-va politkatorzhan i ssyl'poselentsev, 1932), 352; Purvis, *Emmeline Pankhurst*, 28.

100. "Women's Freedom League," *Common Cause,* 1 July 1909, 8.

101. Rosen, *Rise Up*, 118.

102. Radzinowicz and Hood, "The Status of Political Prisoner in England," 1474.

103. Ibid.

104. Purvis, *Emmeline Pankhurst*, 88.

105. *Votes for Women*, 16 July 1909, 934.

106. Ibid.

107. Hobhouse and Brockway, *English Prisons To-Day*, 256, 260–62, 274.

108. For example, see *Votes for Women* issues: 16 July 1909, 934; 23 July 1909, 971, 977; and 30 July 1909, 1014.

109. For example, *Votes for Women*, 30 July 1909, 1014.

110. "Suffragette Joan of Arc," *Leeds Mercury*, 19 April 1909, 3.

111. The same image appeared in the *Illustrated London News* on 24 April 1909.

112. Tickner, *Spectacle of Women*, 83; *Votes for Women*, 23 August 1912, 765.

113. *Votes for Women*, 23 July 1909, 977; Pugh, *March of the Women*, 193.

114. Tickner, *Spectacle of Women*; *Votes for Women*, 6 August 1909, 1043.

115. *Votes for Women*, 30 July 1909, 1014.

116. C. J. Bearman, "An Army without Discipline? Suffragette Militancy and the Budget Crisis of 1909," *The Historical Journal*, 50, 4 (2007), 880.

117. Hollingsworth, "Society of Friends," 62.

118. Pankhurst, *The Suffragette*, 436.

119. "The Repression in Russia," *The Times*, 2 August 1909, 8.

120. "The Tsar's Visit," *The Times*, 2 August 1909, 7.

121. "The Tsar at Cowes," *The Times*, 6 August 1909, 8.

122. J. F. Geddes, "Culpable Complicity: The Medical Profession and the Forcible Feeding of Suffragettes, 1909–1914," *Women's History Review*, 17, 1 (March 2008), 79–94.

123. E. Sylvia Pankhurst, *The Suffragette Movement* (London: Longmans, Green and Co., 1931), 319.

124. "Mr. Asquith at Birmingham," *The Times*, 18 September 1909, 9.

125. *Parliamentary Debates*, Commons, Fifth Series, 1909, vol. 8, 923–35.

126. H. N. Brailsford and Henry W. Nevinson, "To the Editor of *The Times*," *The Times*, 5 October 1909, 8.

127. Bearman, "An Army," 886.

128. Ibid., 881.

129. See the cover of *Votes for Women*, 28 Jan. 1910, reproduced in Vernon, *Hunger*, 66.

130. Bearman, "An Army," 886.

131. Ibid., 887.

132. F. W. Pethick-Lawrence, *Fate Has Been Kind* (London: Hutchinson and Co., 1943), 93.

133. Emmeline Pankhurst, "Speech Delivered at the Dinner at the Connaught Rooms in Honour of the Released Prisoners" (1911), in Cheryl R. Jorgenson-Earp, ed., *Speeches and Trials of the Militant Suffragettes* (Madison: Fairleigh Dickinson University Press, 1999), 144; Rosen, *Rise Up*, 156–59.

134. *Votes for Women*, 12 April 1912, 444.

135. Richard Garnett, *Constance Garnett: A Heroic Life* (London: Sinclair-Stevenson, 1991).

136. Figner, *Memoirs*, 190–94, 218–27; David Garnett, *The Golden Echo* (New York: Harcourt, Brace and Co., 1954), 119–20; Garnett, *Constance Garnett*, 298.

137. Hartnett, *The Defiant Life of Vera Figner*, 198.

138. *Votes for Women*, 12 April 1912, 444. For a summary of this strike, see Hartnett, *The Defiant Life of Vera Figner*, 164–66.

139. "Suffragist Prisoners," *The Times*, 17 April 1912, 3.

140. Rosen, *Rise Up*, 165.

141. Ibid., 171.

142. Memorandum by Herbert Smalley, 31 Dec. 1912, British National Archives, PCOM 7/355.

143. Ibid.

144. Pugh, *March of the Women*, 212.

145. Purvis, *Emmeline Pankhurst*, 296.

146. Ibid., 299.

147. Hartnett, *The Defiant Life of Vera Figner*, chapters 10–11.

148. Figner, *Memoirs*, 193–94.

149. Ibid., 220–21.

150. Ibid., 224.

151. Ibid., 223–25.

152. Vera Figner, *Les Prisons Russes* (Pully-Lausanne: Imprimerie des Unions Ouvrières, 1911), 28, 30, 31–32, 34.

153. Pankhurst, *The Suffragette*, 436.

154. "Speech by Lady Constance Lytton at the Queen's Hall, 31 January 1910," in Jorgenson-Earp, *Speeches and Trials*, 108–9; Sandra Stanley Holton, "Manliness and Militancy: The Political Protest of Male Suffragists and the Gendering of the 'Suffragette' Identity," in *Men's Share? Masculinities, Male Support and Women's Suffrage in Britain, 1890–1920*, ed. Angela V. John and Claire Eustance (London: Routledge, 1997), 122, 124.

155. Holton, "Manliness and Militancy," 110–11.

156. Ibid., 122; Pugh, *March of the Women*, 262–64.

157. *Votes for Women*, 30 July 1909, 1014.

158. For example, "Suffragist Violence: Mrs. Fawcett's Appeal to Cabinet Ministers," *The Times*, 5 December 1911, 7; Mayhall, *Militant Suffrage Movement*, 105.

159. Pugh, *March of the Women*, 206–10. Regarding "terrorists," see Mayhall, *Militant Suffrage Movement*, 107.

160. Rosen, *Rise Up*, 235.

161. Christopher Fletcher, Laura E. Nym Mayhall, and Philippa Levine, eds., *Women's Suffrage in the British Empire* (London: Routledge, 2000).

162. Mohandas Gandhi, "London: Suffragettes," 30 July 1909, *Collected Works of Mahatma Gandhi*, vol. 9 (Delhi: Government of India, 1983), 325.

163. James D. Hunt, *An American Looks at Gandhi* (New Delhi: Promilla and Co., 2005), 103–04.

164. Mohandas Gandhi, *The Mind of Mahatma Gandhi*, ed. R. K. Prabbu and U. R. Rao (Ahmedabad: Navajivan Publishing House, 2002), 36; Joseph Alter, *Gandhi's Body: Sex, Diet, and the Politics of Nationalism* (Philadelphia: University of Pennsylvania Press, 2000), 28–52.

165. Mohandas Gandhi to George Joseph, 12 April 1924, in *The Collected Works of Mahatma Gandhi*, vol. 23 (Delhi: Government of India, 1983), 420.

CHAPTER 3. A SHARED SACRIFICE: HUNGER STRIKES
BY IRISH WOMEN AND MEN, 1912–1946

1. George Kennan, *Siberia and the Exile System*, vol. 2 (New York: The Century Co., 1891), 271–72.

2. For example, "Story of Siberian Exile," *Ballinrobe Chronicle*, 7 March 1890, 2.

3. For example, "Revolutionary Signs in Russia," *Freeman's Journal*, 19 December 1910, 6; "Brutality in Russian Prisons," *Leitrim Observer*, 23 February 1912, 2.

4. Leah Levenson, *With Wooden Sword: A Portrait of Francis Sheehy-Skeffington, Militant Pacifist* (Boston: Northeastern University Press, 1983).

5. W. B. Yeats, "The Stare's Nest by My Window," in W. B. Yeats, *The Poems: A New Edition*, ed. Richard J. Finnernan (New York: Macmillan, 1983), 205, 596.

6. M. J. Kelly, *The Fenian Ideal and Irish Nationalism* (Woodbridge: The Boydell Press, 2006), 179–236; Charles Townshend, *Easter 1916: The Irish Rebellion* (Chicago: Ivan R. Dee, 2006), 28–59.

7. Margaret Ward, "Gender: Gendering the Irish Revolution," in *The Irish Revolution, 1913–1923*, ed. Joost Augusteijn (London: Palgrave, 2002), 172.

8. See, for example, Louise Ryan, "'Furies' and 'Die-hards': Women and Irish Republicanism in the Early Twentieth Century," *Gender and History*, 11:2 (July 1999), 256–75.

9. Sarah Benton, "Women Disarmed: The Militarization of Politics in Ireland, 1913–23," *Feminist Review*, 50 (1995), 148–72; Peter Hart, *The I.R.A. at War, 1916–1923* (Oxford: Oxford University Press, 2003), 122.

10. Maryann Valiulis, "Power, Gender, and Identity in the Irish Free State," *Journal of Women's History*, 6:4/7:1 (Winter/Spring 1995), 117–36.

11. Louise Ryan, "'In the Line of Fire': Representations of Women and War (1919–1923) through the Writings of Republican Men," in Louise Ryan and Margaret Ward, *Irish Women and Nationalism: Soldiers, Women and Wicked Hags* (Dublin: Irish Academic Press, 2004), 45–61.

12. P. S. O'Hegarty, *The Victory of Sinn Fein* (Dublin: The Talbot Press, 1924), 102–5.

13. George Sweeney, "Irish Hunger Strikes and the Cult of Self-Sacrifice," *Journal of Contemporary History*, 28:3 (July 1993), 421–37; George Sweeney, "Self-Immolative Martyrdom: Explaining the Irish Hungerstrike Tradition," *Studies: An Irish Quarterly Review*, 93:371 (Autumn 2004), 337–48, and other essays. Also see William Irwin Thompson, *The Imagination of an Insurrection: Dublin, Easter 1916* (New York: Oxford University Press, 1967).

14. Sweeney, "Irish Hunger Strikes," 425.

15. William Butler Yeats published the poem "Sixteen Dead Men" in 1921. Charlotte Fallon asserts that republican men ignored the origins of the hunger strike in the suffragette movement and disparaged women's strikes in chauvinistic terms. See Charlotte Fallon, "Civil War Hunger Strikes: Women and Men," *Éire-Ireland*, 22:3 (1987), 75–91.

16. Hanna Sheehy Skeffington, "In Mountjoy. My Prison Experiences," *Irish Independent*, 20 August 1912, 4. This article was reprinted in *Votes for Women*, 23 August 1912, 765.

17. See Richard English, *Radicals and the Republic: Socialist Republicanism in the Irish Free State, 1925–1937* (Oxford: Oxford University Press, 1994), 46–47, 62–63.

18. Richard English, *Ernie O'Malley: I.R.A. Intellectual* (Oxford: Oxford University Press, 1998), 91. Also see Fearghal McGarry, *Eoin O'Duffy: A Self-Made Hero* (Oxford: Oxford University Press, 2005), 56.

19. There was a very small number of Protestant hunger strikers in the suffragette and republican movements: for example, Margaret Cousins, Darrell Figgis, and Dorothy Macardle.

20. *Irish Citizen*, 30 May 1914, cited in Diane Urquhart, "An articulate and definite cry for political freedom: The Ulster suffrage movement," *Women's History Review*, 11:2 (2002), 289, endnote 13.

21. Cliona Murphy, *The Women's Suffrage Movement and Irish Society in the Early Twentieth Century* (Philadelphia: Temple University Press, 1989), 88.

22. The WSPU had supported the inclusion of suffrage for Irish women in the home rule bills, believing that granting suffrage to any community of women in the United Kingdom would make it practically impossible for the government to withhold the vote from women in Britain. See Margaret Ward, "Conflicting Interests: The British and Irish Suffrage Movements," *Feminist Review*, 50 (1995), 135–36.

23. For the reasons why various Irish political parties did not support women's suffrage, see Urquhart, 278–79.

24. The women were Marjory Haslar, Kathleen Houston, Maud Lloyd, Jane Murphy, Margaret Murphy, Marguerite Palmer, Hanna Sheehy Skeffington, and Hilda Webb. See *Votes for Women*, 21 June 1912, 622.

25. The Viceroy Lord Aberdeen himself granted additional privileges, seeking to avoid confrontation. See William Murphy, *Political Imprisonment and the Irish, 1912–1921* (Oxford: Oxford University Press, 2014), 14–15.

26. Levenson, *With Wooden Sword*, 128.

27. Margaret Ward, *Hanna Sheehy Skeffington: A Life* (Cork: Attic Press, 1997), 92–93.

28. Hanna Sheehy Skeffington, Prison Notebook, National Library of Ireland (hereafter NLI), ms. 33,618(6). These Irish women were already scheduled for release on 19 August, while their comrades had four months remaining on their sentences. See Ward, "Conflicting Interests," 134.

29. *Irish Citizen*, 25 May 1912, 8. Margaret Cousins, a founding member of the IWFL, had also gained experience in militant protest with the WSPU, and she had been imprisoned for one month in London in late 1910. See *Irish Citizen*, 25 May 1912, 8; James H. Cousins and Margaret E. Cousins, *We Two Together* (Madras: Ganesh and Co., 1950), 169, 179–81. For other Irish women who participated in WSPU protests, and who served time in British prisons, see Ward, "Conflicting Interests," 130–31; Cliona Murphy, 91–92.

30. *Irish Citizen*, 25 May 1912, 8; Cliona Murphy, *Women's Suffrage Movement*, 91.

31. Aberdeen accepted the recommendation of Sir John Irwin, chairman of the Visiting Justices Committee. See transcript of the Coroner's Inquest into the Death of Thomas Ashe, National Archives of Ireland (hereafter NAI), DE2/507, 6.

32. *Votes for Women*, 23 August 1912, 765.

33. Rosemary Cullen Owens, *Smashing Times: A History of the Irish Women's Suffrage Movement, 1889–1922* (Dublin: Attic Press, 1984), 63–64; William Murphy, *Political Imprisonment*, 21; Ian Miller, *A History of Force Feeding: Hunger Strikes, Prisons and Medical Ethics, 1909–1974* (London: Palgrave Macmillan, 2016), 70–74.

34. Hanna Sheehy Skeffington, "Reminiscences of an Irish Suffragette" (1941), in *Votes for Women,* ed. Andrée Sheehy Skeffington and Rosemary Owens (Dublin: E. and T. O'Brien, Ltd., 1975), 22, 24.

35. In January 1913 Margaret Cousins, Barbara Hoskins, Margaret Connery, and Mabel Purser were arrested for breaking windows in Dublin Castle and sentenced to hard labor in

Mountjoy in the second division. The women were transferred to Tullamore Prison, where on 2 February they began a successful hunger strike for transfer to the first division. See William Murphy, *Political Imprisonment*, 23–25. In June 1913 Marguerite Palmer, Dora Ryan, and Annie Walsh of the IWFL went on hunger strike in Tullamore for five days and gained release under the Cat and Mouse Act. See *Irish Citizen*, 21 June 1913, 34; Marguerite Palmer, "The Tale of the Tullamore 'Mice, '" *Irish Citizen*, 26 July 1913, 76–77. In November 1913 Hanna Sheehy Skeffington of the IWFL went on strike and was released unconditionally after five days. See Ward, *Sheehy Skeffington*, 117–21. In April 1914 Dorothy Evans and Madge Muir of the WSPU went on hunger strike while on remand in Belfast and were released unconditionally. Also in April, Mabel Small of the WSPU went on hunger strike and was released after four days under the Cat and Mouse Act. For these three strikes, see *Irish Citizen*, 25 April 1914, 388; Ward, "Conflicting Interests," 141. In May 1914 Kathleen Houston of the IWFL went on hunger strike and was released unconditionally after five days. See *Irish Citizen*, 9 May 1914, 404. In June 1914 Muir and Miss Larmour conducted a hunger and thirst strike of six days at Crumlin Gaol before being released unconditionally. See *Irish Citizen*, 13 June 1914, front page. In August 1914, Evans, Lilian Metge, Miss Wickham, and Miss Carson were released unconditionally from Belfast Jail after a hunger and thirst strike. See *Irish Citizen*, 22 August 1914, front page.

36. Ward, "Conflicting Interests," 140–41.

37. Ward, *Hanna Sheehy Skeffington*, 127.

38. The photograph was published in the *Irish Citizen* on 9 May 1914.

39. Ward, *Hanna Sheehy Skeffington*, 127.

40. I have borrowed the term *conflicting interests* from Margaret Ward's fine essay.

41. James Connolly, *The Re-Conquest of Ireland* (Dublin: New Books Publications, 1972), 41.

42. *Irish Citizen*, 3 October 1914, quoted in Levenson, *With Wooden Sword*, 167–68.

43. *Irish Citizen*, 5 July 1913, 53.

44. James Connolly, *Between Comrades: Letters and Correspondence, 1889–1916*, ed. Donal Nevin (Dublin: Gill and Macmillan, 2007), 672; Recollections of Nora Connolly O'Brien, in *Survivors*, ed. Uinseann MacEoin (Dublin: Argenta, 1980), 193–94.

45. W.K. Anderson, *James Connolly and the Irish Left* (Dublin: Irish Academic Press, 1994), 21.

46. Padraig Yates, *Lockout: Dublin, 1913* (New York: Palgrave, 2000), 373–74.

47. Dermot Keogh, *The Rise of the Irish Working Class* (Belfast: Appletree Press, 1982), 220–25.

48. Ibid., 226.

49. William Murphy makes the larger, important point that republican prison protests after the Rising became effective only after republicans adopted the suffragettes' tactics, although some were reluctant to acknowledge this. Murphy, *Political Imprisonment*, 83–84.

50. Letter from Ellen "Nell" Humphreys, undated, recalling experiences of her son, Richard, in 1916. University College Dublin Archive (hereafter UCD), P106/563.

51. Townshend, *Easter 1916*, 319–20; Sean O'Mahony, *Frongoch: University of Revolution* (Dublin: FDR Teoranta, 1987), 59, 104, 126–27. W.J. Brennan-Whitmore, *With the Irish in Frongoch* (Dublin: The Talbot Press, 1917), 132–33.

52. The Earl of Longford and Thomas P. O'Neill, *Eamon de Valera* (Boston: Houghton Mifflin Co., 1971), 53–54; Seán McConville, *Irish Political Prisoners, 1848–1922: Theatres of War* (London: Routledge, 2003), 518–20.

53. Longford and O'Neill, *Eamon de Valera*, 55.

54. McConville, *Irish Political Prisoners*, 532, footnote 72.

55. J. Anthony Gaughan, *Austin Stack: Portrait of a Separatist* (Dublin: Kingdom Books, 1977), 76–77; Murphy, *Political Imprisonment*, 84–86.

56. MacEoin, *Survivors*, 84.

57. For a summary of Ashe's strike and death, see Murphy, *Political Imprisonment*, 83–88.

58. McConville, *Irish Political Prisoners*, 614.

59. For descriptions of the funeral procession and burial, see Album of Press Clippings, 1916–1918, NLI, ms. 25,588; Sean O'Luing, *I Die in a Good Cause: Thomas Ashe, Idealist and Revolutionary* (Tralee: Anvil Books, 1970), 182–92.

60. Kelly, *The Fenian Ideal*.

61. Transcript of the Coroner's Inquest into the Death of Thomas Ashe, NAI, DE2/507.

62. Joost Augsteijn, *From Public Defiance to Guerrilla Warfare* (Dublin: Irish Academic Press, 1996), 65.

63. Ibid., 84.

64. McConville, *Irish Political Prisoners*, 612–19.

65. Tomás Mac Conmara, *Days of Hunger: The Clare Volunteers and the Mountjoy Hunger Strike of 1917* (Ballyvalley, Killaloe, County Clare: Dallán Publishing, 2017).

66. William Murphy uses different records from the National Archives to determine a different number of prisoners on hunger strike in this period. See Murphy, *Political Imprisonment*, 99.

67. Ibid., 94–103.

68. Stuart Mews, "The Hunger-Strike of the Lord Mayor of Cork, 1920: Irish, English and Vatican Attitudes," in *The Churches, Ireland and the Irish*, ed. W. J. Sheils and Diana Wood (Oxford: Basil Blackwell, 1989), 386.

69. Charles Townshend, *The British Campaign in Ireland, 1919–1921* (Oxford: Oxford University Press, 1975), 5.

70. Murphy, *Political Imprisonment*, 108.

71. Ward, *Sheehy Skeffington*, 214–16.

72. See tables in Hart, *The I.R.A. at War*.

73. Hopkinson, *The Irish War*, 86–87.

74. Townshend, *The British Campaign*, 76.

75. McConville, *Irish Political Prisoners*, 720–21.

76. Townshend, *The British Campaign*, 76.

77. Hopkinson, *The Irish War*, 28.

78. Hart, *The I.R.A. at War*, 84.

79. Frank Gallagher, *Days of Fear* (New York: Harper Brothers, 1929), 54.

80. Mark Sturgis, *The Last Days of Dublin Castle: The Mark Sturgis Diaries,* ed. Michael Hopkinson (Dublin: Irish Academic Press, 1999), 1–10.

81. The division was under the direct command of Brigadier-General F. P. Crozier and then Brigadier-General E. A. Wood until it was demobilized in 1922. D. M. Leeson, *The*

Black and Tans: British Police and Auxiliaries in the Irish War of Independence (Oxford: Oxford University Press, 2011), 32–38.

82. Mo Moulton, *Ireland and the Irish in Interwar England* (Cambridge: Cambridge University Press, 2014), 31–134.

83. It is noteworthy that the government had been transferring troublesome Irish prisoners to England for over a year. MacSwiney was one of 424 such transfers in 1920. See Murphy, *Political Imprisonment*, 175.

84. Hopkinson, *The Irish War*, 87.

85. Terence MacSwiney, *Principles of Freedom* (New York: E. P. Dutton and Co., 1921), 173.

86. Terence MacSwiney's speech upon becoming the lord mayor of Cork, UCD, P48B/485.

87. Francis Costello, *Enduring the Most: The Life and Death of Terence MacSwiney* (Dingle, Co. Kerry: Brandon, 1995), 197–98; Charlotte H. Fallon, *Soul of Fire: A Biography of Mary MacSwiney* (Cork: Mercier Press, 1986), 46.

88. Terence MacSwiney, "Message from the Lord Mayor of Cork to Irish Prisoners on hunger-strike in Cork Gaol", undated, UCD, P48B/435.

89. Terence MacSwiney, "Message from the Lord Mayor of Cork to Irish Prisoners on hunger-strike in Cork Gaol", undated, UCD, P48B/436 and 437.

90. Paige Reynolds, "Modernist Martyrdom: The Funerals of Terence MacSwiney," *Modernism/Modernity*, 9:4 (2002), 547–50.

91. Paige Reynolds, *Modernism, Drama, and the Audience for Irish Spectacle* (Cambridge: Cambridge University Press, 2007), 139–55.

92. Hopkinson, *The Irish War*, 86–87, 95; Murphy, *Political Imprisonment*, 190.

93. For an excellent, creative treatment of MacSwiney's strike, see Reynolds, *Modernism, Drama, and the Audience for Irish Spectacle*, 116–55

94. William Murphy, "Dying, Death and Hunger Strike: Cork and Brixton, 1920," in *Death and Dying in Ireland, Britain and Europe: Historical Perspectives*, ed. James Kelly and Mann Ann Lyons (Dublin: Irish Academic Press, 2013), 297–316.

95. "A Huge Gathering: 40,000 Persons Voice the Claims of Ireland," *Irish Independent*, 1 November 1920, 5.

96. Michael Silvestri, *Ireland and India: Nationalism, Empire, and Memory* (New York: Palgrave Macmillan, 2009).

97. MacSwiney, *Principles of Freedom*, 114–30.

98. Máire MacSwiney Brugha, *History's Daughter: A Memoir from the Only Child of Terence MacSwiney* (Dublin: The O'Brien Press, 2006), 18–20. Also see Joanne Mooney Eichacker, *Irish Republican Women in America: Lecture Tours, 1916–1925* (Dublin: Irish Academic Press, 2003).

99. Cosgrave was leader of the Cumann na Gaedhael party that was reconstituted as Fine Gael in 1933.

100. Maire Comerford notes on Mary and Eithne MacSwiney, NLI, ms. 24,896.

101. Letter from Lily O'Brennan to Fan [Fanny Ceannt], 3 December 1922, UCD, P13/11.

102. Copy of letter from W. T. Cosgrave to the archbishop of Dublin, 18 November 1922, NAI, TAOIS/s 1369/9; newspaper clipping, "Miss M. MacSwiney, T. D.," *Irish Independent*, 23 November 1922, NAI, TAOIS/s 1369/9.

103. Patrick Murray, *Oracles of God: The Roman Catholic Church and Irish Politics, 1922–37* (Dublin: UCD Press, 2000), 75–76.

104. Copy of letter from Mary MacSwiney to Edward Byrne, archbishop of Dublin, 5 November 1922, NAI, TAOIS/s 1369/9.

105. Dorothy Macardle's handwritten reflections on Mary MacSwiney for publication in the *Irish Press* upon MacSwiney's death, UCD, P150/1658.

106. Newspaper clipping, *Daily Mirror*, UCD, P150/1658.

107. "Blaze away with your little gun," typescript manuscript by Maighréad and Siobhán de Paor, UCD, P140.

108. Draft memoir by Maire Comerford, 1956, UCD LA18/20.

109. Sinn Féin flyer, UCD, P88/286(11).

110. Reflections of Eithne Coyle, written in 1974. UCD, P61/2.

111. Letters from Austin Stack to Winnie Gordon, 30 October 1923, NLI, ms.22,398.

112. Reflections of Eithne Coyle, written in 1974. UCD, P61/2.

113. Newspaper clipping, "Anniversary Celebrated. Public Meeting in Dublin," *Irish Examiner*, 25 October 1923, 6, NLI, ms. 21,937.

114. Sinn Féin *Daily Sheet*, 7 November 1923, NAI, TAOIS/s 1369/10.

115. Letter from Sighle Humphreys to her family, 23 November 1923, UCD P106/1053.

116. Peter Hart, *The I.R.A. and Its Enemies*. (Oxford: Oxford University Press, 1998), 176, 224.

117. "Kevin Barry," *Sunday Independent*, 12 November 1949, 2.

118. Letter from Emmet Humphreys to his mother, Ellen Humphreys, 26 October 1923, UCD P106/644.

119. Gallagher, *Days of Fear*, 33.

120. English, *Radicals and the Republic*.

121. Ibid., 139.

122. Ibid., 119–20.

123. Ibid., 244–45.

124. Fallon, *Soul of Fire*, 173.

125. The preceding information is drawn from John Maguire, *I.R.A. Internments and the Irish Government: Subversives and the State, 1939–1962* (Dublin: Irish Academic Press, 2008), 10–20.

126. Ibid., 27.

127. Memorandum on political prisoner status prepared for Eamon de Valera, 18 April 1940, NAI, TAOIS/s 11515.

128. Patsy O'Hagan recalled that upon her internment in 1941 she found another twenty republican women imprisoned at Mountjoy. MacEoin, *Survivors* 171.

129. Patsy O'Hagan, for example, despised government officials for arresting her when she was alone at home with two children and for then leaving the children on their own. Ibid., 170.

130. Maguire, *I.R.A. Internments*, 28.

131. Kathleen Clarke, *My Fight for Ireland's Freedom* (Dublin: The O'Brien Press, 1991), 223.

132. Letter from Margaret Pearse to Eamon de Valera, 15 November 1939, NAI, TAOIS/s 11515.

133. Press release from the Government Information Bureau, 1 November 1939, NAI, TAOIS/s 11515.

134. Gallagher, *Days of Fear*, 58.

135. Ronan Fanning, "'The Rule of Order': Eamon de Valera and the I.R.A., 1923–40," in *De Valera and His Times,* ed. John P. O'Carroll and John A. Murphy (Cork: Cork University Press, 1983), 167.

136. The hunger strikers were Séan (Jack) McNeela, John (Jack) Plunkett, Tony D'Arcy, Michael Traynor, Thomas Grogan, and Tomás MacCurtain.

137. Copy of letter from the Republican Prison Council at Mountjoy to the IRA, 11 April 1940, NAI, TAOIS/s 11515.

138. Barry Flynn, *Pawns in the Game: Irish Hunger Strikes, 1912–1981* (Dublin: The Collins Press, 2011), 100.

139. Donal Ó Drisceoil, *Censorship in Ireland, 1939–1945* (Cork: Cork University Press, 1996), 237.

140. Ibid., 234–43.

141. Mary MacSwiney, "The Hunger Strike," press interview, 23 November 1923, NAI, S1369/10.

142. The signatories were Maire Ni Suibhne (Mary MacSwiney), Hanora Murphy, May Delaney, Bridget Fitzgerald, and Gregory Ashe.

143. The signatories were Caitlin Bean Ni Cleirigh, Aine B.E. Ceannt, R.J. Connolly, Neans Bean Ui Rathghaille, Maud Gonne MacBride, and Donagh MacDonagh.

144. "Government and the Hunger-Strikers," *Irish Press,* 25 March 1940.

145. Maguire, *I.R.A. Internments*, 31–32.

146. Ó Drisceoil, *Censorship*, 237.

147. Maguire, *I.R.A. Internments*, 33.

148. Ibid., 34.

149. Ibid., 246–47.

150. Richard English, *Armed Struggle: The History of the I.R.A.* (Oxford: Oxford University Press, 2004), 56.

151. Maguire, *I.R.A. Internments*, 58.

152. Seán MacBride, *That Day's Struggle: A Memoir, 1904–1951* (Dublin: Currach Press, 2005), 81–82.

153. Ibid., 135.

154. "Mr. De Valera Says Mr. Cosgrave Was Right," *Irish Examiner,* 29 May 1946, 5.

155. For thoughtful reflections on the interwar years, see Senia Pestana, *Irish Nationalist Women, 1900–1918* (Cambridge: Cambridge University Press, 2013), 266–71.

CHAPTER 4. BUILDING THE NATION'S TEMPLE: HUNGER
STRIKES AND FASTS BY NATIONALISTS IN INDIA, 1912–1948

1. One finds the head jailor's last name variously spelled Barry or Barrie. For the preceding account of the Cellular Jail, see Peter Heehs, *The Bomb in Bengal: The Rise of Revolutionary Terrorism in India, 1900–1910* (Delhi: Oxford University Press, 1993), 234–35; Ujjwal Kumar Singh, *Political Prisoners in India* (Delhi: Oxford University Press, 1998), 56.

2. V. D. Savarkar, *The Story of My Transportation for Life* (Bombay: Sadbhakti Publications, 1950), 124–25.

3. Sumathi Ramaswamy, *The Goddess and the Nation: Mapping Mother India* (Durham: Duke University Press, 2010).

4. Savarkar, *Story of My Transportation*, 181.

5. On the integration of revolutionaries into the predominantly Gandhian nationalist narrative in recent years, see Durba Ghosh, *Gentlemanly Terrorists: Political Violence and the Colonial State in India, 1919–1947* (Cambridge: Cambridge University Press, 2017); Kama Maclean, *A Revolutionary History of Interwar India: Violence, Image, Voice and Text* (London: C. Hurst and Company, 2015); Taylor C. Sherman, *State Violence and Punishment in India* (London: Routledge, 2010); and Neeti Nair, "Bhagat Singh as 'Satyagrahi': The Limits to Non-Violence in Late Colonial India," *Modern Asian Studies*, 43:3 (May 2009), 649–81.

6. See Nair, "Bhagat Singh as 'Satyagrahi.'" Nair argues persuasively that Singh's ideologies and tactics were far closer to Gandhi's than Gandhi ever cared to acknowledge, and that Gandhi viewed Singh, in particular, as a threat to Congress power.

7. For an excellent, concise treatment of this subject, see Sherman, *State Violence and Punishment in India*, 93–110.

8. This was the Indian Statutory Commission, commonly known as the Simon Commission, after the chairman, Sir John Simon.

9. Maclean, *Revolutionary History of Interwar India*, 162; Kama Maclean, "Imagining the Indian Nationalist Movement: Revolutionary Metaphors in Imagery of the Freedom Struggle," *Journal of Material Culture*, 19:1 (2014), 17–18.

10. Ramaswamy, *Goddess and the Nation*, 34.

11. This quotation is drawn from Maclean's reference to Pinney's work in her essay "Imagining the Indian Nationalist Movement," 28. Also see Christopher Pinney, *Photos of the Gods: The Printed Image and Political Struggle in India* (Delhi: Oxford University Press, 2004), 117.

12. Sherman, *State Violence and Punishment*, 107.

13. Durba Ghosh, *Gentlemanly Terrorists;* Amit Kumar Gupta, "Defying Death: Nationalist Revolutionism in India, 1897–1938," *Social Scientist*, 25:9/10 (September–October 1997), 3–9.

14. Richard Popplewell, *Intelligence and Imperial Defence: British Intelligence and the Defence of the Indian Empire, 1904–1924* (London: Taylor and Francis, 1995).

15. L. P. Mathur, *Kala Pani: History of Andaman and Nicobar Islands with a Study of India's Freedom Struggle* (Delhi: Eastern Book Corporation, 1985), 83–84; S. N. Aggarwal, *The Heroes of the Cellular Jail* (Patiala: Punjab University, 1995), 104.

16. Some writers have observed that Mukherjee was only sixteen or eighteen in 1912. I have chosen to rely on James Campbell Ker, *Political Trouble in India, 1907–1917* (Calcutta: Superintendent Government Printing, 1917), 430. Ker, who drew on intelligence and police records, indicates that Mukherjee was born around 1890.

17. Ker, *Political Trouble in India*, 465; Heehs, *The Bomb in Bengal*, 245; Aggarwal, *Heroes of the Cellular Jail*, 61.

18. Singh, *Political Prisoners*, 57, footnote 109.

19. Savarkar, *Story of My Transportation*, 239.

20. Ibid., 242, 250.

21. Mathur, *Kala Pani*, 84.

22. Ibid.

23. Savarkar, *Story of My Transportation*, 255.

24. Ibid., 367.

25. Maia Ramnath, *Haj to Utopia: How the Ghadar Movement Charted Global Radicalism and Attempted to Overthrow the British Empire* (Berkeley: University of California Press, 2011), 53–54, 59; Sir Michael O'Dwyer, *India as I Knew It, 1885–1925* (London: Constable and Company, Ltd., 1925), 201.

26. Savarkar, *Story of My Transportation*, 374–75.

27. Randhir Singh, *Autobiography of Bhai Sahib Randhir Singh* (Ludhiana, Punjab: Bhai Sahib Randhir Singh Trust, 2000), 70.

28. Ibid., 82.

29. Singh, *Political Prisoners*, 47.

30. Ibid., footnote 73.

31. Singh, *Autobiography*, 92–99.

32. Prasad is food offered in worship to a god, then redistributed to worshippers.

33. Copy of letter from superintendent, Central Jail, Hazaribagh, to the inspector general of prisons, Bihar and Orissa, 9 April 1918, Bihar and Orissa Proceedings, Municipal Dept., Jails, Oriental and India Office Collection, British Library (hereafter OIOC), P/10290.

34. Copy of letter from inspector general of prisons, Bihar and Orissa, to superintendent, Central Jail, Hazaribagh, 13 April 1918, Bihar and Orissa Proceedings, Municipal Dept., Jails, OIOC, P/10290.

35. Copy of letter from undersecretary to the government of Bihar and Orissa, Municipal Dept., to inspector general of Prisons, Bihar and Orissa, 18 May 1918, Bihar and Orissa Proceedings, Municipal Dept., Jails, OIOC, P/10290.

36. Michael Silvestri, " 'The Sinn Féin of India': Irish Nationalism and the Policing of Revolutionary Terrorism in Bengal," *Journal of British Studies,* 39 (October 2000), 454–86; T. G. Fraser, "Ireland and India," in *An Irish Empire?*, ed. Keith Jeffrey (New York: Manchester University Press, 1996), 77–93; Richard Davis, "The Influence of the Irish Revolution on Indian Nationalism: The Evidence of the Indian Press, 1916–22," *South Asia,* 9:2 (1986), 55–68.

37. "Sinn Fein Demonstrations," *Bombay Chronicle*, 25 September 1917.

38. Telegram from viceroy, Home Department, to the secretary of state, 8 August 1920, OIOC, L/PJ/6/1780/7620/21; telegram from government of India, Home Department, to government of Bombay, Judicial Department, 8 August 1920, OIOC, correspondence in Bombay Proceedings, July to August 1920, P/CONF/53.

39. Ramnath, *Haj to Utopia*, 39.

40. Ibid., 110.

41. Thank you to Sudipta Sen for drawing my attention to this distinction between martyr and *shahid*.

42. David Arnold, "The Colonial Prison: Power, Knowledge and Penology in Nineteenth-Century India," in *Subaltern Studies,* vol. 8, ed. David Arnold and David Hardiman (Delhi: Oxford University Press, 2003), 174.

43. Barindra Kumar Ghose, *The Tale of My Exile* (Pondicherry: Arya Office, 1922), 78–80; Savarkar, *Story of My Transportation*, 413–15.

44. Bankimcandra Chatterji, *Anandamath, or the Sacred Brotherhood*, trans. with an introduction by Julius J. Lipner (Oxford: Oxford University Press, 2005). Note that this author's last name is transliterated in two ways: Chattopadhyay or Chatterji. I have chosen to use the former in the text.

45. Chatterji, 149–51.

46. Chattopadhyay initially composed "Bande Mataram" as a song in 1875. See Sugata Bose, *His Majesty's Opponent: Subhas Chandra Bose and India's Struggle against Empire* (Cambridge: The Belknap Press of Harvard University Press, 2011), 124.

47. Chatterji, *Anandamath*, 299. Lakshmi is the Hindu goddess of prosperity and health. She is the consort of Lord Vishnu and an important aspect of Shaktism embodied in its highest form by Durga.

48. Leonard Gordon, *Bengal: The Nationalist Movement, 1876–1940* (New York: Columbia University Press, 1974), 123. Also see Narasingha P. Sil, "*Bande Mataram*: Bankimchandra Chattopadhyay's Nationalist Thought Revisited," *South Asia*, 25:1 (2002), 121–42,

49. www.aurobindo.ru/workings/sa/01/bande_mataram.eng.pdf, 66 (accessed 11 June 2014).

50. Thank you to Sudipta Sen for explaining to me the particular significance of Bhawani.

51. Harjot Oberoi, *The Construction of Religious Boundaries: Culture, Identity, and Diversity in the Sikh Tradition* (Chicago: University of Chicago Press, 1994), 13–14.

52. Ibid., 17–18, 25.

53. Ibid., 421–26.

54. Ramaswamy, *Goddess and the Nation*, 139.

55. Nicholas Owen, *The British Left and India: Metropolitan Anti-Imperialism, 1885–1947* (Oxford: Oxford University Press, 2008), 67.

56. Sumit Sarkar, *Modern India, 1885–1947* (Madras: Macmillan, 1986), 145.

57. For a list of the accused, see A. G. Noorani, *The Trial of Bhagat Singh: Politics of Justice* (Delhi: Oxford University Press, 1996), 259–60. Regarding the trial and prison protests, see Neeti Nair, "Bhagat Singh as 'Satyagrahi.'"

58. Kamlesh Mohan, *Militant Nationalism in the Punjab* (New Delhi: Manohar, 1985), 187.

59. Sherman, *State Violence and Punishnent*, 101.

60. C. S. Venu, "Jatin Das (The Martyr)" (Madras: C. S. Cunniah, circa 1931), 39, OIOC, PIB 38/1.

61. Nair, "Bhagat Singh as 'Satyagrahi,'" 663; Venu, "Jatin Das," 42.

62. Pinney, *Photos of the Gods*; Ramaswamy, *Goddess and the Nation*.

63. Mary Storm, *Head and Heart: Valour and Self-Sacrifice in the Art of India* (Delhi: Routledge, 2013).

64. Louis E. Fenech, *Martyrdom in the Sikh Tradition: Playing the "Game of Love"* (Delhi: Oxford University Press, 2000), 160.

65. R. C. Temple, "Folklore of the Headless Horseman in Northern India," *Calcutta Review*, 77 (1883), 163.

66. Fenech, *Martyrdom in the Sikh Tradition*, 160.

67. The men pictured around Azad are Bhagat Singh, B. K. Dutt, Raj Guru, Sukhdev, Rajendra Lahiri, Ramprasad Bismil, Roshan Singh, and Ashfaq.

68. Nair, "Bhagat Singh as 'Satyagrahi,'" 665.

69. Gandhi, "The Bomb and the Knife," *Young India*, 18 April 1929, in *Collected Works of Mahatma Gandhi*, vol. 40 (Delhi: Government of India, 1983), 259.

70. Joseph S. Alter, *Gandhi's Body: Sex, Diet, and the Politics of Nationalism* (Philadelphia: University of Pennsylvania Press, 2000), 3–52.

71. Faisal Devji, *The Impossible Indian: Gandhi and the Temptation of Violence* (Cambridge: Harvard University Press, 2012), 6.

72. Ibid., 6–7.

73. Ghosh, *Gentlemanly Terrorists*, 98–138.

74. C. D. O. Prisoners, Nasik Road Central Prison, 1930–31, inspector general of prisons, Bombay Presidency, Poona, Maharastra State Archives.

75. Lisa Trivedi, *Clothing Gandhi's Nation: Homespun and the Nation in India* (Bloomington: Indiana University Press, 2007), 118–47.

76. Ramaswamy, *Goddess and the Nation*, 152.

77. Ker, *Political Trouble in India*, 31–43.

78. Valentine Chirol, *Indian Unrest* (London: Macmillan and Co.,1910), 24–36.

79. Mrinalini Sinha, *Specters of Mother India: The Global Restructuring of an Empire* (Durham: Duke University Press, 2006), 79.

80. Ibid., 88.

81. Ibid., 97.

82. East India (Sedition) Committee, 1918, Report of Committee Appointed to Investigate Revolutionary Conspiracies in India [Cd. 9190] (London: His Majesty's Stationery Office, 1918), 19.

83. Ibid., 17, 47.

84. D. A. Low, *Britain and Indian Nationalism: The Imprint of Ambiguity, 1929–1942* (Cambridge: Cambridge University Press, 1997), 268–302.

85. Sherman, *State Violence and Punishment*, 103.

86. Ibid., 110.

87. Viceroy to Bombay governor, 11 August 1937, in P. N. Chopra, ed., *Towards Freedom, 1937–47*, vol. 1, *Experiment with Provincial Autonomy, 1 January–31 December 1937* (New Delhi: Indian Council of Historical Research, 1985) (hereafter Chopra, *Towards Freedom*, vol. 1), 861.

88. *Bombay Chronicle*, 7 August 1937.

89. Sherman, *State Violence and Punishment*, 106–07.

90. Anderson to Linlithgow, 7 September 1937, Chopra, *Towards Freedom*, vol. 1, 940.

91. Gandhi to Linlithgow via telegram, 27 August 1937, ibid., 896.

92. Chief Commissioner Andaman to Government of India about Suspension of Hunger-Strike by Prisoners, 29 August 1937, ibid., 900.

93. Ibid., 899–901.

94. Gandhi, "Resolution on Ministerial Resignations," 18 February 1938, in *Collected Works of Mahatma Gandhi*, vol. 66 (Delhi: Government of India, 1983), 379.

95. Sherman, *State Violence and Punishment*, 107.

96. Ibid., 108.

97. Ibid., 109.

98. Anderson to Linlithgow, 7 September 1937, Chopra, *Towards Freedom,* vol. 1, 942.

99. Linlithgow to Zetland, 9 September 1937, ibid., 943–44.

100. Linlithgow to Secretary of State Zetland, 7 September 1937, ibid., 937.

101. A.G. Noorani, "Vande Mataram: A Historical Lesson," *Economic and Political Weekly*, 8:23 (9 June 1973), 1042.

102. Tanika Sarkar, "Birth of a Goddess: 'Vande Mataram', 'Anandamath,' and Hindu Nationhood," *Economic and Political Weekly*, 41:37 (16–22 September 2006), 3963.

103. Statement by the Congress Working Committee on *Bande Mataram*, 28 October 1937, Chopra, *Towards Freedom,* vol. 1, 1090. See the first two stanzas in chapter 4 on page 110.

104. Tanika Sarkar, "Birth of a Goddess," 3963.

105. Bose, president of the Bengal Province Congress Committee, to Nehru, 13 December 1937, Chopra, *Towards Freedom,* vol. 1, 1263.

106. Linlithgow to Zetland, 27 October 1937, ibid., 1072–73.

107. Venu, "Jatin Das," 51–52.

108. Eamon de Valera, *India and Ireland* (New York: Friends of Freedom for India, 1920), 20.

109. Mahatma Gandhi, Speech at Prayer Meeting, Calcutta, 23 August 1947, *Collected Works of Mahatma Gandhi*, vol. 89 (Delhi: Government of India, 1983), 80.

110. Dennis Dalton, *Gandhi's Power: Nonviolence in Action* (Delhi: Oxford University Press, 1993), 146.

111. Mahatma Gandhi, "Miracle or Accident?" 16 August 1947, *Collected Works of Mahatma Gandhi*, vol. 89 (Delhi: Government of India, 1983), 48.

112. Mahatma Gandhi, "Statement to the Press," 1 September 1947, ibid., 132.

113. Mahatma Gandhi, "Discussion with Citizens' Deputation," 4 September 1947, ibid., 152.

CHAPTER 5. THE RULE OF EXCEPTIONS: HUNGER
STRIKES AND POLITICAL PRISONER STATUS IN BRITAIN,
IRELAND, AND INDIA, 1909–1946

1. Frank Gallagher, *Days of Fear* (New York: Harper Brothers, 1929), 23–24.

2. Cliona Murphy, *The Women's Suffrage Movement and Irish Society in the Early Twentieth Century* (Philadelphia: Temple University Press, 1989), 101.

3. Barton L. Ingraham, *Political Crime in Europe: A Comparative Study of France, Germany, and England* (Berkeley: University of California Press, 1979).

4. I am drawing this language of governmental rationale from Ujjwal Kumar Singh, *Political Prisoners in India* (Delhi: Oxford University Press, 1998).

5. Mohandas Gandhi, "Hunger Strike," *Harijan*, 19 August 1939, *Collected Works of Mahatma Gandhi* (Delhi: Government of India, 1983), 87.

6. Dáil Debates, 9 November 1939, http://debates.oireachtas.ie/dail/1939/11/09/00018 .asp (accessed 2 June 2011).

7. Sir Evelyn Ruggles-Brise, *The English Prison System* (London: Macmillan and Co., 1921), 2. For an overview of this era in British prisons, see Martin Wiener, *Reconstructing the Criminal: Culture, Law, and Policy in England, 1830–1914* (Cambridge: Cambridge University Press, 1990).

8. Regarding the three prison divisions, see Stephen Hobhouse and A. Fenner Brockway, *English Prisons To-Day* (London: Longmans and Co., 1922), 214–29; and Leon Radzinowicz and Roger Hood, "The Status of Political Prisoner in England: The Struggle for Recognition," *Virginia Law Review*, 65:8 (December 1979), 1458–59.

9. Whipping was not entirely prohibited within the judicial and penal systems. See Ruggles-Brise, *The English Prison System*, 20. Regarding corporal punishment in general, see ibid., 80. Regarding suicide, see Hobhouse and Brockway, *English Prisons To-Day*, 550.

10. Ruggles-Brise, *The English Prison System*, 5, 188–89.

11. Memorandum by the governor of Holloway Prison, "The treatment of suffragette prisoners since 1 March 1912," March 1912, British National Archives, Kew (hereafter BNA), PCOM 8/228.

12. Hobhouse and Brockway, *English Prisons To-Day*, 220. Regarding the growing burden of suffragist militants upon British courts and prisons, see Radzinowicz and Hood, "The Status of Political Prisoner in England," 1460.

13. A small number of working-class suffragists, such as Annie Kenney, were relegated to the Third Division.

14. June Purvis, *Emmeline Pankhurt:A Biography* (London: Routledge, 2002), 117–18.

15. See chapter 1 page 55.

16. A later survey of the English prison system in 1921 found that medical officers were conscientious, but that their numerous daily duties rendered their work hurried and cursory, even when they were not managing hunger strikes. Hobhouse and Brockway, *English Prisons To-Day*, 256, 260–62, 274.

17. C.J. Bearman, "An Army without Discipline? Suffragette Militancy and the Budget Crisis of 1909," *Historical Journal*, 50:4 (2007), 880–81.

18. Sir E. Ruggles-Brise (chair of Prison Commission) to Sir Edward Troup, October 1909, BNA, HO 144/1042/183256.

19. Winston Churchill to Sir Edward Troup, 28 February 1910, BNA, HO 144/1042/183256.

20. Ian Miller, *A History of Force Feeding: Hunger Strikes, Prisons and Medical Ethics, 1909–1974* (London: Palgrave Macmillan, 2016), 49.

21. Memorandum by Herbert Smalley, 31 December 1912, BNA, PCOM 7/355.

22. Memorandum on Prisoners (Temporary Discharge for Ill-Health) Bill, 28 April 1913, BNA, HO 45/10699/234800.

23. Governor of Aylesbury Prison to Home Office, 9 April 1912, BNA, HO 144/1205 /221999.

24. Agnes Savill, C. Mansell Moullin, and Sir Victor Horsley, "Preliminary Report on the Forcible Feeding of Suffrage Prisoners," *British Medical Journal*, 31 (31 August 1912), 505.

25. Sean O'Luing, *I Die in a Good Cause: A study of Thomas Ashe, Idealist and Rvolutionary* (Tralee, County Kerry: Anvil Books, 1970), 170–75.

26. Reports from Prison Medical Officer, R.G. Dowdall, regarding prisoners at Mountjoy to Chairman, General Prisons Board, 7 October 1917 and 14 October 1917, National Library of Ireland (hereafter NLI), ms. 31,777.

27. *The Death of Thomas Ashe: A Full Report of the Inquest* (Dublin: J.M. Butler, 1917), British Library, 9508 f7.

28. Memorandum by Sir Ernley Blackwell, 19 March 1918, BNA, HO 144/1490/356124.

29. For an example, see Memorandum by Sir Bryan Donkin, Director of Convict Prisons and Medical Advisor to the Prison Commissioners, 15 December 1912, BNA, PCOM 7/355.

30. Hobhouse and Brockway, *English Prisons To-Day*, 256, footnote 8.

31. Opinion by Law Officers of the Crown on Forcible Feeding of Prisoners, 15 July 1920, BNA, CJ 4/850.

32. The five men who died on hunger strike between 1917 and 1920 were as follows: The Irish republican Thomas Ashe, in 1917; the English conscientious objector W. E. Burns, in 1918; and the Irish republicans Mick Fitzgerald, Terence MacSwiney, and Joseph Murphy in 1920.

33. Memorandum on Prisoners (Temporary Discharge for Ill-Health) Bill, 28 April 1913, BNA, HO 45/10699/234800. Note that fifty-seven suffragists were on hunger strike at the same time on 25 June 1912. For locations, see Minute by Sir Edward Troup to Secretary of State, 25 June 1912, BNA, HO 144/1195/220196(504–670).

34. Peter Hart, *The IRA and Its Enemies* (Oxford: Oxford University Press, 1998), 56.

35. Sir E. Ruggles-Brise, Chairman of the Prison Commission, to Sir Edward Troup, October 1909, BNA, HO 144/1042/183256.

36. Chief Secretary to the Lord Mayor of Dublin, 6 March 1918, NLI, Ms. 35,294/2.

37. Max S. Green, Memorandum on Forcible Feeding, 9 November 1918, BNA, CO 906/18.

38. In November 1918 Thomas MacCurtain and others went on hunger strike in Cork and were released after less than a week under the Cat and Mouse Act. Cork Public Museum, MacCurtain Papers, D9:6, L1966:147.

39. Joost Augusteijn, *From Public Defiance to Guerilla Warfare: The Experience of Ordinary Volunteers in the Irish War of Independence, 1916–1921* (London: Irish Academic Press, 1998), 195.

40. File of reports on MacSwiney hunger strike, Summary B, BNA, HO 144/10308.

41. Prime Minister David Lloyd George's public statement on MacSwiney's hunger strike made at Lucerne on 25 August 1920, BNA, HO 144/10308.

42. Peter Hart, ed., *British Intelligence in Ireland, 1920–21: The Final Reports* (Cork: Cork University Press, 2002), 24–25.

43. Transcript of the Coroner's Inquest into the Death of Thomas Ashe, National Archive of Ireland (hereafter NAI), DE2/507, p. 5.

44. Government press release on behalf of Cosgrave, 13 November 1922, NAI, TAOIS/s 1369/9.

45. Tim Pat Coogan, *The IRA* (New York: Palgrave, 2002), 142.

46. Michael D'Arcy died on 16 April and John McNeela died on 19 April. The last of the other strikers gave up on the day of McNeela's death, having been assured of concessions that they never, in fact, received.

47. *Bombay Government Gazette*, 24 December 1919, Home Dept. (Spl), 60-D (b) Political Prisoners, 1919–20, Maharastra State Archives, Mumbai, India.

48. Singh, *Political Prisoners*, 32. For a summary discussion of the war-time detention measures, see ibid., 29–31.

49. Taylor C. Sherman, "State Practice, Nationalist Politics and the Hunger Strikes of the Lahore Conspiracy Case Prisoners, 1929–39," *Cultural and Social History*, 5:4 (2008), 499; Singh, *Political Prisoners*, 32–33, 40–42.

50. Singh, *Political Prisoners*, 88–92.

51. "The Indian Jails Committee, 1919–20, And Its Results" (1924), Oriental and India Office Collection, British Library (hereafter OIOC), L/PO/6/46B, 4, 11.

52. Regarding hunger strikes in Bihar, Bengal, and on the Andamans, see Singh, *Political Prisoners*, 49–50, 53. Regarding the Bombay Presidency and Bengal, see Telegram from Viceroy, Home Department, to the Secretary of State, 8 August 1920, OIOC, L/PJ/6/1780 /7620/21; Telegram from Government of India, Home Department, to Government of Bombay, Judicial Department, 8 August 1920, OIOC, Correspondence in Bombay Proceedings, July to August 1920, P/CONF/53.

53. David Arnold, "The Colonial Prison: Power, Knowledge and Penology in Nineteenth-Century India," in *Subaltern Studies*, vol. 8, ed. D. Arnold and D. Hardiman (Delhi: Oxford University Press, 2003),174.

54. Teertha Mandal, *The Women Revolutionaries of Bengal, 1905–1939* (Calcutta: Minerva, 1991), 119–20.

55. Singh, *Political Prisoners*, 103–5.

56. Regarding the case of Pir Mahbub Shah, see correspondence in "Khilafat Agitation in Sind," Maharastra State Archives, Home Dept. (Special), 355 H, 1920.

57. See, for example, Letter from the Acting Inspector-General of Prisons to the Secretary to the Government of Madras, Law Department, 30 May 1934, OIOC, L/PJ/8/491.

58. Letter from the Government of Bombay to the Home Dept., 18 July 1934, OIOC, L/PJ/8/491.

59. Regarding debates over whipping, see Home Dept., ser. no. 1135, file 3841 I, 1923: Whipping, Maharastra State Archives.

60. The major statutes and ordinances regarding whipping in India were as follows: Whipping Act, 1909; Criminal Law (Amendment) Act, 1923; Whipping (Burma Amendment) Act, 1927; Bengal Whipping Act, 1936; Bombay (Emergency Powers) Whipping Act, 1941; Penalties (Enhancement) Ordinance, 1942; and the Abolition of Whipping Act, 1955.

61. Nasser Hussain, *The Jurisprudence of Emergency* (Ann Arbor: University of Michigan Press, 2003).

62. Copy of letter from G. W. Clements, Superintendent, Central Jail, Coimbatore, to the Inspector General of Prisons, 15 October 1921, enclosed in Letter from Government of Madras to Government of India, Home Department, 4 November 1921, OIOC, L/PJ/6 /1780/7620/21.

63. Ibid. Also see copy of telegram from Viceroy, Home Department, to the Secretary of State for India, 8 February 1922, OIOC, L/PJ/6/1780/7620/21.

64. Copy of letter from G. W. Clements, Superintendent, Central Jail, Coimbatore, to the Inspector General of Prisons, 15 October 1921; extract from the journal of the Medical Officer at Coimbatore, 18 October 1921. Both documents are enclosed in letter from Government of Madras to Government of India, Home Department, 4 November 1921, OIOC, L/PJ/6/1780/7620/21.

65. Extract from the journal of the Medical Officer at Coimbatore, 18 October 1921; copy of letter from Superintendent, Coimbatore, to the Inspector General of Prisons, 19 October 1921, OIOC, L/PJ/6/1780/7620/21.

66. Extract from journal of the Medical Officer, Coimbatore, 18 October 1921, enclosed in letter from Government of Madras to Government of India, Home Department, 4 November 1921, OIOC, L/PJ/6/1780/7620/21.

67. Copy of letter from Acting Secretary to the Government of Madras to the Secretary to the Government of India, Home Department, 23 December 1921, OIOC, L/PJ/6/1780/7620/21.

68. See chapter 2.

69. Minute by Lord Lytton, 20 December 1921, OIOC, L/PJ/6/1780/7620/21.

70. Minute by Lord Lytton, 15 February 1922, on copy of telegram from Viceroy, Home Department, to Secretary of State, 8 February 1922, OIOC, L/PJ/6/1780/7620/21.

71. Copy of telegram from Viceroy, Home Department, to Secretary of State, 8 February 1922, OIOC, L/PJ/6/1780/7620/21.

72. Letter from Sir Malcolm C. C. Seton, Assistant Under Secretary of State, to J. E. Ferard, Secretary, Judicial and Public, 18 April 1922, OIOC, L/PJ/6/1780/7620/21.

73. Confidential letter from HO, Whitehall to Under Secretary of State, 12 May 1922, OIOC, L/PJ/6/1780/7620/21.

74. Mary Leigh had sued Herbert Gladstone, the home secretary, and various prison officials for forcibly feeding her while she was on hunger strike. More specifically, Leigh had claimed damages for assault, and she had sought an injunction.

75. See enclosure with the confidential letter from HO, Whitehall to Under Secretary of State, 12 May 1922, OIOC, L/PJ/6/1780/7620/21.

76. Telegram from Viceroy to Secretary of State, 6 February 1935, OIOC, L/PJ/8/491.

77. See chapter 4, pages 112–15.

78. Application from Bhagat Singh to Inspector-General of Prisons, Punjab, Lahore, 17 June 1929, contained in Punjab Legislative Council Debates, 25 November 1929, OIOC, L/PJ/6/1972.

79. Regarding media coverage and the prisoners' symbolic status, see Sherman, "State Practice," 499–501.

80. Letter from the Under Secretary, Home Office, to the Under Secretary, India Office, 28 August 1929, BNA, HO 144/21930.

81. Copy of telegram from Viceroy, Home Dept. to Sec of State for India, 29 July 1929, OIOC, L/PJ/6/1972.

82. F. A. Barker, "Twenty Years of Penal and Prison Reform in India," *Howard Journal of Criminal Justice*, 6:1 (1941), 55.

83. Ibid., 56.

84. The three prisoners who died were Mahabir Singh, Mankrishna Nama Das, and Mohit Mohan Maitra.

85. Superintendents had authority to order the whipping of C class prisoners. Superintendents wishing to whip A and B class prisoners needed the authorization of the local government. The inspectors general recommended instead that superintendents should in these cases require the authorization of a district magistrate. Proceedings of the Fifth All-India Conference of Inspectors-General of Prisons, New Delhi, January 15–19 1934, OIOC, L/PJ/8/487, 6–7.

86. It is probable that the emphasis on segregation came from Barker. He had been transferred temporarily to Port Blair in 1933, following the deaths of three strikers, to serve as an experienced consultant on hunger strikes. See memorandum from Lt.-Col. F. A. Barker to the Secretary to the Government of India, Home Department, 22 June 1933, OIOC, L/PJ/8/484.

87. Proceedings of the Fifth All-India Conference of Inspectors-General of Prisons, New Delhi, OIOC, L/PJ/8/487, 9.

88. Letter from the Government of the United Provinces to the Home Department, 25 October 1934, OIOC, L/PJ/8/491.

89. Letter from the Government of Bombay to the Home Department, 18 July 1934, OIOC, L/PJ/8/491.

90. Letter from the Government of Bengal to the Home Department, 11 July 1934, OIOC, L/PJ/8/491.

91. Letter (No.F.-104/33) Jails, Government of India, Home Dept., from T. Sloan, Joint Secretary to the Government of India, Home Department, to Local Governments, 29 November 1934, OIOC, L/PJ/8/491.

92. Letter (No.F.-104/33) Jails, Government of India, Home Dept., from T. Sloan, Joint Secretary to the Government of India, Home Department, to Local Governments, 29 November 1934, OIOC, L/PJ/8/491.

93. Subsequently, Winston Churchill's wartime cabinet expressed similar concerns. See cabinet meeting minutes, 17 August 1942, BNA, CAB 65/27/29.

94. Jawaharlal Nehru, *India and the World* (London: George Allen and Unwin, Ltd., 1936), 112.

95. Ibid., 141.

96. Statistics on Whipping, OIOC, L/PJ/8/493.

97. For relevant scholarship, see works by Satadru Sen, Clare Anderson, David Arnold, and Taylor Sherman.

98. "The Indian Jails Committee, 1919–20, and Its Results" (1924), OIOC, L/PO/6/46B, 5, 14.

99. "Report of the Departmental Committee on Corporal Punishment," appendix 4 (London: H.M. Stationery Office, 1938), 141, BNA, CAB 24/27.

100. File on prisoner John Fury, BNA, HO 144/21791.

101. Letter from Secretary to the Governor General to the Under Secretary of State for India, P and J Dept., 13 May 1940, OIOC, L/PJ/8/491.

102. Wm. Roger Louis, *Imperialism at Bay* (Oxford: Oxford University Press, 1987).

103. Regarding British views on Gandhi's fasts, see Tim Pratt and James Vernon, "'Appeal from This Fiery Bed . . . : The Colonial Politics of Gandhi's Fasts and Their Metropolitan Reception in Britain," *Journal of British Studies*, 44:1 (2005), 92–114. Regarding critical US media coverage of whipping in India, see, as examples, the following articles in the *New York Times*: "Hindu Boy Picket Sentenced to Lash," 29 January 1932; "Rioting Wanes in India," 22 October 1936; "India's Revolt Hangs Fire," 13 August 1942.

104. Cabinet meeting minutes, 17 August 1942, BNA, CAB 65/27/29.

105. See chapter 3.

106. Michael Silvestri, "'The Sinn Féin of India': Irish Nationalism and the Policing of Revolutionary Terrorism in Bengal," *Journal of British Studies*, 39:4 (October 2000), 479.

107. Memorandum by the Secretary of State for Dominion Affairs for the Cabinet, 25 May 1946, BNA, CAB 129/10.

EPILOGUE

1. John Stuart Mill, *On Liberty and Other Writings*, ed. by Stefan Collini (Cambridge: Cambridge University Press, 1999), 13–14.

2. Mohandas Gandhi, "Notes: Ireland and India," *Collected Works of Mahatma Gandhi*, vol. 22 (Delhi: Government of India, 1983), 17–18.

3. C. S. Venu, "Jatin Das (The Martyr)" (Madras: C. S. Cunniah, ca. 1931), 31, British Library, Oriental and India Office Collection, PIB 38/1.

4. Leith Passmore, "The Art of Hunger: Self-Starvation in the Red Army Faction," *German History*, 27:1 (2009), 32–59.

5. Ralph Armbruster-Sandoval, *Starving for Justice: Hunger Strikes, Spectacular Speech, and the Struggle for Dignity* (Tucson: University of Arizona Press, 2017).

6. Padraig O'Malley, *Biting at the Grave: The Irish Hunger Strikes and the Politics of Despair* (Boston: Beacon Press, 1990). Also see Allen Feldman, *Formations of Violence: The Narrative of the Body and Political Terror in Northern Ireland* (Chicago: University of Chicago Press, 1991); Thomas Hennessey, *Hunger Strike: Margaret Thatcher's Battle with the IRA, 1980–1981* (Dublin: Irish Academic Press, 2014).

7. "Hunger Strike Set," *New York Times*, 11 May 1960, 9; Nelson Mandela, *Long Walk to Freedom* (New York: Little Brown and Co., 1994), 423.

8. Regarding hunger strikes in South Africa, see Fran Buntman, *Robben Island and Prisoner Resistance to Apartheid* (Cambridge: Cambridge University Press, 2003).

9. "Hunger Strikers in 'Solitary,'" *New York Times*, 24 March 1951, 13.

10. "Hijacker on Hunger Strike," *New York Times*, 4 February 1970, 36.

11. "Zimbabwe Says That Bishop Has Ended His Fast," *New York Times*, 11 November 1983, A5.

12. "Trade Center Terrorist Ends Hunger Strike under Threat," *New York Times*, 30 January 1999, B6.

13. Banu Bargu, *Starve and Immolate: The Politics of Human Weapons* (New York: Columbia University Press, 2014), 13. Also see David Mizner, "Starving for Justice," *The Nation*, 4 December 2013 https://www.thenation.com/article/starving-justice/ (accessed 18 August 2017).

14. Mary Bosworth, *Inside Immigration Detention* (Oxford: Oxford University Press, 2014), 191.

15. A. Naomi Paik, *Rightlessness: Testimony and Redress in U.S. Prison Camps since World War II* (Chapel Hill: University of North Carolina Press, 2016), 195.

16. See, for example, the excellent, pioneering work of Banu Bargu.

BIBLIOGRAPHY

ARCHIVES

British Library
    Oriental and India Office Collection
        India Office Public and Judicial Department Records
        Proceedings and Consultations
        Proscribed Publications (Hindi)
        Secretary of State for India: Private Office Papers
Cork Public Museum
    MacCurtain Papers
Maharastra State Archives, Bombay
    Home Department
    Home Department (Special)
Museum of London
    Women's Social and Political Union Collection
National Archives of Ireland
    Dáil Éireann: Secretariat Files
    Department of the Taoiseach
    General Prisons Board
National Archives of the United Kingdom
    Cabinet
    Colonial Office
    Home Office

Home Office and Northern Ireland Office
    Prison Commission and Home Office Prison Department
National Library of Ireland
    Ceannt and O'Brennan Papers
    Máire Comerford Papers
    Hanna Sheehy Skeffington Papers
    Austin Stack Papers
University College Dublin Archives
    Máire Comerford Papers
    Maighréad and Siobhán de Paor Papers
    Eamon de Valera Papers
    Sighle Humphreys Papers
    Terence MacSwiney Papers
    Lily O'Brennan Papers
    Eithne Coyle O'Donnell Papers
    Dr. James Ryan Papers

WORKS CITED

Government Publications

British Parliamentary Debates, Fifth Series
Dáil Éireann Debates, http://debates.oireachtas.ie/dail/
East India (Sedition) Committee, 1918. Report of Committee Appointed to Investigate Revolutionary Conspiracies in India [Cd. 9190]. London: His Majesty's Stationery Office, 1918.

Periodicals and Other News Media

Ballinrobe Chronicle	*Manchester Guardian*
Bombay Chronicle	*Punch*
British Broadcasting Corporation (BBC)	*Review of Reviews*
Cable News Network (CNN)	*Sunday Independent*
Common Cause	*The Anglo-Russian*
Daily Mirror	*The Guardian*
Daily News	*The Independent*
Free Russia	*Irish Independent*
Freeman's Journal	*The Nation*
Illustrated London News	*New Review*
Irish Citizen	*New York Times*
Irish Examiner	*New York Times Magazine*
Irish Independent	*Review of Reviews*
Irish Press	*The Times*
Leeds Mercury	*Times of India*
Leitrim Observer	*Votes for Women*

Published Primary Sources: Articles, Books, and Reports

The Death of Thomas Ashe: A Full Report of the Inquest. Dublin: J. M. Butler, 1917.

"The Fasting Cure." *British Medical Journal*, 1, no. 2632 (10 June 1911): 1379–80.

"The Welsh Fasting Girl." *British Medical Journal*, 2, no. 469 (25 December 1869): 685–88.

Andrews, C. S. *Dublin Made Me*. Dublin: The Lilliput Press, 2008.

Barker, D. A. "Famine Relief in India." *Economic Review* (July 1913): 245–62.

Barker, F. A. "Twenty Years of Penal and Prison Reform in India." *Howard Journal of Criminal Justice*, 6, no. 1 (1941): 52–59.

Benedict, Francis. *The Influence of Inanition on Metabolism*. Washington, DC: Carnegie Institution of Washington, 1907.

Benedict, Francis. *A Study of Prolonged Fasting*. Washington, DC: Carnegie Institution of Washington, 1915.

Brennan-Whitmore, W. J. *With the Irish in Frongoch*. Dublin: The Talbot Press, 1917.

Breshkovskaia, Katerina. *Hidden Springs of the Russian Revolution*, edited by Lincoln Hutschinson. Stanford: Stanford University Press, 1931.

Buckley, Margaret. *The Jangle of the Keys*. Dublin: James Duffy and Co., 1938.

Campbell, Joseph. *"As I Was among the Captives": Joseph Campbell's Prison Diary, 1922 1923*. Cork: Cork University Press, 2001.

Carpenter, Mary. *Reformatory Schools for Children of the Dangerous and Perishing Classes, and for Juvenile Offenders*. Cambridge: Cambridge University Press, 2013.

Chatterji, Bankimcandra, *Anandamath, or the Sacred Brotherhood*, translated and edited by Julius J. Lipner. Oxford: Oxford University Press, 2005.

Chesterton, George Laval. *Revelations of Prison Life*, vol. 2. New York: Garland Publishing, 1984.

Chirol, Valentine. *Indian Unrest*. London: Macmillan and Co., 1910.

Chopra, P. N., ed. *Towards Freedom, 1937–47*, vol. 1, *Experiment with Provincial Autonomy, 1 January–31 December 1937*. New Delhi: Indian Council of Historical Research, 1985.

Clarke, Kathleen. *My Fight for Ireland's Freedom*. Dublin: The O'Brien Press, 1991.

Connolly, James. *The Re-Conquest of Ireland*. Dublin: New Books Publications, 1972.

Connolly, James. *Between Comrades: Letters and Correspondence, 1889–1916*, edited by Donal Nevin. Dublin: Gill and Macmillan, 2007.

Cousins, James H., and Margaret E. Cousins. *We Two Together*. Madras: Ganesh and Co., 1950.

Dal', Vladimir Ivanovich. *Tolkovyi slovar' zhivogo velikorusskogo iazyka*. 1880–82 Reprint, Moscow: Gosizdat, 1955.

De Valera, Eamon. *India and Ireland*. New York: Friends of Freedom for India, 1920.

Deutsch, Leo. *Sixteen Years in Siberia*. New York: Dutton, 1903.

Figner, Vera. *Les Prisons Russes*. Pully-Lausanne: Imprimerie des Unions Ouvrières, 1911.

Figner, Vera. *Polnoe sobranie sochinenii v semi tomakh*, vol. 3. Moscow: Izd-vo Vses. ob-va politkatorzhan i ssyl'poselentsev, 1932.

Figner, Vera. *Memoirs of a Revolutionist*. DeKalb: Northern Illinois University Press, 1991.

Gallagher, Frank. *Days of Fear*. New York: Harper Brothers, 1929.

Gandhi, M. K. *Satyagraha in South Africa*. Ahmedabad: Navajivan Publishing House, 2003.

Gandhi, M.K. *The Collected Works of Mahatma Gandhi*, multiple volumes. Ahmedabad: Navajivan Publishing House, 1983.'

Ghose, Barindra Kumar. *The Tale of My Exile*. Pondicherry: Arya Office, 1922.

Gonne, Maude. "The Famine Queen." In *Irish Writing: An Anthology of Irish Literature in English, 1789–1939*, edited by Stephen Regan, 183–84. Oxford: Oxford University Press, 2004.

Griffiths, Major Arthur. *Fifty Years of Public Service*. London: Cassell and Company, 1904.

Hart, Peter, ed. *British Intelligence in Ireland, 1920–21: The Final Reports*. Cork: Cork University Press, 2002.

Hobhouse, Emily. *Report of a Visit to the Camps of Women and Children in the Cape and Orange River Colonies*. London: Friars Printing Association, 1901.

Hobhouse, Stephen, and A. Fenner Brockway. *English Prisons To-Day*. London: Longmans and Co., 1922.

Hobson, J. A. *Imperialism: A Study*. Ann Arbor: University of Michigan Press, 1965.

Hutchison, Robert. *Food and the Principles of Dietetics*. 3rd edition. New York: William Wood and Company, 1911.

Hutchison, Robert. *Food and the Principles of Dietetics*, revised by V. H. Mottram and George Graham. London: Edward Arnold and Co., 1948.

Jorgenson-Earp, Cheryl R., ed. *Speeches and Trials of the Militant Suffragettes*. Madison: Fairleigh Dickinson University Press, 1999.

Josh, Sohan Singh. *My Tryst with Secularism: An Autobiography*. New Delhi: Patriot Publishers, 1991.

Kennan, George. "Exiles at Irkutsk." *The Century* 37, no. 15 (1889): 502–11.

Kennan, George. *Siberia and the Exile System*, vol. 2. New York: The Century Co., 1891.

Kennedy, Bart. *The Hunger Line*. London: T. Werner Laurie, 1908.

Ker, James Campbell. *Political Trouble in India, 1907–1917*. Calcutta: Superintendent Government Printing, 1917.

Keys, Ancel. "Human Starvation and Its Consequences." *Journal of the American Dietetic Association*, 22 (July 1946): 582–87.

Keys, Ancel. *The Biology of Human Starvation*, 2 vols. Minneapolis: University of Minnesota, 1950.

Kropotkin, Prince. *The Terror in Russia: An Appeal to the British Nation*. London: Methuen and Co., 1909.

Lusk, Graham. *The Elements of the Science of Nutrition*. Philadelphia: W. B. Saunders Co., 1906 and 1928.

Lytton, Constance, and Jane Wharton. *Prisons and Prisoners: Some Personal Experiences*. London: Heinemann, 1914.

MacEoin, Uinseann, ed. *Survivors*. Dublin: Argenta Publications, 1980.

MacSwiney, Terence. *Principles of Freedom*. New York: E. P. Dutton and Co., 1921.

Mandela, Nelson. *Long Walk to Freedom*. New York: Little, Brown and Co., 1994.

Mansergh, Nicholas, ed. *The Transfer of Power, 1942–7*, vol. 3. London: Her Majesty's Stationery Office, 1971.

Morel, E. D. *King Leopold's Rule in Africa*. London: Heinemann, 1904.

Nash, Vaughn. *The Great Famine and Its Causes*. London: Longmans, Green, and Co., 1900.

Nehru, Jawaharlal. *India and the World*. London: George Allen and Unwin., Ltd., 1936.

Nevinson, Henry. *The Dawn in Russia*. London: Harper and Bros., 1906.

O'Dwyer, Sir Michael. *India as I Knew It, 1885–1925*. London: Constable and Company, 1925.

O'Hegarty, P. S. *The Victory of Sinn Fein*. Dublin: The Talbot Press, 1924.

O'Mahony, Sean. *Frongoch: University of Revolution*. Dublin: FDR Teoranta, 1987.

O'Malley, Ernie. *The Men Will Talk to Me: Kerry Interviews*. Cork: Mercier Press, 2012.

Pankhurst, E. Sylvia. *The Suffragette*. New York: Sturgis and Walton Co., 1911.

Pankhurst, E. Sylvia. *The Suffragette Movement*. London: Longmans, Green and Co., 1931.

Pethick-Lawrence, F. W. *Fate Has Been Kind*. London: Hutchinson and Co., 1943.

Poole, Ernest. "Katharine Bereshkovsky: A Russian Revolutionist." *The Outlook* 79 (January–April 1905): 78–88.

Pyarelal. *The Epic Fast*. Ahmedabad: Navajivan Publishing House, 2007.

Rollins, Hyder E. "Notes on Some English Accounts of Miraculous Fasts." *Journal of American Folklore*, 34 (1921): 357–76.

Rosair, H. Basil. "Nineteen Months' Hunger Strike." *The Lancet*, 227 (4 April 1936): 778–79.

Ruggles-Brise, Sir Evelyn. *The English Prison System*. London: Macmillan and Co., 1921.

Savarkar, V. D. *The Story of My Transportation for Life*. Bombay: Sadbhakti Publications, 1950.

Savill, Agnes, C. Mansell Moullin, and Sir Victor Horsley. "Preliminary Report on the Forcible Feeding of Suffrage Prisoners." *British Medical Journal*, 31 (31 August 1912): 505–8.

Scott, the Reverend J. E. *In Famine Land: Observations and Experiences in India during the Great Drought of 1899–1900*. New York: Harper and Brothers Publishers, 1904.

Sinclair, Upton. *The Fasting Cure*. London: William Heinemann, 1911.

Singh, Randhir. *Autobiography of Bhai Sahib Randhir Singh*. Ludhiana, Punjab: Bhai Sahib Randhir Singh Trust, 2000.

Skeffington, Hanna Sheehy. "Reminiscences of an Irish Suffragette (1941)." In *Votes for Women*, edited by Andrée Sheehy Skeffington and Rosemary Owens, 12–26. Dublin: E. and T. O'Brien, 1975.

Stead, W. T. Synopsis of the article "The Revolution of the Twentieth Century," which appeared originally in *The Independent Review*, *Review of Reviews*, 33:194 (February 1906), 163.

Stepniak, Sergius. *Russia under the Tzars*, vol. 1. London: Ward and Downey, 1885.

Sturgis, Mark. *The Last Days of Dublin Castle: The Mark Sturgis Diaries*, edited by Michael Hopkinson. Dublin: Irish Academic Press, 1999.

Temple, R. C. "Folklore of the Headless Horseman in Northern India." *Calcutta Review*, 77 (1883): 158–83.

United Nations High Commissioner for Refugees, London. "Briefing Note: Committee in advance of the visit by the European Committee for the Prevention of Torture and Inhuman or Degrading Treatment or Punishment (CPT), Visit the United Kingdom, 2012," http://www.unhcr.org/en-au/5756ec877.pdf, accessed 20 February 2018.

Ushakov, D. N. *Tolkovyi slovar' russkogo iazyka*. Moscow: Gosizdat, 1935–1940.

Venu, C. S. *Jatin Das (The Martyr)*. Madras: C. S. Cunniah, ca. 1931.

Von Noorden, Carl. *Metabolism and Practical Medicine*. Chicago: W. T. Keener and Co., 1907.

Yeats, W. B. "The Stare's Nest by My Window." In *The Poems: A New Edition*, edited by Richard J. Finnernan, 205. New York: Macmillan, 1983.

Secondary Sources: Articles

Arnold, David. "The Colonial Prison: Power, Knowledge and Penology in Nineteenth Century India." In *Subaltern Studies VIII*, edited by David Arnold and David Hardiman, 148–84. Delhi: Oxford University Press, 2003.

Arnold, David. "British India and the Beriberi Problem, 1798–1942." *Medical History*, 54, no. 3 (July 2010): 295–314.

Bargu, Banu. "The Silent Exception: Hunger Striking and Lip-Sewing." *Law, Culture and the Humanities* (2017), DOI: 10.1177/1743872117709684.

Bearman, C. J. "An Army without Discipline? Suffragette Militancy and the Budget Crisis of 1909." *Historical Journal*, 50, no. 4 (2007): 861–89.

Benton, Sarah. "Women Disarmed: The Militarization of Politics in Ireland, 1913–23." *Feminist Review*, 50 (1995): 148–72.

Carpenter, Kenneth J. "A Short History of Nutritional Science: Part 1 (1785–1885)." *Journal of Nutrition*, 133 (2003): 638–45.

Carpenter, Kenneth J. "A Short History of Nutritional Science: Part 2 (1885–1912)." *Journal of Nutrition*, 133 (2003): 975–84.

Carpenter, Kenneth J. "Nutritional Studies in Victorian Prisons." *Journal of Nutrition*, 136 (2006): 1–8.

Comerford, R. V. "The Land War and the Politics of Distress, 1877–82." In *A New History of Ireland: Ireland Under the Union, II, 1870–1921*, vol. 6, edited by W. E. Vaughn, 26–52. Oxford: Oxford University Press, 1989.

Conlon, Deirdre. "Hungering for Freedom: Asylum Seekers' Hunger Strikes—Rethinking Resistance as Counter-Conduct." In *Carceral Spaces: Mobility and Agency in Imprisonment and Migrant Detention*, edited by Dominique Moran, Nick Gill, and Deirdre Conlon, 133–48. Farnham: Ashgate, 2013,

Cullather, Nick. "The Foreign Policy of the Calorie." *American Historical Review*, 112, no. 2 (April 2007): 337–64.

Daly, Jonathan. "Political Crime in Late Imperial Russia." *Journal of Modern History*, 74 (March 2002): 62–100.

Davis, Richard. "The Influence of the Irish Revolution on Indian Nationalism: The Evidence of the Indian Press, 1916–22." *South Asia*, 9, no. 2 (1986): 55–68.

Fallon, Charlotte. "Civil War Hunger Strikes: Women and Men." *Éire-Ireland*, 22, no. 3 (1987): 75–91.

Fanning, Ronan. "'The Rule of Order': Eamon de Valera and the I.R.A., 1923–40." In *De Valera and His Times*, edited by John P. O'Carroll and John A. Murphy, 160–72. Cork: Cork University Press, 1983.

Fraser, T. G. "Ireland and India." In *An Irish Empire?*, edited by Keith Jeffrey, 77–93. New York: Manchester University Press, 1996.

Geddes, J. F. "Culpable Complicity: The Medical Profession and the Forcible Feeding of Suffragettes, 1909–1914." *Women's History Review*, 17, no. 1 (March 2008): 79–94.

Good, Jane E. "America and the Russian Revolutionary Movement, 1888–1905." *Russian Review,* 41, no. 3 (July 1982): 273–87.

Grant, Kevin. "The Transcolonial World of Hunger Strikes and Political Fasts, c. 1909–1935." In *Decentering Empire: Britain, India, and the Transcolonial World,* edited by Durba Ghosh and Dane Kennedy, 243–69. Hyderabad: Orient Longman, 2006.

Grant, Kevin. "British Suffragettes and the Russian Method of Hunger Strike." *Comparative Studies in Society and History,* 53, no. 1 (2011): 113–43.

Gray, Peter. "Famine and Land in Ireland and India, 1845–1880: James Caird and the Political Economy of Hunger." *Historical Journal,* 49, no. 1 (March 2006): 193–215.

Gupta, Amit Kumar. "Defying Death: Nationalist Revolutionism in India, 1897–1938." *Social Scientist,* 25, nos. 9/10 (September–October 1997): 3–27.

Hall-Matthews, David. "Inaccurate Conceptions: Disputed Measures of Nutritional Needs and Famine Deaths in Colonial India." *Modern Asian Studies,* 42, no. 6 (2008): 1189–212.

Hart, Peter. "A New Revolutionary History." In *The I.R.A. at War, 1916–1923,* by Peter Hart, 3–29. Oxford: Oxford University Press, 2003.

Hollingsworth, Barry. "The Society of Friends of Russian Freedom: English Liberals and Russian Socialists, 1890–1917." *Oxford Slavonic Papers,* vol. 3. Oxford: Clarendon Press, 1970, 45–64.

Holton, Sandra Stanley. "Manliness and Militancy: The Political Protest of Male Suffragists and the Gendering of the 'Suffragette' Identity." In *Men's Share? Masculinities, Male Support and Women's Suffrage in Britain, 1890–1920,* edited by Angela V. John and Claire Eustance, 110–34. London: Routledge, 1997.

Knight, Amy. "Female Terrorists in the Russian Socialist Revolutionary Party." *Russian Review,* 38, no. 2 (April 1979): 139–59.

Lennon, Joseph. "Fasting for the Public: Irish and Indian Sources of Marion Wallace Dunlop's 1909 Hunger Strike." In *Enemies of Empire,* edited by Eóin Flannery and Angus Mitchell, 19–39. Dublin: Four Courts Press, 2007.

Lennon, Joseph. "The Starvation of a Man: Terence MacSwiney and Famine Memory." In *Memory Ireland,* vol. 3, *The Famine and the Troubles,* edited by Oona Frawley, 59–90. Syracuse: Syracuse University Press 2014.

Lennon, Joseph. "'Dreams That Hunger Makes': Memories of Hunger in Yeats, Mangan, Speranza, and Irish Folklore." *Irish University Review,* 47, no. 1 (2017): 62–81.

Lennon, Joseph, and Michael F. Johnson. "A Digital Exploration of Hunger Strikes in British Prisons, 1913–1940." In *The Digital Arts and Humanities,* edited by C. Travis and A. von Lünen, 77–93. New York: Spring Publishing Co., 2016.

MacCullough, J. A. "Fasting (Introductory and Non-Christian)." In *Encyclopedia of Religion and Ethics,* vol. 5, edited by James Hastings, 759–65. Edinburgh: T and T Clark, 1912.

Maclean, A. J. "Fasting (Christian)." In *Encyclopedia of Religion and Ethics,* vol. 5, edited by James Hastings, 765–71. Edinburgh: T and T Clark, 1912.

Maclean, Kama. "Imagining the Indian Nationalist Movement: Revolutionary Metaphors in Imagery of the Freedom Struggle." *Journal of Material Culture,* 19, no. 1 (2014): 7–34.

Mews, Stuart. "The Hunger-Strike of the Lord Mayor of Cork, 1920: Irish, English and Vatican Attitudes." In *The Churches, Ireland and the Irish,* edited by W. J. Sheils and Diana Wood, 385–99. Oxford: Basil Blackwell, 1989.

Miller, Ian. "Food, Medicine and Institutional Life in the British Isles, c. 1790–1900." In *The Routledge History of Food*, edited by Carol Helstosky, 202–7. New York: Routledge, 2015.

Moran, Gerard. "Near Famine: The Crisis in the West of Ireland, 1879–82." *Irish Studies Review*, 18 (Spring 1997): 14–21.

Murphy, William. "Dying, Death and Hunger Strike: Cork and Brixton, 1920." In *Death and Dying in Ireland, Britain and Europe: Historical Perspectives*, edited by James Kelly and Mary Ann Lyons, 297–316. Dublin: Irish Academic Press, 2013.

Murray, John A. "Sir Edward Grey and His Critics, 1911–1912." In *Power, Public Opinion, and Diplomacy*, edited by Lillian Parker Wallace and William Askew, 140–71. Durham: Duke University Press, 1959.

Nair, Neeti. "Bhagat Singh as Satyagrahi: The Limits of Non-Violence in Late Colonial India." *Modern Asian Studies*, 43, no. 3 (May 2009): 649–81.

Nieto-Galan, Agustí. "Mr Giovanni Succi Meets Dr. Luigi Luciani in Florence: Hunger Artists and Experimental Physiology in the Late Nineteenth Century." *Social History of Medicine*, 28, no. 1 (2014): 64–81.

Noorani, A. G. "Vande Mataram: A Historical Lesson." *Economic and Political Weekly*, 8, no. 23 (9 June 1973): 1039–43.

Pratt, Tim, and James Vernon. "'Appeal from This Fiery Bed . . . : The Colonial Politics of Gandhi's Fasts and Their Metropolitan Reception in Britain." *Journal of British Studies*, 44, no. 1 (2005): 92–114.

Radzinowicz, Leon, and Roger Hood. "The Status of Political Prisoner in England: The Struggle for Recognition." *Virginia Law Review*, 65, no. 8 (December 1979): 1421–81.

Reynolds, Paige. "Modernist Martyrdom: The Funerals of Terence MacSwiney." *Modernism/Modernity*, 9, no. 4 (2002): 535–59.

Ryan, Louise. "'Furies' and 'Die-hards': Women and Irish Republicanism in the Early Twentieth Century." *Gender and History*, 11, no. 2 (July 1999), 256–75.

Ryan, Louise. "'In the Line of Fire': Representations of Women and War (1919–1923) through the Writings of Republican Men." In *Irish Women and Nationalism: Soldiers, Women and Wicked Hags*, edited by Louise Ryan and Margaret Ward, 45–61. Dublin: Irish Academic Press, 2004.

Sarkar, Tanika. "Birth of a Goddess: 'Vande Mataram,' 'Anandamath,' and Hindu Nationhood." *Economic and Political Weekly*, 41, no. 37 (16–22 September 2006), 3959–69.

Senese, Donald. "Felix Volkhovsky in London, 1890–1914." In *From the Other Shore: Russian Political Emigrants in Britain, 1880–1917*, edited by John Slatter, 67–78. London: Frank Cass, 1984.

Sil, Narasingha P. "*Bande Mataram*: Bankimchandra Chattopadhyay's Nationalist Thought Revisited." *South Asia*, 25, no. 1 (2002): 121–42.

Silvestri, Michael. "'The Sinn Féin of India': Irish Nationalism and the Policing of Revolutionary Terrorism in Bengal." *Journal of British Studies* 39 (October 2000): 454–86.

Simmons, Dana. "Starvation Science: From Colonies to Metropole." In *Food and Globalization: Consumption, Markets and Politics in the Modern World*, edited by Alexander Nützenadel and Frank Trentmann, 173–92. Oxford: Berg, 2008.

Scanlan, Stephen J., Laurie Cooper Stoll, and Kimberly Lumm. "Starving for Change: The Hunger Strike and Nonviolent Action, 1906–2004." *Research in Social Movements, Con-*

flicts, and Change, 28, ed. Patrick G. Coy. Bingley: Emerald Publishing Group, 2008): 275–323.

Sherman, Taylor C. "State Practice, Nationalist Politics and the Hunger Strikes of the Lahore Conspiracy Case Prisoners, 1929–39." *Cultural and Social History*, 5, no. 4 (2008): 497–508.

Slatter, John. "Among British Liberals: Jaakoff Prelooker and *The Anglo-Russian.*" In *From the Other Shore: Russian Political Emigrants in Britain, 1880–1917*, edited by John Slatter, 49–66. London: Frank Cass, 1984.

Spodek, Howard. "On the Origins of Gandhi's Political Methodology: The Heritage of Kathiawad and Gujarat." *Journal of Asian Studies*, 30, no. 2 (1971): 361–72.

Sweeney, George. "Irish Hunger Strikes and the Cult of Self-sacrifice." *Journal of Contemporary History*, 28 (1993): 421–37.

Sweeney, George. "Self-Immolative Martyrdom: Explaining the Irish Hungerstrike Tradition." *Studies: An Irish Quarterly Review*, 93, no. 371 (Autumn 2004): 337–48.

Tomaszewski, Fiona. "The Tsarist Regime's Manipulation of Public Opinion in Great Britain and France, 1906–1914." *Russian History* 24, no. 3 (Fall 1997): 279–92.

Urquhart, Diane. "'An Articulate and Definite Cry for Political Freedom': The Ulster Suffrage Movement." *Women's History Review*, 11, no. 2 (2002): 273–92.

Valiulis, Maryann. "Power, Gender, and Identity in the Irish Free State." *Journal of Women's History*, 6, no. 4/7, no. 1 (Winter/Spring 1995): 117–36.

Voronina, Tatjana. "Fasting in the Life of Russians (19th–20th Centuries)." *Acta Ethnographica Hungarica* 51, nos. 3–4 (2006): 235–55.

Ward, Margaret. "Conflicting Interests: The British and Irish Suffrage Movements." *Feminist Review*, 50 (1995): 127–47.

Ward, Margaret. "Gender: Gendering the Irish Revolution." In *The Irish Revolution, 1913–1923*, edited by Joost Augusteijn, 168–85. London: Palgrave, 2002.

Worobec, Christine. "Lived Orthodoxy in Imperial Russia." *Kritika*, 7, no. 2 (Spring 2006): 329–50.

Secondary Sources: Books

Aggarwal, S. N. *The Heroes of the Cellular Jail*. Patiala: Punjab University, 1995.

Alter, Joseph. *Gandhi's Body: Sex, Diet, and the Politics of Nationalism*. Philadelphia: University of Pennsylvania Press, 2000.

Anderson, W. K. *James Connolly and the Irish Left*. Dublin: Irish Academic Press, 1994.

Armbruster-Sandoval, Ralph. *Starving for Justice: Hunger Strikes, Spectacular Speech, and the Struggle for Dignity*. Tucson: University of Arizona Press, 2017.

Arnold, David. *Colonizing the Body*. Berkeley: University of California, 1993.

Augusteijn, Joost. *From Public Defiance to Guerilla Warfare: The Experience of Ordinary Volunteers in the Irish War of Independence 1916–1921*. Dublin: Irish Academic Press, 1996.

Badcock, Sarah. *A Prison without Walls? Eastern Siberian Exile in the Last Years of Tsarism*. Oxford: Oxford University Press, 2016.

Bargu, Banu. *Starve and Immolate: The Politics of Human Weapons*. New York: Columbia University Press, 2014.

Beasley, Rebecca, and Philip Ross, eds. *Russia in Britain, 1880–1940: From Melodrama to Modernism*. Oxford: Oxford University Press, 2013.

Beresford, David. *Ten Men Dead: The Story of the 1981 Irish Hunger Strike*. London: Harper Collins, 1994.

Bose, Sugata. *His Majesty's Opponent: Subhas Chandra Bose and India's Struggle against Empire*. Cambridge: Harvard University Press, 2011.

Bosworth, Mary. *Inside Immigration Detention*. Oxford: Oxford University Press, 2014.

Brugha, Máire MacSwiney. *History's Daughter: A Memoir from the Only Child of Terence MacSwiney*. Dublin: The O'Brien Press, 2006.

Bynum, Caroline. *Holy Feast and Holy Fast*. Berkeley: University of California Press, 1987.

Carpenter, Kenneth J. *Protein and Energy: A Study of Changing Ideas in Nutrition*. Cambridge: Cambridge University Press, 1994.

Chattopadhyaya, B. D. *The Concept of Bharatavarsha*. Ranikhet: Permanent Black, 2017.

Chaudhary, Zahid R. *Afterimage of Empire: Photography in Nineteenth-Century India*. Minneapolis: University of Minnesota Press, 2012.

Clements, Barbara. *Bolshevik Women*. Cambridge: Cambridge University Press, 1997.

Coogan, Tim Pat. *The I.R.A.* New York: Palgrave, 2000.

Corbett, Mary Jean. *Representing Femininity: Middle-Class Subjectivity in Victorian and Edwardian Women's Autobiographies*. New York: Oxford University Press, 1992.

Costello, Francis. *Enduring the Most: The Life and Death of Terence MacSwiney*. Dingle: Brandon, 1995.

Cunningham, Philip J. *Tiananmen Moon: Inside the Chinese Student Uprising of 1989*. New York: Rowman and Littlefield, 2014.

Dalton, Dennis. *Mahatma Gandhi: Nonviolent Power in Action*. New York: Columbia University Press, 1993.

Daly, Jonathan W. *Autocracy under Siege: Security Police and Opposition in Russia, 1866–1905*. DeKalb: Northern Illinois University Press, 1998.

Davis, Mike. *Late Victorian Holocausts: El Niño Famines and the Making of the Third World*. London: Verso, 2001.

Devji, Faisal. *The Impossible Indian: Gandhi and the Temptation of Violence*. Cambridge: Harvard University Press, 2012.

Eichacker, Joanne Mooney. *Irish Republican Women in America: Lecture Tours, 1916–1925*. Dublin: Irish Academic Press, 2003.

Engel, Barbara Alpern, and Clifford N. Rosenthal. *Five Sisters: Women against the Tsar*. New York: Routledge, 1992.

English, Richard, and Cormac O'Malley. *Prisoners: The Civil War Letters of Ernie O'Malley*. Dublin: Poolbeg, 1991.

English, Richard. *Radicals and the Republic: Socialist Republicanism in the Irish Free State, 1925–1937*. Oxford: Oxford University Press, 1994.

English, Richard. *Ernie O'Malley: IRA Intellectual*. Oxford: Oxford University Press, 1998.

English, Richard. *Armed Struggle: The History of the I.R.A.* Oxford: Oxford University Press, 2004.

Fallon, Charlotte H. *Soul of Fire: A Biography of Mary MacSwiney*. Dublin: Mercier Press, 1986.

Fenech, Louis E. *Martyrdom in the Sikh Tradition: Playing the "Game of Love."* Delhi: Oxford University Press, 2000.

Fiske, Lucy. *Human Rights, Refugee Protest and Immigration Detention.* London: Palgrave, 2016.

Fletcher, Ian Christopher, Laura E. Nym Mayhall, and Philippa Levine, eds. *Women's Suffrage in the British Empire: Citizenship, Nation, and Race.* London: Routledge, 2000.

Flynn, Barry. *Pawns in the Game: Irish Hunger Strikes, 1912–1981.* Wilton: The Collins Press, 2011.

Fogel, Robert William. *The Escape from Hunger and Premature Death, 1700–2100.* Cambridge: Cambridge University Press, 2004.

Garnett, David. *The Golden Echo.* New York: Harcourt, Brace and Co., 1954.

Garnett, Richard. *Constance Garnett: A Heroic Life.* London: Sinclair-Stevenson, 1991.

Gaughan, J. Anthony. *Austin Stack: Portrait of a Separatist.* Dublin: Kingdom Books, 1977.

Ghosh, Durba. *Gentlemanly Terrorists: Political Violence and the Colonial State in India, 1919–1947.* Cambridge: Cambridge University Press, 2017.

Gordon, Leonard. *Bengal: The Nationalist Movement, 1876–1940.* New York: Columbia University Press, 1974.

Grant, Kevin. *A Civilised Savagery: Britain and the New Slaveries in Africa, 1884–1926.* New York: Routledge, 2005.

Grant, Kevin, Philippa Levine, and Frank Trentmann, eds. *Beyond Sovereignty: Britain, Empire and Transnationalism, c. 1880–1950.* New York: Palgrave Macmillan, 2007.

Gray, Peter. *Famine, Land and Politics: British Government and Irish Society, 1843–50.* Dublin: Irish Academic Press, 1999.

Green, Barbara. *Spectacular Confessions: Autobiography, Performative Activism, and the Sites of Suffrage, 1905–1938.* New York: St. Martin's Press, 1997.

Gupta, Manmathnath. *They Lived Dangerously: Reminiscences of a Revolutionary.* Delhi: People's Publishing House, 1969.

Hart, Peter. *The I.R.A. and Its Enemies.* Oxford: Oxford University Press, 1998.

Hart, Peter. *The I.R.A. at War, 1916–1923.* Oxford: Oxford University Press, 2003.

Hartnett, Lynn Ann. *The Defiant Life of Vera Figner: Surviving the Russian Revolution.* Bloomington: Indiana University Press, 2014.

Heehs, Peter. *The Bomb in Bengal: The Rise of Revolutionary Terrorism in India, 1900–1910.* Delhi: Oxford University Press, 1993.

Hilton, Boyd. *The Age of Atonement: The Influence of Evangelicalism on Social and Economic Thought, 1785–1865.* Oxford: Clarendon Press, 1988.

Hopkinson, Michael. *The Irish War of Independence.* Montreal: McGill-Queen's University Press, 2002.

Hughes, Michael. *Diplomacy before the Russian Revolution: Britain, Russia, and the Old Diplomacy, 1894–1917.* New York: St. Martin's Press, 2000.

Hunt, James D. *An American Looks at Gandhi.* New Delhi: Promilla and Co., 2005.

Hussain, Nasser. *The Jurisprudence of Emergency.* Ann Arbor: University of Michigan Press, 2003.

Ingraham, Barton L. *Political Crime in Europe: A Comparative Study of France, Germany, and England.* Berkeley: University of California Press, 1979.

Kelleher, Margaret. *The Feminization of Famine: Expressions of the Inexpressible?* Durham: Duke University Press, 1997.

Kelly, M. J. *The Fenian Ideal and Irish Nationalism.* Woodbridge: The Boydell Press, 2006.

Kenney, Padraic. *Dance in Chains: Political Imprisonment in the Modern World.* Oxford: Oxford University Press, 2017.

Keogh, Dermot. *The Rise of the Irish Working Class.* Belfast: Appletree Press, 1982.

Kiely, Declan, ed. *The King's Threshold: Manuscript Materials by W. B. Yeats.* Ithaca: Cornell University Press, 2005.

Kumar, Pramod. *Hunger-strike in Andamans: Repression and Resistance of Transported Prisoners in Cellular Jail, 12 May–26 June 1933.* Lucknow: Martyrs Memorial and Freedom Struggle Research Centre, 2004.

Leeson, D. M. *The Black and Tans: British Police and Auxiliaries in the Irish War of Independence.* Oxford: Oxford University Press, 2011.

Lennon, Joseph. *Irish Orientalism: A Literary and Intellectual History.* Syracuse: Syracuse University Press, 2004.

Levenson, Leah. *With Wooden Sword: A Portrait of Francis Sheehy-Skeffington, Militant Pacifist.* Boston: Northeastern University Press, 1983.

Longford, The Earl of, and Thomas P. O'Neill. *Eamon de Valera.* Boston: Houghton Mifflin Co., 1971.

Louis, Wm. Roger. *Imperialism at Bay.* Oxford: Oxford University Press, 1987.

Low, D. A. *Britain and Indian Nationalism: The Imprint of Ambiguity, 1929–1942.* Cambridge: Cambridge University Press, 1997.

MacBride, Seán. *That Day's Struggle: A Memoir, 1904–1951.* Dublin: Currach Press, 2005.

Mac Conmara, Tomás. *Days of Hunger: The Clare Volunteers and the Mountjoy Hunger Strike of 1917.* Ballyvalley, Killaloe, County Clare: Dallán Publishing, 2017.

Maclean, Kama. *A Revolutionary History of Interwar India: Violence, Image, Voice and Text.* London: Hurst and Company, 2015.

Maguire, John. *IRA Internments and the Irish Government: Subversives and the State, 1939–1962.* Dublin: Irish Academic Press, 2008.

Majumdar, R. C., *Penal Settlement in Andamans.* New Delhi: Government of India, 1975.

Malia, Martin. *Russia under Western Eyes.* Cambridge, Mass.: Harvard University Press, 1999.

Mandal, Teertha. *The Women Revolutionaries of Bengal, 1905–1939.* Calcutta: Minerva, 1991.

Mathur, L. P. *Kala Pani: History of Andaman and Nicobar Islands with a Study of India's Freedom Struggle.* Delhi: Eastern Book Corporation, 1985.

Mayhall, Laura E. Nym. *The Militant Suffrage Movement.* Oxford: Oxford University Press, 2003.

McConville, Seán. *Irish Political Prisoners, 1848–1922: Theatres of War.* London: Routledge, 2003.

McGarry, Fearghal. *Eoin O'Duffy: A Self-Made Hero.* Oxford: Oxford University Press, 2005.

Miller, Ian. *A History of Force Feeding: Hunger Strikes, Prisons and Medical Ethics, 1909–1974.* London: Palgrave Macmillan, 2016.

Mohan, Kamlesh. *Militant Nationalism in the Punjab.* New Delhi: Manohar, 1985.

Morris, A. J. Anthony. *Radicalism against War, 1906–1914*. Totowa: Rowman and Littlefield, 1972.

Moulton, Mo. *Ireland and the Irish in Interwar England*. Cambridge: Cambridge University Press, 2014.

Mukherjee, Janam. *Hungry Bengal: War, Famine and the End of Empire*. Oxford: Oxford University Press, 2015.

Murphy, Cliona. *The Women's Suffrage Movement and Irish Society in the Early Twentieth Century*. Philadelphia: Temple University Press, 1989.

Murphy, William. *Political Imprisonment and the Irish, 1912–1921*. Oxford: Oxford University Press, 2014.

Murray, Patrick. *Oracles of God: The Roman Catholic Church and Irish Politics, 1922–37*. Dublin: UCD Press, 2000.

Noorani, A. G. *The Trial of Bhagat Singh: Politics of Justice*. Delhi: Oxford University Press, 1996.

Oberoi, Harjot. *The Construction of Religious Boundaries: Culture, Identity, and Diversity in the Sikh Tradition*. Chicago: University of Chicago Press, 1994.

Ó Drisceoil, Donal. *Censorship in Ireland, 1939–1945*. Cork: Cork University Press, 1996.

Ó Gráda, Cormac. *Black '47 and Beyond*. Princeton: Princeton University Press, 1999.

Ó Gráda, Cormac. *Famine: A Short History*. Princeton: Princeton University Press, 2009.

O'Luing, Sean. *I Die in a Good Cause: Thomas Ashe, Idealist and Revolutionary*. Tralee: Anvil Books, 1970.

O'Malley, Padraig. *Biting at the Grave*. Boston: Beacon Press, 1990.

Owen, Nicholas. *The British Left and India: Metropolitan Anti-Imperialism, 1885–1947*. Oxford: Oxford University Press, 2008.

Owens, Rosemary Cullen. *Smashing Times: A History of the Irish Women's Suffrage Movement, 1889–1922*. Dublin: Attic Press, 1984.

Pestana, Senia. *Irish Nationalist Women, 1900–1918*. Cambridge: Cambridge University Press, 2013.

Pinney, Christopher. *Photos of the Gods: The Printed Image and Political Struggle in India*. Delhi: Oxford University Press, 2004.

Popplewell, Richard. *Intelligence and Imperial Defence: British Intelligence and the Defence of the Indian Empire, 1904–1924*. London: Taylor and Francis, 1995.

Prabhu, R. K., and V. R. Rao, eds. *The Mind of Mahatma Gandhi*. Ahmedabad: Navajivan Trust, 2002.

Pugh, Martin. *The March of the Women*. Oxford: Oxford University Press, 2000.

Purvis, June. *Emmeline Pankhurst: A Biography*. London: Routledge, 2002.

Rabe, Volker. *Der Widerspruch von Rechtsstaatlichkeit und strafender Verwaltung in Russland, 1881–1917*. Karlsruhe: Verlag M. Wahl, 1985.

Ramaswamy, Sumathi. *The Goddess and the Nation: Mapping Mother India*. Durham: Duke University Press, 2010.

Ramnath, Maia. *Haj to Utopia: How the Ghadar Movement Charted Global Radicalism and Attempted to Overthrow the British Empire*. Berkeley: University of California Press, 2011.

Reynolds, Paige. *Modernism, Drama, and the Audience for Irish Spectacle*. Cambridge: Cambridge University Press, 2007.

Riasanovsky, Nicholas, and Mark D. Steinberg. *A History of Russia*, 7th edition. Oxford: Oxford University Press, 2005.

Rosen, Andrew. *Rise Up, Women!* London: Routledge and Kegan Paul, 1974.

Ruud, Charles, and Sergei Stepanov. *Fontanka 16: The Tsars' Secret Police*. Montreal and Kingston: McGill-Queen's University Press, 1999.

Sarkar, Sumit. *Modern India: 1885–1947*. Madras: Macmillan India, 1983.

Schrader, Abby. *Languages of the Lash: Corporal Punishment and Identity in Imperial Russia*. DeKalb: Northern Illinois University Press, 2002.

Sen, Amartya. *Poverty and Famines*. New Delhi: Oxford University Press, 1981.

Seton-Watson, Hugh. *The Decline of Imperial Russia, 1855–1914*. London: Methuen and Co., 1952.

Sherman, Taylor C. *State Violence and Punishment in India*. London: Routledge, 2010.

Silvestri, Michael. *Ireland and India: Nationalism, Empire and Memory*. New York: Palgrave Macmillan, 2009.

Singh, Ujjwal Kumar. *Political Prisoners in India*. Delhi: Oxford University Press, 1998.

Sinha, Mrinalini. *Specters of Mother India: The Global Restructuring of an Empire*. Durham: Duke University Press, 2006.

Slatter, John, ed. *From the Other Shore: Russian Political Emigrants in Britain, 1880–1917*. London: Frank Cass, 1984.

Stites, Richard. *The Women's Liberation Movement in Russia: Feminism, Nihilism, and Bolshevism, 1860–1930*. Princeton: Princeton University Press, 1978.

Storm, Mary. *Head and Heart: Valour and Self-Sacrifice in the Art of India*. Delhi: Routledge, 2013.

Taylor, A. J. P. *The Troublemakers*. London: Pimlico, 1993.

Thompson, William Irwin. *The Imagination of an Insurrection: Dublin, Easter 1916*. New York: Oxford University Press, 1967.

Tickner, Lisa. *The Spectacle of Women: Imagery of the Suffrage Campaign, 1907–1914*. Chicago: University of Chicago Press, 1988.

Townshend, Charles. *The British Campaign in Ireland, 1919–1921*. Oxford: Oxford University Press, 1975.

Townshend, Charles. *Easter 1916: The Irish Rebellion*. Chicago: Ivan R. Dee, 2006.

Trivedi, Lisa. *Clothing Gandhi's Nation: Homespun and the Nation in India*. Bloomington: Indiana University Press, 2007.

Tucker, Todd. *The Great Starvation Experiment: Ancel Keys and the Men Who Starved for Science*. Minneapolis: University of Minnesota Press, 2008.

Vandereycken, Walter, and Ron Van Deth. *From Fasting Saints to Anorexic Girls: The History of Self-Starvation*. New York: New York University Press, 1994.

Vernon, James. *Hunger: A Modern History*. Cambridge: Harvard University Press, 2007.

Ward, Margaret. *Hanna Sheehy Skeffington: A Life*. Cork: Attic Press, 1997.

Whelehan, Niall. *The Dynamiters: Irish Nationalists and Political Violence in the Wider World, 1867–1900*. Cambridge: Cambridge University Press, 2012.

Wiener, Martin. *Reconstructing the Criminal: Culture, Law, and Policy in England, 1830–1914*. Cambridge: Cambridge University Press, 1990.

Winick, Myron. *Hunger Disease: Studies by the Jewish Physicians in the Warsaw Ghetto*. Chichester: John Wiley, 1979.

Yates, Padraig. *Lockout: Dublin,* 1913. New York: Palgrave, 2000.

Zweiniger-Bargielowska, Ina. *Managing the Body: Beauty, Health, and Fitness in Britain, 1880–1939.* Oxford: Oxford University Press, 2010.

Secondary Sources: Dissertations

Hartnett, Lynn Ann. "Perpetual Exile: The Dynamics of Gender, Protest, and Violence in the Revolutionary Life of Vera Figner (1852–1917)." PhD dissertation, Boston College, 2000.

Phillips, Ben. "Political Exile and the Image of Siberia in Anglo–Russian Contacts Prior to 1917." PhD dissertation, University College London, 2016.

INDEX

Kerensky, Alexander, 65
Kerr, Harriet, 33–34
Keys, Ancel, 39. *See also* starvation
Khan, Munshi, 34–35
khilafat movement, 140
Kilmainham Gaol, 89–92
Kilroy, Jack, 96
Kipling, Rudyard: and *Kim* (1900–1901), 6; and
    White Man's Burden (1899), 17, 152
King's Threshold, The (1904, 1920). *See* Yeats,
    William Butler
Korf, Governor General Baron, 47
Kovalevskaia, Maria, 48
Kovalskaia, Elizabeth, 47–49
Kravchinskii, Sergius, 42–43, 46–47, 49, 51–52
Krishak Praja Party (KPP), 103–104, 121, 123, 126
Kropotkin, Peter, 51
Kropotkin, Sophie, 54

Lahore Prison, 106
Lambert, F. A. Heygate, 81
Larkin, James, 81
law, 10, 44, 156; and formulation of British gov-
    ernment policy on hunger strikes, 10–11, 19,
    130–131, 134–135, 142–143; and political crime,
    4–5, 130; and the responsibility of prison
    medical officers for hunger strikers, 13, 32,
    60, 72, 108, 134–135, 142–143, 145–146, 148. *See
    also* criminalization; forcible feeding; *Leigh v.
    Gladstone* (1909); political prisoner status
Lawlor, Mrs. George, 97
Leigh, Mary, 60, 63, 77
Leigh v. Gladstone (1909), 60, 63, 134, 142–143.
    See also forcible feeding; law
Lennon, Joseph, 45
Levanzin, Agostino, 26
Lewes Prison, 81, 83
liberalism: challenged by hunger in protest, 4–5,
    11, 13, 18–20, 63, 68, 72, 126, 129, 146, 149,
    152–156; and the government's duty to com-
    bat hunger, 11, 13–18, 153; and violence, 5, 126,
    152–153. *See also* fasting; hunger strike
life reform movement, 23, 27–29. *See also* Had-
    ley, Hopton
Linlithgow, Lord, 40–41, 122–123
lip sewing, 5, 153
Lloyd George, David, 64, 86, 136–137, 150
London Russian Hertsen Circle, 53
Lowe, Dr. William, 82, 134
Lyallpur District Jail, 37
Lynch, Jeremiah, 95, 138

Lytton, Lady Constance (*alias* Jane Wharton):
    hunger strikes by, 20, 141; and hunger strike
    medal, 57*fig.*, 58*fig.*, 59
Lytton, Lord, 141–143. *See also* India Office

MacBride, John, 93
MacBride, Maude Gonne, 16–17, 93, 96
MacBride, Sean, 93, 97–98
MacCurtain, Thomas, 86–87
MacCurtain, Tómas, 96
MacDonald, James Ramsey, 53
Maclean, Kama, 102
Macready, Sir Nevil, 86
MacSwiney, Annie, 89, 90, 93
MacSwiney, Mary, 35, 94–96, 126–127; hunger
    strikes by, 89–90, 93, 137; and Joan of Arc,
    89–91
MacSwiney, Muriel, 89
MacSwiney, Sean, 94, 97–98
MacSwiney, Terence, 35, 92, 94; as inspiration
    for Indian revolutionaries, 9, 109, 143–144;
    hunger strikes by, 9, 20, 26, 31, 36, 84, 86–88,
    130, 136, 141–142, 149–150; on gender roles,
    89; on sacrifice, 87
Maffey, Sir John, 151
Mahabharata, 18
Malia, Martin, 44
Manchester Guardian, 31, 53–54, 63
manslaughter. *See* medical officer, prison
Markievicz, Countess Constance, 78, 79*fig.*, 80
Mary (Christ's mother): and hunger strikes by
    Irish republican women, 38, 75, 89–90, 91*fig.*
    See also Catholicism; hunger strike
Masterman, Charles, 61
Masyukov, 47–48
Mayhall, Laura, 45
Mayo, Katherine, 119. *See also* Mother India
McCarthy, Charles, 138
McCarthy, Richard, 95, 138
McCaughey, Seán, 97–98, 150–151
McGrath, Patrick, 95, 97, 137
McKenna, Reginald, 55, 63, 65
McKinley, President William, 46
McNeela, John (Jack), 96–97
medical officer, prison, 4, 97–98, 107–108, 135;
    and challenges posed by hunger striking,
    32, 55, 60, 65, 132, 140; and deference to class
    hierarchy, 20, 32, 65, 133; and diagnosis of
    starvation, 23, 25, 30–35, 40–41; difficulty
    in hiring and retaining, 134; and the dif-
    ficulty of forcible feeding, 133–134, 140; and

www.ingramcontent.com/pod-product-compliance
Lightning Source LLC
Chambersburg PA
CBHW030320270326
41926CB00010B/1437